All My Love, Chad

The WWII Love Letters of Private Charles D. Crouchley

Assembled by J.P. Potter

Order this book online at www.trafford.com
or email orders@trafford.com

Most Trafford titles are also available at major online book retailers.

Printed in Victoria, BC, Canada.

ISBN: 978-1-4269-2598-6 (soft)
ISBN: 978-1-4269-2599-3 (hard)

Library of Congress Control Number: 2010901384

*Our mission is to efficiently provide the world's finest, most comprehensive book publishing
service, enabling every author to experience success. To find out how to publish your book, your
way, and have it available worldwide, visit us online at www.trafford.com*

Trafford rev. 1/29/2010

 www.trafford.com

North America & international
toll-free: 1 888 232 4444 (USA & Canada)
phone: 250 383 6864 ♦ fax: 812 355 4082

Camp Devens, Mass.
August, 19, 1943

Dearest Bedie:

We certainly have had a hectic time since our arrival here at camp. The train coming up from New Haven was very dirty because of the smoke and cinders coming in through the open doors.

Lew, Dave, Gene and I played set-back for 15 games and Gene and I won 25 cents (8 games to 7).

We pulled in at Devens about 1:00 p.m. and were sent through the mill. We got 2 big brown canvas bags bigger than my brown zipper bag and were given our winter or O.D. uniform (shirt, 2 pants, jacket, winter underwear, winter sox, woolen cap) Besides that we got a plastic helmet, raincoat, sun-tan pants, shirts, cap, and necktie, toilet articles, towels, Soldiers' Manual and a lot of other incidentals.

We all got shots in the arm for typhoid and some of the fellows were sick. Fortunately, my arm was only a little sore.

Today we had our mechanical aptitude test, radio aptitude test, and general intelligence tests. We saw a film explaining the organization of the Army and then had lunch.

This P.M. we had our interviews with personnel officers and men for our placement. I told my interviewer about my Biology and said I preferred work in the Medical Corps. Whether I get such an assignment is in the lap of the authorities.

I am enclosing a copy of my application for dependency benefits for you. Please keep it in case the War Dept. should lose the copy they have.

It is only a few minutes to lights-out so I will close. Take good care of yourself and tell the folks I will have more time to write later.

I am thinking of you. Keep your chin up and remember you have all my love.

Your Kutsie bug.

Chad.

P.S. Better not write to me until you hear more about my assignment to a training center. C.

August 25, 1943

Dear Petunia:

Since my first letter to you things have slowed down a bit. Friday, Saturday, and Sunday were the busiest days. Friday we got up at 4:30 a.m., as usual, and went down to the company day room where Gene, Dave, Lew and I were picked for junk yard detail. We got on a truck with about 10 others and were taken down to what looked like a repair shop with a big wooden enclosure in back of it. There we were split up into groups and assigned to different jobs. First we cleaned up around the outside of the shop picking up salvageable lumber, glass bottles, and metal. Dave worked inside the shop repairing cots. They fixed cots all day while Lew and I were in a group out in the junk yard. We sorted over old metal, wire, and lumber and raked up the stuff to be thrown away. Saturday we were introduced to military drill and learned the various facings. My two greatest difficulties were to decipher the various barks, grunts and other military jargon which non-coms and their assistants use in issuing commands, and to move my big feet around in the sandy soil of the drill ground. You wouldn't recognize my shoes. They make my feet look really large. Sunday Morning, after reporting for detail I found that I was going to be introduced to the joys of K.P. duty. Our detail went down to the mess hall right after cleaning up and were assigned to our various jobs. For about three hours I helped clean pots and pans. The pans had to be scraped and soaked and took a lot of elbow grease. At lunch I helped serve coffee. This is done by the chain system with the milk and coffee spigots open all the time. As soon as a cup had enough milk init, it was shoved under the coffee faucet. By doing that we kept up a steady chain of coffee cups moving. That time we served about a couple thousand cups. During the afternoon we went into the cold roomf or cheese and bologna. The idea of the red stamps involved made my dizzy. During supper, another fellow and I served hot tea. After supper we cleaned up, swept the floor and left things for the night crew to take over. Monday and today Dave and I didn't have too much to do. Monday morning Gene Casagrande was shipped out. We have very strict order from our commanding officer not to say anything in our letters about destinations so I can't say anything about where he is going.

Several nights we went down to the Service Club where we played cards. Our rivalry was pretty even. The boys tell me I'm eally catching on to high-low-jack fast. One night we went down to a dance given by the U.S.O. at Robbins Pond within the fort area. It was so crowded that I don't see how they danced. We went up on the balcony and watched the jitterbugs' antics. Lew had a couple of dances with one of the chaperones who was very nice looking.

We have met two boys from Ridgefield so far, John DeBenigno and Bob Myers. They helped us a lot in getting the real low-down on how things are done.

Dave and I are still together although we never can tell when we will be shipped off for basic training. Since the Army seems to need signal corps and medical corps men the chances are good we will soon be separated.

The set-up here is very unsettling psychologically, because the men all seem to be just waiting for their shipping orders. Everyday new men come in and, within a week, fellows like us who have been here a week feel like old hands.

Tomorrow Dave and I are going down to the doctor for our second shots in the arm. These will be stronger thatn the first one. If I don't have any more of a sore arm than I had with the first one I'll be doing alright.

I'm beginning to realize the disadvantages of sleeping alone. Sunday night some of the married men who had just seen their wives came into the barracks talking about the emotional kick they got out of it. I found it hard to get to sleep that night.

The fellows in G-3-Down are a pretty good bunch. Many of them are married men and are pretty steady. However, there are a few wild ones whose language consists of using that word (----_ you don't like, about every other word. There is one young fellow who was shipped out Monday who has "----ed" more people than would be physically possible. By and large most of them are honest and the only thing I have had lifted so far is that metal soap dish. I bought another and put my name on it. Some fellows have been careless and left watches and money around, to their regret. If we play cards we keep to ourselves because there are some old army men among us who would like nothing better than to shear a nice fleecy lamb. The officer's are very careful to warn new-comers to keep their money out of sight and not to loan money to anyone.

Our moral education has been well taken care of by a stirring appeal by the chaplain. You know the line about "she could be your own sister." This was followed by a film depicting the horrors of syphilis and clap. They didn't spare any details to impress the men with the necessity of leaving loose women alone. In this army the only one who will look out for you is yourself.

When you told me Thursday night that you had sent me a shoe kit I kept looking for it in the mail but it hasn't arrived yet. Perhaps it would be best not to send me anything because the prices for things in the Post Exchange (PX) are much cheaper than those in civilian life and, besides, I can get many things you won't find in Ridgefield stores anymore.

Tell the gang I am thinking of them and wishing them well. I wrote to the Red Cross, Rotary Club, and Teachers' Assoc. I sent cards to Leve & Mary, Karl & Dot, Lyman & Ruth, Harold & Alice, and Grace. Remember me to Cliff and tell him I will try to write soon. I hope he has a new biology teacher. Tell mother and dad I will write soon; also Ralph and Ruth.

I am afraid the shoes Ralph gave me are going to be too tight when I start carrying a pack on my back. I will bring them home when I have leave (Lord knows when that will be). Remember me to the bunch in the bank.

I miss you sweetheart but don't worry I will be doing my damnedest to see you just as soon as I can possibly manage it.

All my love,
Chad

September 2, 1943

Dearest Bedie:

This note is the second I have written you. The first was lost in the shuffle this morning so it wasn't mailed. I take back all I said about life at Ft. Devens. This place is like a nut-house. You feel like a squirrel in a cage.

We left Devens about 3:40 p.m. Monday in day coaches which had just a hole-in-the floor type toilet with no washing bowls or place to get drinking water but a small cooler in each car. We crossed Mass. to the Hoosac Tunnel and then to Troy and Albany. By that time it was night and we traveled across N.Y. State to Buffalo and saw Lake Erie in the a.m. We were a sorry sight trying to sleep in day coaches. I got cramps in my legs. We crossed Ohio to Cincinnati all day Tuesday and got some sleep crossing Tennessee to Alabama. We arrived at Ft. McClellan Wed. a.m. and started the merry-go-round.

Don't worry about me, Bedie. Gradually I'll get toughened up to this army life. Tell mother and Dad that I'll try to write just as soon as we are less restricted, and life settles down to a more regular routine.

Please send me 12 wire coat hangers as soon as you can. I need them badly. Then I can stop living out of a canvas barracks bag. I will write you more soon about our training here.

With all my love,

Chad.

P.S. Be sure to use the address on envelope

Dearest Petunia:

This marks the end of my first real week in the army and I thought it would never end. Last Sunday we were running around from pillar to post getting equipment and listening to advice from our officers but today we have the day to ourselves. It's a grand feeling to celebrate, I got up at 6:30 a.m. and went up to the latrine and did my laundry. Our fatigue suits (work suits made of green herring bone twill) get absolutely filthy during the week and by Saturday they could walk down the company street all by themselves. Socks and handkerchiefs get sweaty and filled with this damn Alabama red dust which old-timers say makes the gooiest stickiest mud. They say it sticks to your shoes just like chewing gum. Last Sunday we hung our laundry up on a wire in back of our hut but Lt. Behan, our platoon commander, darn near broke his Adam's apple on it so he ordered it taken down. Today I hung my stuff on a string between huts out of the way. This Alabama sunshine dries your clothes in about an hour. This afternoon Bill Dunn, a nice fellow from Mass., and I decided to do some exploring so we came down to the service club where I am writing this.

During the week we have had a pretty strenuous schedule. We received our rifles and proceeded to learn the intricacies of their mechanism. We haven't shot them yet and probably won't for several weeks yet. Friday we concentrated on aiming the rifle properly and I got a couple of good marks. The thing is done by marking a target with a pencil when you think you are on the bulls-eye. You take three dry shots this way and your pencil marks on the target have to be near enough together to be covered by the end of a lead pencil. The distance is 50 ft. We also have had a lot of practice in doing the manual of arms. It's practically a criminal offense to place a rifle on the ground or to drop it.

We also received our gas masks and were instructed in the proper method of putting them on. Along with this we had a lecture on chemicals. Every night this week we have had something or other to keep us busy until time for lights out. Several nights were devoted to movies about gas warfare, conduct of war prisoners, and sex hygiene. We were plenty glad to hit the hay.

We have had more practice in making full field packs and pitching tents. You remember the saying about Army pup tents. It's true, every word of it.

Soon we will be going out on hikes, then the dogs will bark. Any where you look in this place you see hills in the distance. Climbing them takes the wind out of you. There is one bitch of a hill called T5 which darn near gives the boys heart failure when we head for it.

I received the coat hangers, magazines and Brownies Friday. The boys who sampled them said they were as good as their mothers make. They tasted super - super. I also received the shoe kit from Fort Devens. Speaking of mail, the boys gasped when they saw me reading the 23 page letter you wrote. I doubt whether I will ever have the time to reciprocate. During the week days letter writing is almost an impossibility. We have very little time between blasts of that damn whistle and the shout "Second Platoon, Fall In!" I received letters from Ralph and Zeke. I hope to write answers this P.M. This A.M. I received the very legal-looking absentee ballot. I'll fill it out and get it back in time.

I was sorry to hear about Dot and Bill Winthrop. The thing has probably gone so far now that it will mean a breakup. I hope that Karl's business and political career does not suffer. Ridgefield would be greatly improved by Bill's permanent absence.

Ralph told me about Ed. Villareal and I feel that if I keep my nose clean and attend to business in this basic training, I will get my chance in the Medical Corps. There is, of course, the fact that I haven't had much chemistry but, with some extra training, I thing I could do the work. I realize by now that my chances for a commission are about nil but there is always the chance of winning a noncommissioned officer's stripes.

Last week I met Dave Moore in the Post Exchange and we talked for a few minutes. However, we don't see each other during the day's work since he is in a different company. I may get a chance to drop into his barracks tonight.

I was glad to get Levi's address and will write him soon. Also thanks for Mr.. Horton's address.

Frankie Bassett certainly got a royal snub. It tickled me to think of him striding up and down, chewing his nails. If he keeps it up he will cook his own goose in Ridgefield.

Ralph is getting to be quite a politician. Maybe he could use that rubber hose on a few of our ward-hecklers.

Those income tax forms sound formidable. I think I'd rather climb T5 than tackle one of them. You know I never was very good at figures.

Give my love to Mother-Bedient and remember me to Grace, Cliff, and Grandma. Remember me to Lyman and Ruth, Joe and Ellen and the people at the bank.

Don't get all tuckered out with the canning, Bedie. By this time, the cellar must look like a Grange Canning exhibit.

Keep well, sweetheart, and be patient with me. I won't be able to write as often as I would like to. Sunday is the best time for me to really sit down and put my disjointed thoughts on paper.

All my love to you, my sweet, and ten thousand kisses in the soft little hollow under your ear. And ten thousand more quivery ones on your sweet lips. I love you with all my heart and soul.

Your Chad

P.S.   Tng. Bn + Training Battalion
         I.R.T.C. + Infantry Replacement Training Center

Better not send me newspapers. We have them in our day room - Life magazine good.

Thursday, September 16, 1943

Dearest Petunia:

By some strange fate it rained this evening and the officers called off the movies which were scheduled for us. Up to now we have had movies or lectures which have taken up our evenings until the bugle blows the call to quarters and lights out.

Today we went out on our first hike. We marched about 5 miles out to the southwest where we had classes in extended drill. This involved breaking up into squads and walking through underbrush and through pine forest until our tongues were hanging out. We had show from a field kitchen set up in the open under the pine trees. During the afternoon we had more extended order drill. All the movements are controlled by hand signals which we have to know. The way a squad is made up every man has to be able to step into any job in the squad.

We marched back to camp in the middle of the afternoon. Some of the boys had their asses dragging when they pulled into camp. Right after that we had to line up for tetanus shots but fortunately my name wasn't called so I dashed up to the latrine for a shower. Boy! Did that feel good. Last week, Thursday, I had a typhoid shot and a small pox vaccination in the left arm and a tentanus shot in the right arm. It made me feel just as though I had spring fever, hot, listless and somewhat nauseated. However in about two days I was feeling better. Right now I think my physical condition is improving. The only thing that causes me much trouble is my catarch in the nose in throat.

I am afraid my letter is to much self centered but I have gotten into the habit of thinking a lot about myself. This is pretty general among the boys. After a while you get into the habit of blowing off steam by bitching

This P.M. we had mail call and I got your letter of Monday night the 13th. I know how hard it must be for you to wait for days to hear from me. Except on Sundays, any time I can get for writing a letter has to be snatched. Tonight's chance to write was like finding a gold mine. Certainly our separation is tougher on you because you have to bear the brunt of keeping things going at home and here I am stuck in this hot hole for 15 more weeks, not able to help you or tell you how much I love you or comfort you.

It is now about 8:30 and I still have to make my bed and clean up my dirty mess kit. Today we had to drag our cots out into the street so they could be "aired." The sad part is that every time a squad of men marches through the street they raise a cloud of dust which settles all over our cots. That's army life.

Good night, sweetheart, with kisses on both your blue eyes and a little nip at the end of your perky little nose.

Chad

Dearest Bedie:

The date shows what a time I have keeping track of the days of the week. We live so close to our daily routine that the outside world seems far away.

Tonight we stole a march on the rest of the boys and mopped up our floor and cleaned the windows so that we had some free time before lights out. So in this letter I will try to catch up on some of the tag end of questions that I haven't taken up.

I still have the famous leather bag and find it useful since it is so sturdy. I have had to explain several times that I haven't visited the many places that the labels show.

About Dave Moore's many letters to Alice. The only way I can figure that his is able to write so often because he goes up to his company's day room after lights out. Usually by that time of night I am so pooped that I couldn't do a letter justice. Not that my letter writing efforts have been so wonderful so far.

You mentioned the possibility of our seeing each other some time in October or November. The only town available is Anniston which is about 7 miles from camp; a town of about 10,000 people, not very pretty and the hotels charge big city rates for small town service. I leave it up to you. Any town would be paradise if only you were with me.

Thanks for the Readers' Digest. I received a card confirming the subscription today.

I will execute the power of attorney for the insurance and send it up. If you want to use it you can go ahead. I will keep the cards.

Harvey Keeler's letter was very interesting. I am enclosing it.

Give my regards to Elsa Hartmann and the Dixons and tell them that I will drop them a line next Sunday.

So far I haven't come across a Joe Casajza although there are four platoons in our company, nearly 200 men I haven't learned more than about 50 names.

You mentioned the Brownies being stiff and expressed the wish for something else pretty stiff. Well, this morning I woke up with the nicest main mast you ever saw. The salt peter must be wearing off or my glands must be working over time.

Whistle has blown for lights out so sweet dreams, my dear.

Saturday, P.M. the 18th

Well, here I am again with some spare time. Today we had four hours of marksmanship up on top of TA5 (that damned hill I told you about before.) We learned how to hold our rifles from a kneeling position, a squatting position, and the erect position. This P.M. for 2 hours we got ready for inspection, cleaning our rifles, shoes, clothes etc. About ten after two when we all were on tenterhooks two lieutenants strode into our hut and proceeded to look us over. One of them noticed a bulge in my shirt and asked me whether I was pregnant. I explained to him that the bulge was my money pouch but he still insisted that I suck in my guts so that my profile would be more military. After the officers got through with us, our sergeant went over us with a fine toothed comb and had some pointed remarks to make about the condition of our rifles, clothes, and hut. Some of the boys were "gigged" which means that they are slated for special details such as K.P. or some other dirty job.

During the last two periods of the afternoon we had bayonet drill followed by instruction in recognizing American, British, and Russian tanks.

Now for some more unfinished topics. I still have enough money. I don't spend more than 25 cents a day. There isn't a great deal to spend money on. I usually splurge on a pint of ice cream which costs 15 cents. Mom's mouth must be watering by now.

I forgot to mention that I received the carrot. It certainly was a strange specimen. I showed it to some of my buddies and they got a big kick out of it.

I got a letter from Art Dingee and was sorry to hear that the boys still haven't had a scoutmaster assigned to them. I hope they get some one pretty soon so that they can get the log cabin finished up.

I got a letter from Ruth Anderson. She writes so much like her conversation that it was just like some of the bull sessions about local political and social topics we used to have back home.

I have forgotten Cousin Lois' address. I really ought to write to her soon or she will think I am snubbing her.

You asked about the food here. Some days we do very well but on other days we don't eat very much and a great deal of food is wasted. By and large there is plenty to eat. The only thing is that we get quite a lot of fried food.

Can you get a small padlock with a key? Sometimes I want to leave things in my foot locker and would feel better if I had a lock for it. Not that the fellows in our hut are dishonest but the huts are open and anyone can come in if they want.

Another thing we need is to get a door latch like the old-fashioned door latches which work with a thumb plate on the outside and on inside latch.

(a crude sketch I admit, but you know what I mean.)

Let me know how much it costs and I will collect from the boys.

Sunday, A.M., September, 19th, 1943

Brrrr. What a morning, I woke up late, about 6:30, and it was cold and raw and raining like hell. I slept under 2 wool blankets and had a terrible time getting warm even though I work my field jacket. We are getting into the rainy season and it will probably rain every day now for about a month.

During our fifth week of training we are going to be out on the range, (Sept. 28- Oct. 10) getting experience firing our rifles. After firing a rifle you have to clean it every night for 3 nights. So we are going to be pretty busy boys until the second week in October.

About xmas time we will probably be out in the Morrisville area camping out in our pup tents. Then we graduate from our basic training on Jan. 2, 1944. Pretty gloomy prospect. Yesterday our commanding officer gave us a talk about our chances of getting out of the Infantry. He said that when orders come through for a certain number of men they take a whole unit and ship them out. Things don't look so good for me getting into the medical corps.

Last week we had gas mask drill. We marched out about 2 miles to the gas chamber. First we went into the chamber with our masks on and when we got headed for the door we were told to take our masks off. It was tear gas so you can imagine we didn't waste anytime getting out. The next time we went in we had to put our masks on after we got into the chamber. We moved! The drill was to impress us with the value of our masks. It did!

Well my darling, I have to quit and wash my clothes, then back to letter writing.

All my love, Bedie, and a nice warm snuggle on this cold morning.

Chad

P.S. The boys are telling jokes and that reminds me of a joke one of the officers told the other day. It seems that the Norse god Thor, god of thunder and lightening, grew weary of life in Valhalla and decided to go down to earth and see how life was down there. So he descended to earth, met a nice blonde and took her to a hotel room. Being a mighty man, he put the Devil in hell 28 times.

In the morning he was sorry for the girl he thought that, in all justice, he ought to explain that he was not like mortal men so he said to the girl, "young lady, I am sorry I was so passionate last night and I should tell you who I am. I am thor." "Hell!" The girl said, "You're Thor, I'm so damned thor I can hardly pith."

Dear Bedie:

Don't fall over. Yes, I found time to sneak in two letters to you in one day. This morning before dinner I received your letter of the 16th. After dinner I went down to the hospital with another fellow to visit one of the boys who has ulcers on his leg. We stayed for a while and looked around. They have a very nice P.X. and a big recreation room. Also steam heat.

I am going to see our sergeant about the schedule for October and November. I know that we will be out on the firing range during our fifth week so we probably won't be straightened out until the 10th of October. As soon as I find out definitely I will write so that you and Alice can get your heads together.

I was asking today about the number of men at ft. McClellan and learned that there are about 50,000 men here. The barracks certainly look as though they were built long ago. They are drafty and since the windows have to be left open the wind picks up the dust and it drifts right through the screens onto our blankets.

I was certainly surprised to hear about Madge. It doesn't seem possible that she would get mixed up with another man. This war has certainly jumbled people's emotional life.

Some of the boys have angry, red spots on their arms from the small pox vaccinations but my arm didn't react any more than any ordinary series of scratches. All I have left now are the tetanus shots which sting like hell for about 15 minutes then you are O.K.

I suppose by now that Brownie is quite a proud fellow. He ought to be a good bookkeeper for the flock. You haven't mentioned much about getting eggs. How are the red pullets coming along?

I forget to include Harvey Keeler's letter this A.M. So I made sure this time by putting it in the envelope first.

It is really getting blustery and raw now with the wind blowing through the cracks around the windows. Well, Petunia, I have to clean up my shoes and get ready for tomorrow so here's a nibble at the tips of your ears and a pat on your fanny. Then a nice, warm snuggle up against your back with both hands around your little round nubbins and my main mast right between your legs.

All my love,
Chad

Sunday, September 26, 1943

My Dearest:

This week has been quite eventful. Tuesday we had a ten-mile hike out to Miller's Hill, the same place we went last week. We carried our full field packs which consist of a blanket, half a pup tent with a pole, 5 pegs, and length of rope, a rain coat and a shovel with a mess kit on top in a small canvas case. After we have had some more hikes we will carry this pack plus an overcoat and extra shoes, socks and underwear; also our toilet kits. Yesterday we had another hike out to the same place with combat packs which are much lighter, while we were out there we practiced running full tilt and flopping on our bellies with our rifles at the ready. We also learned about patrolling and using cover and concealment. About 24 men would go out and hide themselves up in trees, behind bushes and in the grass. The other 24 men would turn their backs while the first group was hiding and then would turn around to see whether the first group was successfully concealed. In most cases not more than 5 or 6 men could be discovered. When the instructors put on special camouflage suits painted with splotches of brown and green, we had great difficulty in finding them. - On the way back we marched about 2 miles at a cadence of about 160 to the minute which is almost double time and were we pooped. However they slowed down and we had a chance to recover. Last evening we had a regimental parade with all the big wigs in the reviewing stand. As far as I could see we marched just as well as many of the groups that have been training for 10 weeks.

Today my letter-writing program took a severe jolt. This morning I caught up with my laundry because last Sunday was so bad with wind and rain that I couldn't get much done. I also visited the hospital to see how the fellow with ulcers on his leg is getting out. We (Gene Eckerty and I) spent quite a lot of time there and came back too late for evening chow.

Your mention of sirloin steak made my mouth water. We don't get good meat more than about twice a week. However my weight hasn't suffered any and I feel much better than when I first came here. I weigh about 160 lbs. when I subtract about 8 lbs. of clothing. My cough is about gone although I use plenty of handkerchiefs with my catarch.

If I get a chance to check up on Clyde McCaslin I will do so but for the next ten or twelve days I am going to be pretty busy. Next Wednesday we go out on the firing line. Each day we will start out early in the morning and spend all day away from camp. We get back late each night, clean our guns and get ready for the next days firing.

About the thumb latch. I know it seems fantastic but it is very difficult to get much done around here. Some of the boys complained to their sergeant about a leaky roof and the sergeant laughed and told them to report it to the chaplain. In other words the old brush-off. So I thought that if you could get a latch it would save us a lot of headaches. I still have an extra tute of Molle- shaving cream so I won't need any more for a long time. Did you say chocolate cake? Holy Smokes! I'm slobbering.

Last night I saw Dave Moore over at the PX and he promised to find out about his program. I will let you know as soon as we can get our heads together on something definite.

I wish I could put my hands on your tummy and keep it nice and warm while you are going through the pip, then I could snuggle up close and kiss your shoulders and neck.

All my love sweetheart and take good care of yourself.

Chad

Sunday, October 3, 1943

My dearest snuggle-bunny:

By this time I feel as guilty as hell because I certainly have been a frizzle as a letter writer. I even broke my promise to try to get in a letter before we went out on the firing range. As for getting my absentee ballot filled out and set that was just a pipe dream of mine. We all have been busier than the proverbial one-armed paperhanger. Last Tuesday we had to get our rifles ready and full field packs made for going out Wednesday. Bright and early Wed. A.M. we started out for Defendam Range (about 1 1/2 rules out) and were ready to shoot just as the sun was coming up. I was in the 10th or last order of firing so was not scheduled to shoot until that afternoon. Sgt. Shepherd put me on the firing line all morning picking up empty cartridges. I had to walk up and down right behind the men who were firing and bend over, as one corporal says, "keeping my ass up and my head down." Each time a rifle went off you get the blast of the concussion and the fumes from the burning gun powder. By that afternoon I had a splitting headache, the first I've had in a long time. You remember my bilious headaches. I went up to fire my rifle and made out pretty well with a score of 88 which is more than qualifying . I didn't care whether I hit the target or not because I wanted to get away as far as possible. I was quite surprised though to find that the rifle doesn't kick as much as some shot guns.

Thursday we went out to Miller's Hill and ran our asses off learning more about open squad formations. Fortunately we haven't had to change into our sun-tans because during the time the company is on the firing range we don't have any retreat formation.

Friday we went out on the range and finished our practice shots. I had a much easier day because I was called up to shoot early and loaded ammunition clips in the P.M. So I wasn't around the firing line very long. My total for Wed. and Friday was 157 out of a possible 200. This considered as fair or a marksmanship rating.

Saturday was a fairly easy day except for one period of hand-to-hand combat. Just to show us how soft we were the instructor let us go at it for 1 1/2 minutes. At the end of a minute my partner I were ready to quit. We were gasping for air. When I am in good condition I will probably be able to keep it up for 2-3 minutes. We are learning different holds which are handy to know in case you come up against a man bigger than you.

Today I slept and luxuriated in bed until 6:00 a.m. I did my laundry and cleaned my rifle. We do our laundry on the wooden floor racks of the shower room. You get under the shower, wet your clothing and put in a pile. In the meantime about 8 other fellows are doing the same. You spread your towel or what have you on the floor rack, soap it and scrub it with a stiff brush. When finished you rinse out your clothes and hand them behind the hut on a string which you put up yourself. While the clothes are drying you look out occasionally to see that no misbegotten son of a vandal steals your socks or undershirts. These two articles seem to cause the most difficulty here. We can't buy work socks in the supply room or in the PX. If you possibly can get some gray work socks size 11 1/2 it certainly would help a lot. They are, I would judge part wool and part cotton. Cotton socks are absolutely no good for this type of tramp, tamp, tramping because they get wet and bunch up. They are not elastic enough. Also if you could get some white shorts size 30 it would be swell. All they have here at the PX is the athletic type of shorts which creep up and catch a fellow in what our lieutenant calls "the family jewels." Also those jockey shorts are a khaki color. Hell, it makes a fellow think he has done something in his pants!

Tomorrow we go out on the range for the full day. We will be firing off 9 shots in 51 seconds for record. We won't have a second chance so I hope I do half way decently. During the A.M. I will be in the pit detail. That means that we leave camp with full field packs at 6:00 a.m. and set up the targets. The pits are about 10 ft. deep and we have to crane our necks to see what is happening to the target up above the earth bank which protects us. We pull the targets down and use various signals to indicate the score. When a fellow misses the target entirely we call what is known as "Maggie's Drawers" (a red flag.)

Thanks, darling, for the box of stuff. The chocolate cake was damn good. I haven't been into Anniston yet so I would hardly know how civilized people eat. We have a bunch of chow hounds in our company and, as a result, every one who ever had decent table manners now rushes through his meals so as to get enough to eat. Damn it all, I am going to stop complaining about army life. I guess it must be a habit hear so much of it every day. As a matter of fact I have been very fortunate so far because no bad bugs have caught up with me. Yesterday we had our second tetanus injection. There is one more left. So now I have had shots for typhoid, and tentanus and vaccination for small pox.

This afternoon being Sunday we had only one mail call just before mess. Our usual hours during the week days are between 12 to 12:30 p.m. at 6 & 6:30 p.m. I got your letters of September 29th and 30th and from then on the day seemed brighter. I am going to hear from Sergeant Doherty soon about our schedule for November. Probably there will be plenty of hikes during the month but I don't think will have any long bivouacs.

Much later Sunday

Just back to the hut after going down to the main PX for supper. We cleaned our shoes & polished them and made up our full field packs. Tomorrow is a big day so many of boys are going to bed early. Soon lights out will blow.

About the Oxford Book Co. bill for $3.13. I don't recall exactly but it seems to me that I paid the bill this summer & paid it by check. Look in the checks for August. If not then it is a tag-end that I didn't get cleared up. The books are stored in Mary's room.

Good night, my sweet, I have to close this hodge podge of a letter but I will try to write tomorrow night after we get back the hut.

All my love and a nice smacky kiss

from Chad.

Dearest Bedie:

This will have to be a short one because we have only a few minutes before lights out. Today was a tough one even though we didn't go out on the firing line. This A.M. we went puffing up TA 5 to spend a couple of periods learning about the Browning Automatic Rifle. or B.A.R. The Damn thing weighs 21 lbs. and shoots 550 shots per minute. This P.M. we learned how to take the rifle apart and clean it. So in a few days we will have another little piece of machinery to take care of. Also today we had a class in dirty fighting. This consists of a combination of boxing, wrestling and man-slaughter. About the only things barred are gouging, biting and chewing a man's ear off. The boys in our hut don't take very well to this durty fighting and neither do I. I suppose it is due to the years of training in sports and school in playing fair and not taking advantage of the other fellow.

Tomorrow morning we get up bright and early for our last trials with the firing range using the M rifle. So far I have a score of 75 out of a possible 90 which is a fair standing. Next we slow fire at 200, 300, 500 yards.

Right after mail call this evening I had a talk with Sgt. Doherty and he promised definitely to tell me all he could about our schedule for November. I hope he comes through this week.

You mentioned the rationing program. Our chow is getting worse if anything. Today we had no sugar at one meal and for supper we had no bread so if anybody is getting the food it is probably the men in the fighting forces. At that we are better off than the men in either company A or C because today part of Co. A's men had lunch with us and said that our chow is much better than theirs.

Time for lights out my dearest. So all my love and a nice fluttery kiss from Chad.

To my dearest one with
the perky "go-to-hell" hat:

Now I believe what they say about a woman getting a new hat. That green one must be quite a creation. However, as far as I am concerned, the hat or the dress won't mean as much to me as the sweet little body wearing them. Hurry up, Nov.!

This last week has been quite eventful. We finished our work on the range with the M rifle and had our last class on the mechanics of the Browning automatic. I wound up with a final score of 160 or marksman. Don't get excited, however, because marksman's medals are a dime a dozen in the army. In order to qualify you have to get a score of at least 140. If you don't qualify you are call a bolo. I just missed sharpshooter by 5 points. I don't feel badly (sour grapes maybe) because it might be embarrassing later if some officer looks at my record. If I were a sharpshooter (160-180) or an expert (180-210) he could say that I would be needed in the Infantry and I certainly don't want to be an infantryman. I wouldn't mind being attached to the Infantry in a medical unit or something of that sort.

Thursday we stayed around camp and had classes in the B.A.R., Map making etc. Friday the whole company hiked with light packs out to Miller's Hill where we had classes and practical work in laying and sapping for anti-tank mines. When you sap for mines, you crawl along, bugging the ground, and poke a bayonet or knife into the ground until you strike metal. You have to be careful that you don't poke straight up and down because you might set off the fuze of the mine. Fortunately we had practice mines which had no TNT in them, but if you poked a fuze it would go with a flash and throw a lot of dirt around. Needless to say the boys were very careful.

Yesterday the whole company had a rough day. We stayed in camp and went through the "Blitz" course. We had to climb walls and scaffolds, jump ditches, crawl under barbed wire and fall on our faces. I went through OK until the last obstacle. After crawling under barbed wire, scrunching along on my back, I got up and had to run through a series of shallow pits and then flop on a dirt bank. I flopped all right but landed on a board or something hard because I banged my right knee. It threw me off stride for the rest of the day but it is much better today. I was more fortunate than some because 32 of the boys were casualties with 13 of them in the hospital. Oh, I forget, on Friday, we went into foxholes out at Miller's Hill and had a 14 ton light tank run over us. We curled up at the bottom of the holes and in most cases the tread of the tank rumbled right over the top of the hole. I wasn't looking up so I can't say whether the tank went over my hole or not. Some of the boys had dirt thrown on them by a couple of the playful officers.

Today has been the usual thing with laundry and letter-writing, including letters to Lois, Dad & Mom, Ralph & Ruth, Van Miller etc.

Sgt. Doherty says that Oct. 29th we go out for 14 days on bivouac. That means I will be back in camp the 12th of Nov. Then we have a week to get rested and cleaned up and we go out again. That is as much information as I can get right now and I hope nothing prevents us having that week of Nov. 12th. If it does I'll blow my top off. I don't think I will have too much trouble getting over-night passes because so far, (fingers crossed), I haven't been gigged for any lapses. I hope my good luck holds.

My dear, I dream of holding your white little body in my arms and caressing you from head to foot. It's awfully hard to keep from dreaming and longing for you during the day-time.

I went down to see Dave this P.M. and we agreed to go down to Anniston next weekend (probably Sunday P.M.) to make reservations at the U.S.O. Club for rooms at some private home. I will see him again during the week and make more definite plans about going in to the big town.

Tomorrow we go for our first over-night hike with full field pack. We will go over Bain's Gap which is a slope about 3 miles long into the Talladega Forest area. We will come back sometime Tuesday. I will try to see Dave and write you again during the middle of the week.

This letter is rather jumbled up because I put it down and picked it up again at least six times.

I just remembered some unfinished business. One I think was the subject of garnets. The garnets over in Redding Glen are of very poor quality because they crack up very easily. The best ones around here are found to the north. I think it is Roxbury.

Quite a few of the boys have shower slippers made with wooden soles and web straps across the top. I tried to get some down here but haven't been successful so far. They would be handy because there is a lot of dirt tracked into the dressing room next to the showers and it is easy to get dirt all over your bare feet. I am afraid those rope-soled shoes would be to cumbersome and would mildew because I would have to put them into my foot-locker during the day. We are not allowed to have any slippers etc. under our beds only our extra shoes.

I can get plenty of towels and wash cloths at the PX so don't worry about them. I certainly was glad to hear that you were able to get those sox. They will be a big help. I'm sorry you tramped up and down Danbury's shopping section looking for stuff for me.

The watch is going like a top. I damn near had a fit the other day. During Calisthenics I slipped the watch off my wrist and put in my watch pocket. Somehow the thing slipped down inside my pants and held in place by my leggings. I got back the the hut, missed the watch, searched frantically for it, then took my leggings off and found it.

You can bet that I take special care to feel for my watch now when I take it off. I keep it in my jacket breast pocket which has a flap and a strong button.

Good-night, my sweet, a nice hard smack on your lips, then a gentle little nip at that point on your upper lip, then a fluttery kiss, then to lay out full length on you with my love throbbing inside of me and my passion pounding through my ramrod right up tight between your legs and pressed against that "nicest little place you ever saw to put one." I've got to stop now or the boys will hear an explosion going off here in this corner. I love you, my dear, and I'll never tire of telling you.

Chad

Dearest Bedie:

The big package arrived today and I certainly was glad to get it. Those sox were just the ticket. The bread, jelly, and peanut butter not to mention those candies just hit the spot. Now I feel better about the laundry situation. The rubber-soled bath sandals are just the thing I need because the shower room floor gets pretty dirty.

I received Dad's package of cookies and certainly appreciated them. They went will with my nightly snack of ice cream from the PX.

Well, we dragged our fannies in about 8:30 p.m. from Bain's Gap. Having hurt my knee last week on the obstacle course, I was able to get a ride out in the truck with the supplies. We were crammed into the truck with our rifles sticking out over the tail-board and set out hell-bent-for- election. Since most of the roads are Alabama red clay the dust was something terrific. Our rifles were filthy. Our bivouac area was in a pine forest and the rest of the boys pulled in about 9:30 p.m. We dug our slit trenches and pitched our pup tents. It was quite cold and the ground was pretty hard but I managed to get about five hours sleep. Some of the fellows didn't get much sleep.

Yesterday we went out and dug some fox holes. A fox hole is about 3'x3'x5' (deep). The unfortunate part was that none of the officers bothered to come around to inspect them when they were finished but they gave the order to fill them up again.

During the afternoon we went out and ran a compass course. Our squad was complemented on its map (guess who drew it). After that we had two classes on writing a military message. Then we had chow and rested for a while. About 6:30 p.m. with a full moon coming up we started back. We kept going up, up, and up. We had a 10 minute break, then we went over the crest and started down. We went down for about 3 miles then hit the home stretch. When we got back I was too pooped to even start a letter.

You spoke about looking for the rope-soled shoes. I think that they got so warped that I must have thrown them away.

Take your time with those shorts, my dear, because I can make out nicely with what I have now. I will launder these I have myself so they won't get lost in our company laundry. Just send a few pairs along when you can and I will let you know when I need the rest. Don't get kinks in your back cutting and sewing. You have a tough enough time working over those machines in the bank.

We are now officially in the sixth week of our basic training since they don't count the time spent at Devens. Six Millennia? My dearest, it seems like something you dream about. That weekend at home certainly is far off.

Dave Moore is out on bivouac because everything is very quiet over in Co. D. I think they went out to Bain's Gap. If they did they ought to be dragging in any time right now. It is blowing hard and raining. Tough situation (the army expression is T.S. or tough shit)

I'll try to see Dave just as soon as I can and make arrangements for going into Anniston to reserve rooms for your stay.

Boy! Every time I think of it, I get tingly all over. Right now I'm sitting on something very hard which would fit nicely inside that fur collar you mentioned. A million kisses and all my love,

Chad

Dearest Petunia:

This is a hurried note to bring a little news. This A.M. we have a little time.

15 minutes later - we had to fall out to pledge part of our pay for the War Chest Appeal. By the way, my pay for last month was $4.87 although I don't need much money down here. If I spend 25 cents in one day that is about average.

I didn't get a chance to write last Sunday because Dave and I were in Anniston all day. We went to the U.S.O. and they couldn't help us with rooms until the first of Nov. It seems that the people of Anniston don't like to reserve their rooms very far ahead. So probably Dave will have to do the reserving of the rooms because I think I will be on bivouac. At the U.S.O. they seemed pretty certain that they could get what we wanted.

Yesterday we were on the range firing our M' carbines. They are small rifles of 30 caliber and are pretty accurate up to 300 yards. Last night we went out to Defendam Range where we had a demonstration of effective machine gun fire. It was quiet a show.

In a few minutes we will be going through the infiltration course which means we crawl under barbed wire with machine gun fire directed over our heads. It's pretty safe because the bullets are about a yard over our heads.

This noon we set out with full field packs for Bain's Gap where we will spend tonight and most of tomorrow. I will try to write Wed. night.

All my love, sweetheart.

Chad

Wednesday 9:55 p.m.
October 20, 1943

Dearest Bedie:

Tuesday and Wednesday have been two busy days. After going through the infiltration course we came back to camp and got ready for Bain's Gap. The infiltration course wasn't so bad but was very tiring. We crawled for about 85 yards on our bellies with our rifles and bare bayonets. Where there were curtains of barbed wire we had to crawl on our backs. All the time we had machine gun fire overhead. Occasionally the gunners would set off TNT blasts to simulate grenades and nearly every one was covered with mud from them. When we finished the course we had to get up and charge at and bayonet some burlap dummies.

Out at Talladega Forest we pitched our tents and dug our slit trenches. That night we ran a compass course of about a thousand yards. Our patrol was one of the first ones in so we were chosen for the honor of standing guard duty until late. We shivered and shook for an hour and a half and when we were relived we stumbled back into the bivouac area where there were no lights. I had a hell of a time finding my tent. Finally I settled down to rest on the cold hard ground. About 1:30 a.m. I was so cold with one blanket and a raincoat that I and my tent mate put our two blankets together and lay back to back to keep warm. Today we spent most of the day tramping the hills and after supper headed back for camp. We got back about 9:00 p.m. and shaved and showered. The beds in camp feel like the Ritz compared with Bain's Gap.

Your two letters were delivered out at Bain's Gap. The chow truck brought out the mail. Two bright spots in a long dreary day!

The bread, jelly and peanut butter arrived in A' condition. They were a swell treat. In fact several of the boys cast such longing eyes on them that I made them some sandwiches.

Today I heard some rumors from boys in Company D that gave me the Heeby-jeebies. They told us that some of their fellows wanted to bring their wives down for a while in the middle of November and their lieutenant told them not to make any plans because the whole 25th Battalion would probably be shipped out of McClellan by then. One thing that makes me suspicious is that our company is being rushed along and right now has reached the climax of it's training. I'm keeping my finger crossed. I don't want to worry you needlessly but I know you want to know which way the wind is blowing.

Most of this note has been written by the light of two little night lights one of my buddies has plugged in here in a wall socket. I'm propped up in bed on one elbow scribbling away.

I'm pretty tires and sleepy so I'll close with a pat on your fanny to let you know I want you to roll over on your back. Then I want to lay between your legs with my face on your breast and both hands full of nubbins. Then to creep up a little farther and give you a nice kiss all fluttery. Then to feel your hands grasping my ramrod and helping made an inspection that would end with a flood of love and lingering good-night kisses from your loving husband.

Chad

Sunday, 7:45 p.m.
October, 24, 1943

Dearest Petunia:

Today has certainly been a long drawn-out affair. I was gigged yesterday by our executive officer for having what he called a dirty rifle. I spent about three hours on the damned thing and later when I asked our platoon sergeant to look at it, he said it was O.K. Today I found out that they needed a list of men for dirty work so I guess I was one of the many elected. I had to work in the mess hall most of today so I didn't get much time to sit down and catch up on my correspondence.

Friday we went out on the range to shoot at moving targets and when we came back they read a list of men for guard duty. Sure enough, I was elected. With 15 minutes to prepare for it we picked our asses over to the guard house and got our assignments. I was on the first relief from 5-7 p.m. and 11:00 p.m. - 2 a.m. It wasn't too bad because I was able to get some sleep but walking my post was a cold job.

An interruption. One of the boys just told a good one. He said that rape is impossible because a woman with her dress up can run faster than a man with his pants down. Gave me a good laugh and how I need one.

The package of shorts arrived safely and they certainly look super. Many, many thanks.

I saw Dave Moore right after coming from mess hall and he said that he had a way of getting into Anniston if things got too tough. He also told me that about half of Company D was gigged this weekend. The officers seem to be getting tougher all along the line.

Next week we go out to Bain's Gap for two days. I hope the nights aren't too damned cold. I seem to feel the cold more down here than I ever did at home or while up to Colgate where it went to 30 degrees below. I guess it must be the dampness.

I hope I didn't scare you with my note about the infiltration course. It wasn't really so bad because later we got a chance to see the machine guns from the rear. They were firing way above the heads of the fellows crawling along. A man would have to lose his head completely and jump up full length in order to be in the line of fire.

I've got to close this scribbling and get ready for tomorrow. I'll try to write a better letter tomorrow night if I get the chance.

Lots of kisses and dreams of our meeting again which can't come too soon.

Chad

Tuesday, P.M.
postmarked October 27, 1943

Dearest Bedie:

Just a few lines tonight during free time because by the looks of the schedule there won't be much chance to even get near pen and paper. Tomorrow we go out on the range for practice in shooting at landscape targets and using fire orders. Thursday, P.M. we start out for Bain's Gap and Talladega Forest where we will bivouac until Saturday. While out there we will luxuriate in a bed made on the ground with a raincoat and two blankets. This time we will probably have plenty of marching during the day and guard duty at night. At 3:30 a.m. Saturday we pull down our tents, make full field packs and haul our asses back over the Gap to camp.

Today we were out on the range shooting at moving targets with the Browning automatic rifle. The whole thing was a waste of ammunition because we rushed through the thing and, of course, the B.A.R. shoots so damned fast that you fire off a magazine in short order. After a few days of marching and bivouac we probably will start in on the light machine gun and the mortar.

I have been wading through the letter from the teachers and was very much interested in the school activities. Please explain to Elsa Grace and Cliff that I have a hard enough time keeping up my correspondence with you so, if I get a break Sunday and don't draw table waiter's job the way I did last Sunday, I'll try to get some letters off.

This A.M. we went through the bayonet course jumping ditches and jabbing dummies. I think, however, that we are pretty well caught up on our bayonet work. I hope so, because learning the bayonet is one of the most difficult things in army training.

I forgot to mention that my pay for October was $4.87 because we had to pay insurance rates for three months in order to get caught up. Counting the allotment and laundry charges that brought it out about right. However, my next pay will be more because they will take out only one month's insurance rates.

Several of the boys are having their wives down to visit and are having trouble getting rooms. Dave and I are going to get on the ball this weekend, if we aren't gigged, and see what we can do in Anniston. Sergeant Doherty has left us to go to a non-coms school so we have a new platoon sergeant. I am going to talk to him and see whether I can get more information about our November activities. The other day the non-coms. were talking about our final maneuvers from Dec. 2nd to Xmas. This will just about finish our training. Oh, happy day!

The new socks and shorts are working very well and certainly have saved me a lot of head aches.

I'll stop now because I have to clean up my mess kit for tomorrow.

Lots of kisses, my dear, and plenty of happy dreams of nicer kisses to come.

Chad

Sunday, October 31, 1943

Dearest little sassy-pants:

Here writes one of the poopedest guys in Fort McClellan. As I told you we started out for Talladega Forest over Bain's Gap Thursday afternoon with full field packs. Only this time our packs included an extra blanket and our overcoats. The whole pack weighs about 60 pounds and certainly cuts into the shoulders. After walking (excuse me, marching) for several miles the bones of the feet begin to spread out under the weight. We set up our tents in the bivouac area we used before. Since the maneuver was tactical we had to race against time and light conditions. After supper we went on a night compass problem followed by a stumbling march through the woods back to our bivouac area where we slept three to a tent. I was chosen to awaken the first detail at 5:15 a.m. We went out to meet the chow truck and carried the big pots of food back to the mess area.

Friday we went through a series of problems out in the field. To top it off we went out on guard duty. We pulled in about 10:30 p.m., rolled up in our coats and one blanket, since we had been told to be ready to pull out Sat. a.m. with full packs we had one blanket rolled up inside our shelter half. We awoke at 3:30 a.m. and pulled out for Bain's Gap after eating breakfast in the dark. We got back into camp a little after 8:00 a.m. Gratefully we slipped off our packs and had our feet inspected. I had no blisters but the soles of my feet certainly were sore.

Today Dave and I went out to Anniston and tried to get rooms. We got the same answer. "Come back later." So we are going in Wed. night if possible and according to what the girl at the U.S.O. Club said we ought to have some success.

Just heard a good joke, probably you have heard it before. A Jew was told by a New York specialist that he had a bad case of Rheumatism and that the only cure was to take salt water baths. Immediately the Jew started out for Atlantic City. The next morning he went down to the beach looked at the nice high tide and stuck a toe in to experiment. It was terribly cold so he had the happy idea of getting a pail of water and taking it back to his hotel where it was warmer. An Irish policeman saw him and decided to have some fun so he asked the Jew what he was doing. The Jew explained his sad story. The policeman said, "Well in that case, that bucket of water will cost you twenty-five cents "The Jew tearfully paid and returned to the hotel where be bathed. That afternoon he returned to the beach for more water. However it was low tide and the Jew couldn't believe his eyes so he jumped up and down and shouted, "Mein Gott, vat a business!" Corny, eh? But that is what army life is doing to me. Saturday A.M. when I reached the top of Bain's Gap which by the way, is a climb of over 1500 feet, I was somewhat hysterical. The least little thing that was funny would give me the greatest belly laughs. I suppose i was worn down pretty close the last notch.

Back to business. The rubber-soled slippers are proving to be a great help. They are a little short but certainly keep my feet clean and off the muddy floor.

I am glad Francis Martin found that stuff up at Ridgefield School. Of course, I have a print of the football picture but I was surprised that some one like Jessup hadn't taken the list of Valedictorians. Save that plaque if you can.

The Press is coming regularly as is Life magazine. Both are swell but Life Magazine presents a problem. Do you want me to save them? My space is very restricted so if you want to keep our files intact I will have to mail them back to you. Otherwise I will present them to the Day Room where the boys go to read papers and write letters.

You asked about A.S.T.P. I was called in for an interview along with a lot of other fellows. I had checked Foreign Languages and Medicine as my choices. First they asked me if I could speak French or Italian like a native. I said "No sir, only a good reading knowledge of the languages." Then they asked if I had a letter from an accredited medical school, to which I had to say, "No." So that was that. However I haven't lost hope.

Thank George Rockwell for me but don't let him squeeze your elbow I appreciate the fact that he was thinking of me, however.

If you want to send me anything to eat you could send Milk crackers, Salteens, or something along that line. They make good snacks. Of course jellies are out of the question, now they are rationed but maybe you could manage some more peanut butter.

I just had good news. Some of the fellows were asking me about my trip to Anniston. I reported my bad luck so one of them told me about the Anniston Auto Court just south of the main part of the city. It is a tourist camp with cabins that sound pretty good. They have beds with inner spring mattresses and are equipped with running water. They cost about $2.00 per day. This fellow said that they were very clean. If Dave and I can't manage to get rooms in private homes in Anniston when we go in this week we will go out to the Auto Court and see what we can do. The hotels, of course are out of the question because they charge $5.50 per day for fair rooms and small town service. I hate to keep things up in the air this way but you can realize what a problem it is near a camp of over $50,000 men.

Our program seems to have been changed for November. Instead of spending a long time out on bivouac we probably will have over-night hikes each week. This won't be too bad if we don't get too much of Bain's Gap. About the only definite things for the present seem to be our training in use of the light machine gun and mortar and as far as I know, our maneuvers from December 2nd to just before Xmas.

It's time for light out (9:00 p.m.) so I'll quit now. Oh, I forgot about your question concerning what clothes to bring with you. The days are fairly warm and pleasant except for spells of windy weather. The nights are quite cool so it would be a good idea to bring some warm clothes for evening. Of course, during many of the evenings you won't need any clothing because I'll furnish you with a nice internal heating system which has a good safety valve. I'll hold you real tight and keep you from getting cold. Preliminaries to installation of the heating system will be several thousand nice lingering kisses between your two little nubbins with a proper clasp on the tops of the round white hills. Then a trip down across the valley of your soft little tummy. Then a tour around the nicest place to put one and down your thighs to the dimples on your knees. Then to spread your legs apart and make a tour upward with the steam knocking on the pipes of the heating system. After installation a full head of steam would rapidly be reached. Then the explosion of the safety valve and a blissful give and take of love until my sweetheart gets sleepy and cuddles up in my arms.

Your heating engineer,

Chad

Sunday, November 7, 1943

Dearest Petunia:

I hope this gets home before you leave for Anniston although the telegram outlines the main idea of what happened today.

Things have been pretty hectic here. The main reason seems to be that we are going to have a general's inspection on Nov. 18th. Our entire battalion has been buzzing with preparation. Various details have been painting the latrine, digging ditches, sweeping streets etc. probably during the week the tempo of preparations will be stepped up. Also we have another trip out to Bain's Gap to look forward to.

Friday we went out to Miller's Hill where we pitched our tents. After supper we went out by moonlight on night patrol. We had to follow an Azimuth of 3 degrees through the fields and woods without being discovered by the instructors who had hidden themselves in our path. Saturday morning we spent several hours taking tests on various phases of our individual training. About 10:00 a.m.

We made our full field packs and ran a rat race back to camp to be in time for chow. Sat. P.M. we had two hours of mortar and two hours of light machine gun.

This morning I did my washing of my socks, leggings and cartridge belt. This P.M. I went up and got a pass to go into Anniston. It had been raining hard most of the morning se we had to wear our raincoats. We went into the U.S.O and interviewed the agent for the Traveler's aid. She gave us a good lead which we followed out. The house is fairly small but clean and is on the side of Anniston toward camp. Mrs. Guy McClure of 2216 Gurnee Ave. is the place. She is a very fine type of woman from Texas. The woman at the U.S.O. said that Mrs. McClure is reluctant to rent her rooms for a week or more but that she may be persuaded to relent and rent the rooms for longer than four or five days. The rooms are neat and clean and the beds seem to be all right. The only disadvantage is that the bath is at the rear of the second bed room and anyone in the front room would have to go through the rear room to get to it. However I don't believe this will cause any difficulty. Boy I certainly am looking forward to lying in that bed with you.

Dave and I decided to send the telegram so that we wouldn't be caught short. I am not sure whether we will be able to get in Thursday because we may have a hike out to Bain's Gap planned. Either Dave or I will try to phone Thursday afternoon. Then we may be able to meet you in town or at the Service Club. It is best not to call the Orderly room of Company B because that phone is usually used for company business.

Sweetheart, I can hardly wait until I see you again. I long for the time when I can take you in my arms again and tell you how much I love you. Then I can carry out that little act you like so well. I'll conduct a personal strip tease session after which I will gently let you down on a nice soft bed. Then to do all the thousand and one things I have wanted to do for so long.

Good night, sweetheart, and all my love.

Chad

November 10, 1943
from Pvt. Fred Drager

Hello Mr. Crouchley,

I don't know whether or not you remember me, but I was in your home room and class in 1940. I think you called me Alfred. I have been in the Army about 9 months and just recently came over to the Hawaiian Islands where I am still stationed. I suppose most or all of the fellows I went to school with there are in some branch of the Armed forces. I liked my English teacher very much, but can't think of her name, ditto my French teacher. Will you please give them my best regards and ask them to write if possible? My regards also to Mrs. Kasper. How are things going with you? I'm in the best of health, but of course looking forward to the day I can once again go home.

I liked the school very much while I was there and hated to leave when I did. Give my best regards to all, especially the lad whose father is a patrolman. I'm not sure whether he's still there. Name is Pete. Take care of yourself and write.

Sincerely,
Fred

Dearest Kutsie Bug:

Since you left I have had difficulty in collecting my thoughts and emotions to write you a letter that will make sense. When Dave and I went back to camp we stopped at the Service club I wrote a short letter to Mother and Dad because I knew I couldn't adequately express myself. I wrote them about camp life, the weather and a lot of impersonal topics. Monday and Tuesday were busy days. Tuesday we took a hike out to Miller's Hill with full field pack. We had some problems dealing with raiding parties until about 9:00 p.m. then we started on the run for camp going full tilt. We all arrived pooped out and had coffee and cinnamon buns. Today I was on detail delivering groceries for Thanksgiving. The detail is called the Ration Bread-down. I was on the truck delivering eggs, tomatoes, grapes and lettuce. We stopped at 35 different mess halls. It certainly was tiring to work in a stooped position inside the truck. By the looks of the rations that were handed out the boys are going to eat well tomorrow. There will be turkey with dressing, potatoes and turnips, pumpkin pie, nuts, raisins and hard candy. As a special feature, the officers and their wives are going to eat with us. So the boys will be on their best behavior. Just before dinner we are having a parade. After dinner we are going to have movies. A fairly easy day by the looks except for the men on K.P. and table waiter.

I haven't seen Dave for very long since Sunday. I guess Dave has been pretty busy with night problems, hikes etc. I certainly envied him the chances he had to come into Anniston. I'll never forget the times I did get a chance to come into town to see you. All the dreams we had of being in each other's arms couldn't equal the real thing.

Here I go ending with the same old excuse lights out. Lots of love and them some.

Chad

Sunday, November 28th, 1943

Dearest Petunia:

It has been a busy Sunday with laundry and letter writing. I have been catching up a bit with back correspondence. I wrote Leve and Ralph to Ruth and probably will have a chance to write some more before the day is over. Since Tuesday or Wednesday we will be going out on maneuvers at Morrisville I won't have much chance to write anyone for the next two weeks. Tonight after chow I was over to the PX getting some Pall Malls and was just coming out as a battalion was marching in from Morrisville. They certainly looked pooped out.

We will be out two weeks and will hike about twenty miles to get there. We will carry full field packs with shelter half, tent pole and pegs, two blankets, mess kit and shovel, overcoat, extra pair of shoes, toilet articles, extra suit of fatigues and steel helmet. I think we will be allowed to have fires at night to keep our pup tents warmed up. During the day or night we will have problems dealing with the training of the individual soldier. Part of the schedule calls for an attack on the German Village where we will be fired on by snipers. After returning from Morrisville we will rest up for three days and then will wind up with a week out at Talladega Forest. I hope this will be my chance to spit on Bains Gap for the last time. When we get back from Talladega we will probably be in time for Xmas. Then we clean up our equipment and get ready for shipping.

The day we got back from a demonstration of the machine gun, I think it was Friday, our officers announced that the Air Corps and A.S.T.P. have been closed for the time being. Since meteorology comes under the A.S.T.P. it looks as though the whole lot of us are slated for the infantry. However we won't know much about our classification until after maneuvers.

I am enclosing the V-mail letter from Fred Drager. I remember him in my classes in 1940 but since the letter refers to several of the teachers it might be a good idea to contact them. The English teacher he mentions is probably May Boland and the French teacher is probably Ruth Wills.

I am going to write to Frank T. Hines about the change of name. I will take care of it before we go out on maneuvers.

I'll have to get back to cleaning up for tomorrow so I'll break off.

All my love, sweetheart, with a thousand kisses on your sweet lips and lots of snuggling with your loving husband.

Chad

Monday, November 29th, 1943

Dearest Petunia:

I am dashing off this short note just before lights out because tomorrow will probably be pretty hectic with preparations for going out to Morrisville.

We are going to be allowed to take our comforters in a big roll. Each squad is making up a roll to go out on a truck. So we won't have to add them to the already enormous load we will be carrying.

Today we were told to turn in our O.D. overseas caps to be garnished with the blue piping of the Infantry. So it begins to look even more like the Infantry. However time will tell.

While we are on maneuvers we will have mail call every four days as far as we know now. I will try to get off some notes to you while I am out there. If they won't take in-going mail I'll have to wait until I get back.

At any rate, wish me luck sweetheart, and accept a great big kiss with all my love.

Chad

Sunday, December 5, 1943

Dearest Poultry Expert:

I am writing this from the prone position inside a 4 man pup tent. So far maneuvers have been quite a grind. We spent 4 days in one Bivouac where we went through the German village and had squad tactics and field firing. Last night we moved to another area. So far the weather has been pretty wet. I took a bath this P.M. in a little creek nearby. The Water was plenty cold! Thanksgiving back at camp is now a very pleasant memory. The brief case you mentioned must belong to someone else. Give my love to the family. Tell mother Bedient to take good care of herself and you do the same.

Love,

Chad

December 15, 1943
Wednesday Night

Dearest Bedie:

Well, I made it back to camp! 18 1/2 miles in about 6 hours in the rain. We all were cold and pooped out with feet so numb that we couldn't feel very much. We showered and got the bark off then went out and bought a good meal. Then to blessed bed.

Today was hectic with cleaning rifles and inspection. At mail call I got the package from Ralph and Ruth. While out on Bivouac I got packages from Francis and Daisey and Lyme and Ruth. They certainly were appreciated.

This P.M. we had classes out in the cold. Then we had "pecker parade" (I don't remember whether I have mentioned this before but it is a delightful army custom in which the soldier shows his pecker to an army doctor to see whether he is OK or not).

Also the officers have started talking about shipping out. I suppose after our next bivouac which starts next Saturday we will be moved out to regular Army units. Classifications have been pretty well completed by now and soon we will know what lies in store for us.

Well, the corporal just bawled us out for having lights on so I'll have to quit. I'll try to write tomorrow. All my love and lots of kisses.

Chad

December 25, 1943
Xmas P.M.

Dearest Bedie:

Sixteen weeks are over! Whoopee! Only one more to go. Though our cycle is not over yet there is a great feeling of relief, knowing that there will be no more bivouac at Morrisville or Talladiga and only hikes which return to camp are left. Now I have that off my chest. Here's a great big hug and a kiss for Christmas season. Some fellows were able to dash off short notes while on bivouac but I still don't understand how they did it. So my humble apologies for not keeping up my correspondence better. In the last four weeks we haven't spent more than four or five nights in our own beds back in camp but have been sleeping on the ground out at Morrisville or Talladega. Now to be more coherent and start from where I left off in my last letter (ages ago). After spending three days back in camp after Morrisville. (By the way, we had been told that we would have a lot of free time during those three days but were busier than the devil) we set out once more with full field packs for good old Bain's Gap. This time we were not allowed to have our comforters put in the squad rolls to be taken out by truck but were allowed to have two extra blankets making three per person. We didn't go very far into the Talladega section (only two or three miles above the little blanket of White Plains.) We pitched our tents in the late morning and had chow. During the P.M. we dug our slit trenches and camouflaged our tents etc. Some of us heaped up pine needles and hay. Don Condon and I bunked together and we had two blankets under us and four over us. A couple of nights we had the use of two extra blankets of one of the boys who was confined to quarters back in camp. The nights were pretty cold and a couple were windy. We were allowed to have a big bonfire for the entire company and usually I managed to get my chest or my rear end toasted before going to bed. I slept in my stocking feet and was fairly warm but after walking around for a while in the morning there were frost crystals on the course grass and weeds that grow in this section.

We usually were up in the dark at 0600 and got under way by 0730. The first three days we worked on 16 problems having to do with all the various phases of our training. A lot of the boys already had bad coughs or colds (including myself) and so we weren't too peppy.

The last days up until Friday, were spent on a company problem. This carried out the idea of a continuous movement of men from one terrain feature to another. We used the attack defense, and withdrawal phases. When we had taken and given up the hills for the last time we withdrew. Five of our meals were C ration consisting of two cans of food. The first contains 3 candies, some whole wheat crackers or biscuits and a beverage I really liked with cold water was cocoa although they say the coffee is swell with hot water. The second can contains either hash (beef and some pork, carrots, potatoes etc.) or boiled beans with beef and pork. The portions are large but don't seem to furnish the terrific amount of body heat needed. Speaking of cold, of course, the reason for such unusual temperatures is partly the altitude. When you are in the Talladego section you are surrounded by mountains. As a matter of fact, in going over the famous Gap you go from 920 ft. above sea level to over 2000 ft. and some of the nearby mountains are 2500 or close to 3000 ft.

We came back to camp Friday A.M. and had lunch at camp. That P.M. we began the process of getting rid of hair, beards and dirt. I looked like something out of the wild west and had quite a time getting back to human decency. That night it was bitterly cold and we certainly were thankful that we weren't on bivouac. This A.M. when we awoke we were doubly thankful because it was raining like hell and blowing a gale and the temperature had dropped so that ice was forming on the ground. We dressed in our O.D.'s for Xmas and awaited developments. Finally we were informed that we were going to March down to the Field House to hear dear General Philoon (Lieut. Spitoon, some of the boys call him) who is the commander of the I.R.T.C. we marched down in the rain, listened to the Xmas sermon etc., sang carols etc, but lo and behold, no General. He sent his regrets and best Xmas wishes. We hustled back to our huts, dried out a bit and waited for chow. Our turkey fest was very good and everyone was satisfied. This P.M. I have been cleaning up some of my stuff because this coming week we are going to be told what happens to us and I want to be able to get my things together in a hurry if I have to. A lot of the boys are going to Fort Meade, Md. but, of course, no definite information has been given out. With the R.R.

situation what it is, we may all be herded on to a troop train and shipped en masse to our next unit.

Usually they give you some extra time in which to go on to your home to see your folks so it may be that I will be seeing you before very long. I have enough money to take care of my transportation and as far as I know now the Gov't reimburses you for the expense of shipping to your next unit.

I haven't been getting my hopes up too high because I have finally learned that if you don't expect much you are never disappointed especially where the U.S. Infantry is concerned. But if things do happen so that I can get near home I'll be off like a "big-assed bird" (as the boys say) for dear old Ridgefield and the sweetest blue-eyed little blonde that ever was. I'll make her forget all about the weeks we have been apart and cuddle up to her and keep her warm. I'll kiss her soft eye lids and the little pulsing hollow at the base of her throat. I'll nip her little nose and tips of her ears. I'll burrow into the hollow of her shoulders and cup two nice nubbins in my hands then I'll kiss her little round belly and slide up between her legs with something nice and hard to probe with. Then I'll do what the monk in De Cameron did, "put the devil in hell" for I've a raging fire that's burning in my devil and he's longing to get into hell. I know it has been awfully tough on you, sweetheart, all these dreary weeks but keep up your courage and maybe, if the fates that be are kind, we will be together again before long.

I thought of you constantly this Christmas day and tried to send out to you all my love. I know you understand why I didn't try to phone or telegraph. The offices around camp are swamped and there is so much to be done right here.

I'll sing off now and write more tomorrow. Good night sweetheart, Give my love to the family and wish them good health from me.

You bivouacky husband
Chad

December 27, 1943
Sunday P.M.

Dearest Petunia:

This P.M. I hit the jack pot. Three of your letters in one mail call (Dec. 20th & 22nd). also Xmas cards from Leve and Mary and the Bolands. This A.M. was pretty dark and dreary and those letters were like rays of sunshine.

Everybody was up late this A.M., accumulation of fatigue, I suppose. Very few turned out for breakfast so there was plenty to eat. By now you probably have realized that your husband is a full-fledged chow-hound. I don't know where I get the appetite - After breakfast I got all my laundry together and spent most of the morning in the shower room scrubbing out the dirt and sweat gathered while on maneuvers. Two suits of fatigues, two suits of underwear (one heavy), 15 pairs of socks, 9 handkerchiefs and a bath towel. I used two bars of soap doing it and emerged from the latrine in a triumphant mood. Now I am caught up the laundry situation except for cleaning my web equipment. However I am going to leave that to later because we have more hikes this week. One of the hikes will be a forced march of 24 miles in 8 hours. Probably we will have that about Tuesday.

After dinner I settled down to keep the fire going to dry my clothes and also to write some letters but one of my friends who has been transferred to another battalion came in and told about his experiences on bivouac. He says that his outfit is nowhere near as tough as the 25th. The discipline is easier and the training is much lighter. Now that I have almost finished my basic training I can see that it will mean something in the future to say that I was trained in the 25th Battalion at Fort McClellan. At our Xmas party yesterday our officers and cadre heaped praises upon us and told us that we had completed the toughest training program that had ever been given here. Thank the Lord they don't have much longer to think up things for us to do.

Some of the boys are still trying since yesterday to get calls through to home so I think I was wise though probably inconsiderate in not attempting to phone. It would have been nice to hear your voice again but probably if things work out right we can have that belated New Year's Party you mentioned.

Do you think that you would be a good peter inspector? You would have to sit astraddle a chair and assume a very wise and judicial countenance. I know you could look wise and judicial and could probably straddle a chair but do you think I would stand idly by and let you inspect my peter from a sitting position? Nothing doing. It would have to be in the good old-fashioned way. What the boys would call the inverted prone position. Oh well, I can dream, Can't I?

I suppose by this time the Dapper Dan of Catoonah St. is married. I wonder if he had the same experience as Lord Algy. You remember that joke about the butler saying, "Milord, the trouble seems to be that the Middle is in but the end is out."

Your remarks about Dot and "Fish-eye" Winthrop remind me of the stories about how old Darius used to sneak across the meadows to blow up Maine. I suppose to Dot the stolen sweets taste the best but I'll be damned if I can see how she could bear to be near that slinky S.O.B.

I doubt if I'll have a chance to see Pvt. Cummings because this next week will certainly be a lot like the first week I came here, running around from pillar to post turning in equipment and falling out in the company street every five minutes to hear some officer or non-com. Try to explain in words of two syllables what is going to happen next.

I thought I mentioned receiving the Paul Bunyan package. The mail clerk said that he didn't know how it got through the mails. There is enough there to keep the boys and I nibbling for many evenings. Those socks were a happy thought. They helped to augment my supply for bivouac. And that copy of Esquire! Wow! After examining it minutely I would have been ready for any peter inspection. I could make you yell for mercy.

Your mention of Lou Price certainly has me stumped. The only thing I see is that those maneuvers he is going on are with a regular unit. If his is a P.F.C. or a corporal he must be with a regular unit by now because, strictly speaking, we, who are not through with our basic training, are called trainees and we won't even be called privates until our 17 weeks are up.

I guess I'll break down and buy myself a chauffeur's cap as long as it will please you. Besides being somewhat antagonistic toward them there was the personal problem of finding space enough in a foot locker for one. However, with a little good management, I guess I can find space for me.

Your gluttonous husband hears the chow whistle blowing so I'll sign off with plenty of love and you know what.

Chad

December 31, 1943
Friday P.M.

My dearest wife:

This note cannot make amends for my past neglect, I know, but perhaps I can explain a little of what is happening to me. First let me say that I may have changed my feelings toward everything and everyone but my feelings toward you will never change. The things that have happened to me in the last 17 weeks have made me care very little about what happens. Here, you live from day to day and now that training is drawing to a close we know less and less about our futures.

Yesterday I paid my transportation to New York and back to Washington, D.C. We have to travel on a troop train and we have been told that an airplane is out of the question. We still don't know when we are leaving but we are getting our equipment and some of our clothing turned in to the supply room. Of course the battalion will be pretty well spit up. Some may go out west while others may be shipped east.

Your mention of Dave's letters to Alice while on bivouac certainly puzzles me somewhat. While we were out there we usually got up at six a.m. and didn't get through with our day's work until about 4:30 p.m. This left just about time enough to wash your hands and eat chow. By that time it was dark and if you wanted to write a letter you would have to do it inside your pup tent. I'm sorry, sweetheart, but I wasn't physically capable of doing it. I know I hurt your feelings terribly but please try to understand.

Much later.

I just finished turning in my equipment. Probably tomorrow we will turn in our rifles, bayonets and packs.

After chow the boys had a beer party in the mess hall and some of them are feeling pretty gay. Out sergeant just came in to see us and wish us a Happy New Year. I certainly hope it is one for us both. The happiest moment for me will be when I know this war is over and can walk into your arms and tell you how much I love you.

I received the telegraphic money order of $25. I wrote Dad and Mother and thanked them. Thanks a lot for sending it. It will be handy in case something comes up while I am being shipped. I paid $21.69 yesterday to a company officer for my transportation from here to New York and New York back to Washington.

Several nights I have gone into the telegraphic office to put in a call to you but so many fellows have been ahead of me that I didn't want to risk being away from the company area so long. As things are now fellows are being called right and left to consult about their transportation and shipping orders.

I'll have to quit now, my sweet, to go up and wash my rifle sling, shave and get ready to turn in.

Here's wishing you a Happy New Year with all my love and devotion and the fervent hope that I will be seeing you soon.

Chad

January 17, 1944

Dearest Bedie:

Ed Strait and I had a rugged trip down to Washington. As we went south it seemed to get colder and by the time we arrived in Washington we were very thankful for our overcoats. We took a local train out for Laurel and arrived just as it was getting light. We took a bus over icy roads through rolling country out to Fort Meade. The Fort is very large with hundreds of wooden two-story barracks. We turned in our papers and waited around for an assignment. We had a brief physical exam and then got our barrack assignments. We are now restricted for 72 hours, a sort of quarantine period. I am the only one in the barracks for the 25th Inf. Bn. Although there are many fellows here from the 13th.

Most of them were the fellows in that first car up from McClellan to New York so evidently everything was cut and dried way back several weeks ago.

The atmosphere here is a good deal like that hectic first week at Devens. There is the same uncertainty and desire to get in touch with the folks back home. Of course we all know what Fort Meade is and realize that many of us will probably be sent out of the country before very long. It is a harsh and difficult thing to face but there it is and there is no help for it.

They seem to be quite liberal with weekend passes here and if I am kept on here for a week or more I am going to do my damndest to get to N.Y. The passes are usually issued about 5:00 Saturday P.M. and run until Sunday midnight. The only rub is in making the right train connections so as to get into N.Y. in decent season. We are still trying to figure it out but some of the fellows have train schedules for this line to Laurel and I am going to get more definite information.

If I can work it and am able to get to N.Y. I will phone you and give you some advance warning.

Our parting in N.Y. was tough especially on you who had just got up out of a sick bed. Know my dear, that I love you with all my heart and miss you more than words can tell. I am looking forward to the chance to see you again for a few hours although I don't dare get my hopes up too high and you musn't count on it as a certainty, my sweet, because you know by now what can happen. Here's hoping I can manage.

With all my love
Chad

January 24, 1944

Dearest Bedie:

Sunday night certainly must have been tough on you with all the crowds shoving and pushing to get on the trains. I hope you were able to get a seat. The train going down to Ft. Meade was loaded with service men and even though I went down to the platform early I was just able to get on the platform of one of the cars. I got back to camp with plenty of time to spare and turned in my pass. One of the boys hasn't turned up yet so he is A.W.O.L. that will probably mean more stringent regulations for the rest of us.

Today's program was quite easy. We had two movies, a lecture, some scouting and patrolling, physical training and dismounted drill. Tomorrow will probably be plenty tough. We are going out for a problem involving overhead fire something like the problem I told you about that we had on maneuvers. I spent most of this evening scrubbing my mess equipment, canteen, and canteen cup. They are the devil to get clean when brand new because they have a protective coating over the metal.

There is so much talk around the barracks now about being shipped out that it seems to be the only thought on the fellows' minds. It begins to look now that we will be alerted soon so our hopes of another week-end together don't look too good. However I plan to phone you Thursday or Friday, most likely it will be Friday.

Personally, I have a feeling in my bones that we aren't going to be around Ft. Meade much longer. As the week progresses we will begin to know more about it so my rambling are just a lot of conjecturing.

I am looking forward to getting a letter telling me how you are after the strenuous week-end. All my love, sweetheart. Take good care of yourself and get as much rest and sleep as you can. Excuse the sloppy writing. I am perched on my bunk with the fellow up above jiggling around. Must sign off. I have to shave the "whiskers" off my ugly mug.

Love

Chad

January 25, 1944

Dearest Bedie:

More scribbling to let you know that I came through the overhead firing problem all in one piece with the exception of a bump on the knee which will be OK in a couple of days. We marched out of camp about five miles in an hour and a quarter with no breaks. The ground was frozen hard so we made good time. After getting out there an officer explained the problem which was an infantry attack on an enemy position with the support of all the different kinds of weapons, 60 mm and 81 mm mortars, light and heavy machine guns and 105 mm howitzers. During the morning we had a practice run of the problem then moved back into the woods where we built fires and laid around until chow. After chow we went back waited until 3:30 p.m. About three or four regiments of men marched out to see us run the problem. At 3:30 we started out as skirmishes and moved up to our line in short rushes. On the last rush I was hitting the ground OK when I slipped sideways and landed on my right knee. It hurt like the devil for a while but fortunately we had reached a point where we were supposed to lay low for a while. By the time the mortars, machine guns and howitzers ceased fire my knee felt better. The ground had thawed out by this time and the mud was ankle deep. To complete the problem four tanks went through our lines and attacked the hill. We followed and "took the hill."

One of the boys from B Company at McClellan just came in and we exchanged news about mutual friends. It seemed good to see one of the old gang from B17. It made me feel less like an orphan.

Still now news about shipments although I heard from Rod Ferguson, the fellow who cam in, that Ed Strait is on the alert. There is still a good chance for us to see each other this week-end. I will telephone Thursday night to let you know how things are shaping up. I certainly hope we get at least one more chance to be together.

Take good care of yourself and get as much rest as you can. Give my love to the family and tell them I am thinking of them.

All my love to you and you know what.

Love Chad

January 26, 1944

Dearest Wife of Mine:

I received your letter this P.M. and was sorry to read that the trip and weekend were so tiring for you. I was afraid that the whole thing would be too much right after having the flu. I wasn't really on the ball as far as getting a room was concerned. I should have thought of the U.S.O. but somehow or other my mind wasn't functioning on all cylinders. If this weekend turns out all O.K. I should be able to get to New York and see you.

The officers and non-coms are already talking about weekend passes so I presume that there are no shipping orders for us yet. One of the corporals said that our shipping orders had come through but that they had been cancelled. I had a feeling that there might be something in the wind this week but I guess the wind changed. Probably tomorrow or Friday we will be allowed to put our names in for weekend passes.

Today we had lots of close-order drill and bayonet training, a couple of movies. We had squad problems this afternoon. I was one of the "enemy" posted near a simulated ammunition dump. Being an outpost I had to lie on the ground. It was tough finding a spot that was comparatively dry.

Tomorrow we have more drill and bayonet work and in the P.M. we have more squad problems out in the woods.

Take good care of yourself and try to get rested up. Remember me to Mother Bedient and give her my love. All my love to you, sweetheart.

Chad

Dearest Bedie:

I am dashing off a few lines this P.M. while on duty as barrack's guard. Tonight we are going out on a hike to work some problems in the use of the compass so I know I'll be too tired to write then. Being a barrack's guard means that you stay in the barracks and sweep the floors, clean the wash bowls and latrine floor and get rid of any rubbish that may accumulate. The morning is quite busy but the P.M. is quiet although a lieutenant may come in for an inspection at any time.

The trip down from Katonah was O.K. Riding in trains is getting to be quite an old story. In the last five months I guess I have spent more time on trains than at any other time in my life. I had plenty of time to get over to Penn. Station and to get a bite to eat. The train I had to catch was the 6:25 p.m. for Odenton. By chance I got a seat with three other fellows from my barracks. One of them was a Tennessean who was all excited about the big city and another was an Italian boy who is in love with a girl in New York. So you can see that time passed quickly. We signed in at the orderly room about 11:30 p.m. even after stopping in a little place in Odenton where we got coffee and hot dogs. I was pretty tired so 5:30 a.m. came around too soon for me. However, not have to got out in the cold with the company today has given my feet a little rest so that tonight's problems won't be so bad.

This morning I was pretty busy around the barracks but this p.m. things slowed up enough for me to wash out some socks and underwear and write this letter.

How is Dave Moore? I certainly hope he doesn't have a bad case of strep throat because they really leave you feeling like a dish rag for quite a while.

This A.M. at reveille there were four fellows who are A.W.O.L. and according to the first sergeant things will probably be pretty tough for them. They can be tried under the 28th article of war if there is evidence to show actual intention of remaining absent. However in most cases, A.W.O.L.'s get about six months at hard labor and lose half their pay.

Some of the fellows are getting their slips of acknowledgment for the additional voluntary allotments they made to their folks. I'll probably get mine soon. I thing I told you about increasing my allotment to you from $22 to $32. We will probably be paid this P.M. or tomorrow so I'll have plenty of money for another weekend trip if I stay. Rumors are starting again about being shipped. It is getting to be an old army custom. They say that when a group is actually shipped out the rumors fly thick and fast. Oh well, we are beginning another cycle leading up to next Sat. and Sunday. As the days go by the pressure will increase. The Army administration acts on the assumption that soldiers are like little children. To me, however, the rewards for compliance are thrilling. I don't think we ever were in closer physical harmony than this last weekend. It doesn't seem that one time could be better than another but that seems to be the way it is.

Much later - Tues. A.M. 11:00 things certainly happened fast. Just as I was peacefully scribbling away one of the boys came in and informed me that I was wanted at the orderly room. The first sergeant told me to get into my O.D.'s and report for guard duty. Another fellow, named Bryce, and I went on guard duty at 5:00 p.m. It was plenty cold and windy and the sandy soil whipped up easily in your eyes. When we came off duty they allowed us to sleep late. Then we had to get up and clean the barracks.

The boys are starting rumors again this morning about being alerted but so far, as usual, there is nothing definite. Some fellows seem to delight in starting the rumor factory going again.

I'll close now what started to be a short note. Take good care of that cold and try to get plenty of sleep and drink lots of water. All my love, Sweetheart and here's hoping. Chad

P.S. When I went to check up on my pay the lieutenant told me that the Army has me down on the records for $3.75 each month for war bonds. So they took five payments out of this months pay. That left me with no pay for January. The lieutenant wanted to know whether you had ever received a bond. I told him I had never signed anything about bonds and that I would ask you if you had ever received anything concerning it. What I am going to do is to agree to the payment for one bond and cancel the rest. Somewhere along the line the Army system slipped a cog. Let me know whether you have had any word about a bond.

Love

Chad

February 2, 1944

Dearest Bedie:

I had just mailed my last letter to you when the whole company was called out to hear a special announcement. Of course, there was only one thing that could happen and it did. We were sent down to the Day Room where they read the articles of war to us and put us on alert. However they cancelled it this morning and left us high and dry. Right now we are back on the old rumor wagon and are hoping and praying for the coming weekend. The sergeant told us that nine fellows in our barracks will have to stay in. I'm doing my best to be a good boy.

This A.M. we went through a series of problems. First we had the Close Combat Course where we fired on surprise targets. Then we ran the attack course on the German Village. After that we had a class in booby traps. Then we went into the pits and threw had grenades. This P.M. we had drill work and classes in the Bazooka and the carbine.

Tonight we had to clean the barracks and wash windows then clean our rifles so the evening was pretty well gone by the time I started this note.

If the fates will it, the weekend will be a happy one for me. However I have learned by now not to expect much and to be very grateful when something extra special really does happen. By extra special I mean another chance to take you in my arms and tell you how much I love you.

Chad

February 3, 1944

Dearest Bedie:

About five minutes before lights go out and I'll have to make it short. The pass situation is cleared up and the nine fellows in our barracks who have to stay have been picked. I did some plain and fancy praying and sure enough they were answered. I am going to try to make the same train as last week and hope to be home about the same time.

I tried to call you tonight to tell you the good news but there was such a gang ahead of me that I couldn't get the call in. So I am hoping that this reaches you in time. I'll try to call tomorrow night however but in any case this letter ought to be in Ridgefield before I start home.

Right now I am just living for that happy moment when I can see you again.

Love,
Chad

February 7, 1944

Dearest Bedie:

I'm getting to be a regular commuter and, according to the unofficial word that is passing around, our group will probably be around for another weekend. My luck has been almost phenomenal and if everything continues in the same lucky streak I will have another chance for a weekend pass. However, the week is still young. By Thursday or Friday we will know more definitely about our chances.

I reached the Penn. Station just in time to get a good seat on the 7:25. Also I met the same three fellows from my barracks so we came back together. On the way down my nose began to feel stuffed and swollen so I am now nursing a cold. I have been taking pills for it and am going to bed early.

Today I was on a detail to work the targets on the range for a group of officers who were firing the carbine. It was quite cold and windy so that didn't help my cold much. However, we quit early this P.M. and came back to the barracks where we laid around until retreat.

I'll quit this really short letter now and get ready for bed. I hope your cold is better. Try to get plenty of sleep. Sweet dreams, my little snuggle bug.

Chad

February 15, 1944

Dearest Bedie:

Just a short note to tell about the hectic times here. Yesterday we checked and double-checked our duffle bags and clothing. We worked until about 9:30 p.m. then laid down to catch some bunk fatigue.

This A.M. we were inspected by the colonel and put our duffle bags away until we are shipped. This P.M. we will have the usual army physical exam. We have to stay in our barracks until we are called out and have to stay ready to go any minute.

I found a small box in which I put some dirty clothing, soxs, handkerchiefs etc. I am going to give it the mail clerk to have him mail it home.

The trip down Sunday was tough. The Penn. R.R. had some old cars for their special to Odenton. We sat in a converted baggage car which was very drafty.

It certainly was tough leaving this time. In a way we have been very fortunate to have week-ends together but it has been hard on both of us physically and emotionally. However I would have been plenty down-hearted if I had missed any of those weekends.

I have grabbed this chance to write because I don't know when I'll get a chance to write again. We may have a long train trip ahead of us.

All my love, sweetheart, and take good care of yourself.

Chad

February 16, 1944
Somewhere in Africa

Dearest Bedie:

At last I have a chance to sit down and write you from the "Dark Continent". At the last camp "Somewhere on the eastern coast" we had very little if any chance to get in touch with home folks. Everything from Camp Meade on was very "hush-hush". During the trip across the Atlantic I found myself to be a better sailor than I thought I was. I also developed one hell of an appetite. On our arrival I was interested to note that the natives of this section are much the same as those I have seen snap shots of. However it was a pleasure to see green grass and trees in leaf. This place is only a temporary stop-off. Soon we will be on our way again.

I still have your letters of Feb. 10th and 13th with me and treasure them. Especially the latter. We probably won't be together again for a long time but at least we have the memory of four perfect weekends.

Please reassure Mother and Dad and Ralph and Ruth. Give my love to them and to Mother Bedient. When you write either use air mail or V-mail, preferably the latter.

All my love, sweetheart. Don't worry and take good care of yourself.

Love,

Chad

February 17, 1944

Dearest Bedie:

I have had plenty of trouble in the past writing letters but this one takes the cake. We are not allowed to give any information which might show our present location, our numbers, how we came, or any description of the camp.

The trip was quite tiring and we finally arrived "somewhere on the eastern coast." There will be no phone calls or weekend passes for security reasons.

We had our stuff packed in duffle bags and fortunately I was able to locate my bag right away. We finally got to bed after having chow. This A.M. we were awakened at 6:00 a.m. and were informed that the entire barracks was on K.P. duty. However it was a false alarm so we went back to catch forty winks.

We cleaned up the latrine then had our clothing checked. This P.M. has been pretty quiet due to the fact that we are all restricted to barracks.

The PX and Service club are quite near although we haven't had a chance to go there yet.

The chow is plentiful and so far pretty good. K.P. duty here is quite a chore since they feed so many men and I suppose by tomorrow our barracks will be elected.

My cold is much better although I have the same trouble with catarach.

Take care of yourself, sweetheart. Don't forget that I want you to keep your health above all things. Get plenty of rest.

All my love,
Chad

Friday, February 18, 1944

Dearest Bedie:

We are still being processed although things aren't too rushing here. Certainly not as hectic as when I was processes at McClellan. There the cadre were blowing whistles every five minutes.

Last night we were still restricted because of some mix-up about K.P.s our first day here.

This A.M. we marched over to the theatre to see a training film which, mirable dicter, was one we hadn't seen before. Most of the training films have been seen by the fellows two or three times. I suppose they want to make sure that the subject of the film sinks in.

This P.M. we had an injection for this a routine matter in the Army. After a certain length of time the shots have to be removed. My arm stung for about ten minutes but now it feels alright.

After getting the shots we had to clean up the barracks and wash the windows. They use soft coal around here and everything gets sooted up.

I hope Mother and Dad aren't too much upset by my recent change of address. Mother's health has been rather shaky since she had that bad cold.

I had a chance to talk with Ralph and Ruth the last time I was home. I was admiring their living room and liked the paint job Ralph did on the ceiling. He used a special type of paint which I remember seeing somewhere before. It was an odd shade of blue with a greenish cast. I think he called it Diana Room Blue.

I am well and eating like a horse. I wouldn't be surprised if I were over my usual weight. I'll sign off now sweetheart, with all my love and you know what.

Chad

March 20, 1944

We have been moving around a lot but now are settled down for a while in sunny Italy, I am well and have recovered pretty well from the cold I had in the States. We are stationed somewhere on the Anzio Beach head which is just a very small dot in the big picture of the war. Spring is on its way here and the winter cold and rain is about over. I am going to write more this afternoon.

All my love.

Chad

March 20, 1944

Dearest Bedie:

I am writing this from somewhere on the little area known as the Anzio Beach head. As you can see I have finally been assigned to a regular unit in the U.S. Army instead of existing in the great company of infantry replacements. The way we were moved around steadily from place to place made it almost impossible to settle down to writing a letter. As for receiving mail, I certainly will be glad when it catches up with me. Out trip took us from Casablanca to Oran through very interesting country with mountain sides carpeted with orange, red, and purple flowers. The people of North Africa are much the same as you remember them only more so. Spring is slowly but surely coming now and the days are much warmer. My cold is much better. Give my love to Dad and Mother C. and Mother B. Remember me to the folks. Every time I get a chance I look at your picture and wish my love to you across the seas.

Love,
Chad

March 22, 1944

Dearest Bedie:

 I am writing this from a slit trench where we have our pup tent set up. We dig slit trenches here for protection from a chance long shot from Jerry. This morning was rather wet, but the sun obligingly came out and gave us a chance to air out our blankets. The fellow with me is very much interested in model railroads and we have had a lot of good sessions talking about life back in the States. We are getting additional training since our regimental commander is a great believer in indoctrinating the men before having them join their units. This afternoon we are going to take showers and enjoy the luxury of hot water again. I am looking forward to receiving back mail from the States and catching up with the news from home. Be sure to tell Dad and Ralph to use V-mail when they write.

All my love, sweetheart,

from Chad

March 23, 1944

Dearest Bedie:

Another chance to write a brief note before we take up our evening chores of getting rations etc. Yesterday we all had showers and a rare change into clean under clothing. It felt great to be clean again after taking sponge baths out of a steel helmet. This morning we had more instruction and this afternoon we went on a short hike. The nights are cold here and you can bet we really curl up in our blankets. Many of the fellows here have small folders and snapshots of their folks and I was wondering if you could send me some snap shots of yourself and any pictures you would like to include to remind me of some of the happy times we have had together. How is Mother B? Give her my love Remember me to Grace, Cliff, and Grandma. How are the chickens progressing? I'll bet you're quite a farmer by now. Remember me to the Dixons and the Hartmanns.

All my love,
Chad

March 25, 1944

Dearest Bedie:

I found this morning to my surprise that somewhere along the line I had lost track of the days as they went sliding by and had lost a day. So this letter is at least dated properly. Our short period of instruction is now over so that except for special details, there isn't a great deal of activity. This morning I took advantage of the opporutnity and rearranged my duffle bag. while we were in a camp near Oran I got rid of a lot of extra stuff I knew I would not have any occasion to use. For instance I turned in my O.D. blouse because it certainly wouldn't fit into the picture here. I suppose by now that the blustery, rainy days are coming to Ridgefield and that the oil burner doesn't go on so much. Over here we burn the remains of K ration boxes and a sort of bamboo like grass which is found all over the beach head. Soon however it will be getting warmer, I hope.

All my love, sweetheart, and don't forget to send the snapshots.

Love,
Chad

March 26, 1944

Dearest Bedie:

Having secured a pencil with a softer lead, I feel a little more sure that these V-Mail letters will be legible when they finally arrive in the States. There isn't very much to write about anyway so I may sound pretty infantile. Back at McClellan there were always a lot of training activities which I could use for letter writing. Five days later - Well I'll pick up where I left off and finish this letter. Since I started this we have been doing a lot of detail. Our sergeant finally was able to get us hot chow but, of course, during the day we had K rations for lunch. We got back to our area late and sometimes didn't get much chance to do more than make our beds. In our new area we have very little to do other than keep our equipment in shape. To be continued in another letter.

Love,

Chad

March 31, 1944

My dearest heart:

My letter of the 26th certainly was a disjointed affair but I am using this sheet to carry on the story. We finally moved away from our previous area and joined our companies. I took off the O.D. shirt and pants to which I had been wearing since leaving the States and put on a brand new suit. Of course my present needs are just clean underwear and socks which I carry in my light pack. We are enjoying hot chow again although when we do go into the lines we will eat K rations again. I have done guard duty a couple of times and have spent quite a lot of time keeping my rifle in good condition.

Sand and rust are the chief difficulties in keeping any piece of equipment clean. Some of the old fellows receive V-mail and we new fellows are all hoping for the day when our mail will catch up with us. That will be a red letter day.

All my love,
Chad

April 4, 1944

My Dearest heart:

Since I wrote you last we have been pretty busy moving around. Fortunately sunny Italy is beginning to live up to its reputation so we are not bothered much by rain and mud. However, when it does rain here it really does get muddy. I haven't told you much about a foxhole so I will give you a general idea of what one is like. It is a rectangular hole about 10 ft. long, 6 ft. across, and 3 ft. deep and is lined on the bottom with sticks covered with old cardboard packing cases. Most of the top is covered over with polls, dirt and brush. Usually two fellows sleep together in the hole using the buddy system. The boys set great store on the mail the receive. Many of them don't begin to get their mail until they have been around here about a month so I guess I will have quite a while to wait before my letter catch up with me. Be sure to use V-mail or if you really want to give your pen free swing use air mail. I haven't any Easter cards with me but here is wishing you a Happy Easter with lots of love and you know what,

Chad

April 6, 1944

My dearest Bedie:

Having just finished my breakfast at the outrageous hour of 1:30 p.m. I thought I ought to get busy and write a letter. In the past my letter haven't been of the type to arouse your libido because I have always been conscious of the fat that a third person, be he sergeant or lieutenant, will have to read my letters to you and can sort them. Knowing my nature you also know what effect that has on my expressing my thoughts about us. However in the past few weeks I have found myself recalling the many happy hours we spent together during the winter and spring of 1934. I remember especially some of the trips we took over to Redding Glen and one night on the ledge near the falls at Devil's Den. Then I think about the many nights you sent me home reluctantly after we had been drinking port wine. Do you remember how we drank it? Port wine served like that would be heaven right now although I would want it in more roomy quarters. I hope you don't mind the reminiscences but I was just in the mood.

Love

Chad

April 6, 1944

Mi Dulse Corazon:

   this is the second installment of my letter to you on a sunny April afternoon. My salutation shows the Spanish influence of my foxhole buddy a boy of Mexican decent. Gradually I am learning some Spanish words and I find them a lot like the Italian and French. The nights are getting somewhat warmer so my New England blood is beginning to thaw out a bit. I am well and so far have still escaped the colds which plaque my sinus. During the night I wear a wool-lined pair of overalls and my field jacket. We have all turned in our over coats since they are too bulky. I suppose that you have a perky little hat for Easter. Is it like the go-to-hell hat you wore when you can down to Anniston. I sure would like to see it and kiss the little nose under it. Don't forget to send me the snapshots of you. Give my love to Mother bedient and tell Tippie to be a good little girl and play with Bussie. Remember me to the Whites, Dixons, and Hartmanns.

All my love,
Chad

April 7, 1944

Mia Carrissima Sposa:

Having slept like a log I feel just like writing a letter to my sweetheart. The sun is beating in at the southern exposure of our foxhole and is really very warm. My companion is busy answering a letter which was written to him late in January and which he just received last night. From that you can see that my mail will probably be around by the end of this month or early in May. That red letter day seems a long way off. Maybe I ought to tell you about our famous K rations. The breakfast consists of powdered coffee, lump sugar, 2 kinds of hard crackers, a can of egg and pork, a bar of assorted fruits, chewing gum and 4 cigarettes. The piece de resistance of dinner is a can of cheese and the drink is powdered lemon which no one uses. The supper unit however is better with canned beef and pork loaf and a bar of chocolate. These rations are pretty concentrated and of course, they fill the bill where it is often impossible to get hot chow. We get lots of insect visitors in the form of red ants which are after our sugar supply. Give my love to the family and don't forget the snap shots. All my love to you, sweetheart.

From
Chad.

April 16, 1944

My Dearest Bedie:

I am writing this from a quiet area after having been "up" as the boys call it. I am O.K. and considerably cleaner then I was a few days ago. Of course conditions are nowhere near what they were in February and March. Dampness does however create a problem in keeping equipment from rusting. From now on I am going to have to watch my Ps and Qs because I am now a part of an honor platoon which is supposed to represent the enlisted men of our unit at all ceremonial occasions. Yes, we still have manual of arms and drill here in a combat zone. I was talking to some fellows who came overseas with our group and they said they were receiving mail, so, happy days may soon come for me when I will start receiving your letters. A magazine or newspaper which would be picked up in an idle moment and hurriedly scanned is minutely read here, even the little articles. Give my love to the family and remember me to the gang. Remember that our love for each other is abiding. I keep you in my heart always.

Chad

April 19, 1944

Dearest Bedie:

I received your letter #28 on the 17th and since I have been rather busy I though I would wait to see if the air mail letter you sent at the same time would arrive but as far it hasn't come. According to the number I certainly have a lot of mail on its way to me. Probably those with A.P.O. #15155 will take quite a while to reach me. One of the fellows was telling me that he is still getting letters which were written in January. You can't imagine the thrill I got when I was handed your letter. I'll bet I read it over 5 or 6 times in the space of two hours. While writing this it just got the incoming mail, a copy of the Press dated Feb. 24. I'll probably read even the want ads. I'm glad you told me where Freddi Jackson is. I may be able to get to see him soon. I don't know Dave's address because we were separated some time ago. Thank Elsa for me and tell here I will write. My darn pen isn't working right so I guess I'll have to go back to using a pencil. Could you send me a couple of soft pencils and some envelopes. They are had to get. I hope your arches are O.K. All my love, my sweetheart.

From Chad.

April 22, 1944

My Sweetheart:

I was glad to hear that Bobbi R. got his assignment to the Medics. I can't imagine anyone enjoying wading in water up to his chest. Dot Nash seems to be going her own way. Pretty tough on the kids. How is the supply of frozen meat up in the cold storage plant lasting. I'll bet that sausage taste good. That joke about the holly hock was swell. Tell Horace I enjoyed it. I suppose by now that Mrs. Runan has made up her mind about the Candlewood lot. Sounds like a sensible thing to get rid of the lot. I had a letter from Ruth Crouchley and enjoyed the bit about Ralph taking the boys on a hike. I can sympathize with him. My feet certainly have taken enough of a beating in the last 6 months. Tonight I was assigned new duties as a sort of messenger. I may even get a chance to use my ability to use a typewriter. I read your letter over and over and dream of the happy day when the good Lord will let us be together again. I love you, my sweet, and long for you. Be of good courage. Love to all and especially to my dear heart.

Chad

April 22, 1944

My dearest sweetheart:

Last night I was wandering around our company area disconsolately because I didn't get any mail when one of the boys told me that he had picked up my mail and had placed it on my dugout. What a letter! 11 pages mailed on Feb. 21st before I left the states.

Some of the letter is very snooky and raised my blood pressure as well as my morale. We weren't allowed to phone or write just before we left. I don't know how it was in Dave's outfit. Your letter was full of news and I am glad to hear that some of the boys who dodged the draft so long are finally going to learn all about army discipline. Although I don't wish them the hard luck of being shipped out. The other day I was sent to Malaria school - very interesting. About all a man in combat can do though is to take his stabrine pills and use insect repellant. I am now the company Malaria control representative. Most the control work however is done by the Medics and engineers.

Chad

April 27, 1944

My dearest wife:

Last night at mail call, I was bowled over. Nearly all your letter came in a bunch plus some from Elsa and one from Rutch C. The only ones that haven't come in yet are Nos. 9, 10, 11, No. 14, Nos. 16-29 and No. 31. I nearly read my eyes out catching up. Many of your letters made me very humble and ashamed of myself for not writing more often. Back in Africa after we landed we were told that a cable would take a least 6 days longer than V-mail to reach the States so I used V-mail. All through Africa and up until we reached our companies things were pretty hectic and it was very difficult to get a chance to write. I know this is a pretty weak alibi but I do feel very much ashamed of myself. When we were up on the front it was possible in the afternoon to write letters in our foxholes. Now that we are in a rear area with a training program going on letter writing has to be done in snatches. I know a little about how you feel. Life is empty without you by my side but there is an unpleasant job to be done and it may God forbid, take a long time to finish it. Was has done a terrible thing to millions of families all over the world but every day sees us coming closer to the end of this killing.

I told you in a previous letter that I had a different job. Being a runner is a great deal like being a connecting link between the company and the platoon. Up at the front the runner is responsible for maintaining that like but his chief job seems to be concerned with rations and mail. Back here I have had a chance to help out a bit with typing. So far I have kept close to the orderly room to do typing and occasionally take messages. I am no longer on the honor guard since is conflicted with being a runner.

Our chow is quite good though most of it is canned. Once in a while we do get onions or celery. We eat a lot of hard biscuits which seem to help keep our gums healthy.

When I became a runner I moved to another dugout which was much more shallow. I am continually bumping my fool head on the roof sticks. Due to the arrival of so-called Spring we have turned in our woolen underwear and have cut ourselves down to two blankets. However it is still pretty chilly and I throw my field jacket over my shoulders.

If I dig a foxhole out in the side lawn and crawl into it when I get back don't be surprised. You get used to sleeping on the ground that you forget what a bed feels like. However in my dreams I still remember out big double bed with you snuggled down in my arms and me trying to kiss the lobes of your ears. One dream keeps coming back of those blissful days at Lake Katrine, Blue Mountain and Cape Cod. Remember when I lost my britches? I have an awful itch to be traveling too. I'd like to see some of the West and if you feel like doing it I would like to just take off for about a month stopping when and where we liked and getting adjusted to each other again. You would probably become like Alice Moore was when Dave was coming home week-ends. Glad of a chance to say "No" once in a while. But sweetheart I have an awful lot of loving to do when we get together again. All my love with plenty of trimmings.

Chads

Dearest Sweetheart:

Tonight I received Nos. 10 & 11 and laughed like the devil over those jokes about W. Dixon and Mommy Hartmann. There is still quite a lot of the twenties to come.

When I think that I left some Skyrite paper in my duffle bag back at the vineyards where we were first I am mad as hell. They told us that V-mail would be much more satisfactory but I certainly see the advantages of Air mail now. However even air mail is pretty impersonal because of security. Who? When? Where? How? and How Many? Are more or less forbidden subjects.

I'll take this opportunity to write about some of the notes I took while re-reading your letters. I know it makes a letter very sketchy but it also provides topics for me to write about.

I am enclosing the application for my drivers license. Just looking at an operator's license makes me itch to get behind the wheel of a car. This is certainly one time you would find me reluctant to turn back home. Just you and I, rolling along through pleasant American countryside, stopping when we wanted to and lazily taking our own sweet time. At night we would stop at some place with nice surroundings and would be sure to have a nice soft bed without squeaking springs! If possible I would like to stop where we could build a fire at night and lie in each other's arms wrapped up in blankets watching the flames of the fire. Drowsily content to be close to each other. Then we would go to bed to sleep? In close embrace. So many of the boys over here are determined to travel for a while that I'm sure the highways are going to be busy places.

You mentioned a newspaper film projector on the "running board." It is worth saving because it has good lenses. If it is in the way just put it out in Mary's room if you can find a place for it.

The thumb tacks (a million or more) really belong to the scouts. I thought I had put them in the box which I gave to Levio. Charlie Walker bought them with Scout money so they should go the scouts.

Hilda Kuhlmann was mistaken about A.P.O. numbers. They number I had (#15155) was only temporary. All those letters had to come through the Directory Service.

You mentioned that you are taking vitamin pills and that they seem to help you. We take vitamin pills too as well as satabrine pills. Those damn little yellow pills! I'll be glad when I get out of this Malaria region where Madame Anophiles does her dirty work. I'm glad to take the pills however because having Malaria is no picnic. Anything you can do to keep from getting it is welcome. Madame Culex may raise bumps on your skin but she doesn't pack the same wallop as Anophiles.

I received your dollar bill O.K. and will keep it as a sort of starter for that travelling fund we will need in happy days that will come. Over here we use Allied Military Occupation currency or gold seal U.S. currency. However there is little occasion to use money at all except to buy candy etc. when the PX rations are brought around. Today they came and I bought candy, gum a mirror and a writing pad. We get a PX ration on an average of every two or three weeks. Candy cigars and chewing tobacco are the most popular items although I haven't taken to chewing tobacco yet!

Your suggestion about writing Mrs. Nash was a good one. I will probably get a chance to do it soon. I don't blame Karl for feeling morose being saddled to a frigid clothes horse. He must be so in love with her. It's pathetic. If anything like that happened to us I think i would pray for a German 88 to make a quick end of it all. One of the warmest spots in my life is the love I hold for you and there would be nothing left for me if I no longer had your love. I know love goes where it will but I pray dear God that he will give me the strength to make up to you all the heart aches you have suffered while we have been apart. Never mind those stupid people who make remarks about you're being single again. They don't realize how true love between man and woman can be a bond as strong as steel even across three thousand miles of ocean! They are to be pitied because they never had and never will have as much joy together as we have had in the last ten years.

From what you say about the Rev. "Holy Joe" I wondered if he really has read the New Testament and understood the teachings of Jesus. Remember Mary Magdelene? What he is telling his Cathecists about

Mary Belle will color their thinking about her for the rest of her life. No wonder he loses parishioners.

I was sorry to hear about the school losing Van Miller. It's going to be pretty hard to replace him. He had a lot of progressive ideas about education which were not radical and would really work. Sometimes he did go off the deep end as every one does occasionally but he was pretty keen.

Your Easter Sunday comments remind me of my Easter. I was thinking of you and sending my love to you from a foxhole up at the front.

It's getting dark now as I sit here at the opening of my foxhole writing to you in between interruptions. All my love sweetheart, with plenty of good wishes to my beloved

from

Chad

Letter from Don Condon
May 1, 1944

Dear Bedie:

I've just finished writing to Charlie. It was great of you to write such a nice letter to Betty. She quoted a lot of it to me. Was going to write to the old address and see if the letter would be forwarded, so was very pleased to get the correct address.

I am right where Charlie left me - taking more training much the same as we had in the States, and waiting for assignment to a regular outfit. We are in the middle of a farming district, in a beautiful little Valley. The weather we would call summer back home. I wonder what it will be in July! The roses are in full bloom, and there are many wild flowers. It is fun watching the woman carry large bundles on their heads and doing the family wash at the well in the grass. The Arabs were more picturesque, but probably Charlie wrote about them. Am still so thankful that you were in Anniston with Betty.

Sincerely,

Don

May 5, 1944

Dearest Bedie:

I am writing this while seated on a couple of sand bags somewhere on the Anzio front. I am sorry that I wasn't able to write to you sooner but my buddie and I have been making extensive alterations on our shelter.

The night of May 2nd I received another bundle of letters from you and V-mail from Ralph and Ruth C. and Levio. There is a lot of material in them so here goes.

Letter 16. Wow! You must have been plenty mad. Just about that time we were being shoved along one step nearer to the beach head. I would have liked to be home to put out the fire.

Letter 18. We read about the blizzard you had home and wished we could shovel snow instead of fill sand bags. That storm must have been a regular hum dinger though.

Letter 19. In this letter and some others you mention visiting people in Italy. The way the war is now in Italy an ordinary solder doesn't get to see many Italians unless he is in Naples or southern Italy. Around here the Army has evacuated most of the Pizans as they call them. However while I was in a rear area I did get a chance to chat with a very dear friend of the Finches. He looks fine.

Letter 20. You mention sending a pencil and pen set. I don't know about the pen. From page one of this letter you can see that old faithful ran out of ink. A good pencil with plenty of spare soft leads would be invaluable. Money doesn't mean much here. So that is probably why Dave was able to mention such a high price for a pencil and pen set. However please send the set by all means.

Letter 21. If I do get a chance to buy some Italian handiwork I'll pick it up and send it home. They do nice beadwork and carve in cameo. Most of that sort of thing is back in Naples though.

What's this about the Webster scandal? I don't remember hearing about it. Ridgefield wouldn't be natural without some juicy morsel of scandal at least once a year.

Letter 29. I received this letter May 2 so you can see that there is quite a delay - when I was in Naples old Vesuvios seemed peaceful and quiet although, when I got to Anzio our service paper had a big article about the eruption.

So far I haven't been able go see Freddie Jackson. Tell his parents that he is in a good outfit.

You mentioned articles by Ernie Pyle. He has the reputation of appreciating the situation here and has a genuine sympathy for the lot of the infantry men.

Letter 36. I sure would like to be able to visit people in Ancona and Pesero provinces because that would mean that our forces would be beyond Rome. Oh, happy thought.

It certainly is a coincidence that we both thought of snapshots. Maybe there is something to this mental telepathy. I'll be happy when I have some pictures of my darling although I would much rather be carrying the original in my arms.

You mention of the oil burner reminds me of what Boots used to say about preferring a good oil burner to having a man in the house. Maybe she has changed her mind by now.

Letter 37. Thanks for the skyrite paper and air mail envelopes. Its the best paper I have ever used. This pencil I am using is one that I had back at Ft. Meads for marking articles to I hope you'll excuse the illegible scrawl.

Letter 43. Thanks for sending off those packages. The candy will be welcome. As yet I haven't received any packages. The policy is to hold the packages until a unit gets into a rear area. Up at the front a lot of paper lying around makes it easy for the enemy to spot a position. By all means send the lighter. It will come in mighty handy. There are times when our clothing gets very sweaty or wet from other reasons and matches won't light.

I think you are mistaken about salt peter being nitrate of silver. If I remember my chemistry salt peter is called sodium nitrate. It doesn't make any difference as long as the stuff makes a cigarette light.

Tell Elsa that I appreciate the listing of thunder mugs in the British Navy. I can just picture a lunatic cracking himself over the head with one and wondering why is didn't hurt.

Ask Francis if he can get me a knife that has a good blade and a screw driver. I have on Army can opener so that isn't necessary. As for corkscrews I have forgotten how to use one. A loaned my Scout knife to a guy and he ruined it for me. Knives are very useful over here and I would appreciate it.

I'll have to quit now, my love, because it will soon be time to start the nights round of jobs. I am well. Give my love to the family and remember me to the neighbors. My special love to you and prayers that you are well. I love you with all my heart.

Chad

May 8, 1944

Dearest Sweetheart;

You asked sometime ago what I meant by calling you "Mi Corazou." I suppose it was the Spanish influence of my roommate from New Mexico. It means "my heart."

While up in the lines last time I received mail nearly every day so now the only numbers I haven't received are Nos. 9, 17, 24, 35, 39, 40 and 42. The latest one I have received is No. 50.

I am writing this with a pencil I borrowed from one of the runners. So here goes. No 14. I was surprised to hear that the Army would take Lawrence Brudage after all the abuse he has given his stomach with liquor.

No. 22. You mentioned that Dave had time on the boat to write some letters. I had time too but very little space. Our bunks were two by four arrangements which required the use of a shoe horn. During the time we were allowed on deck it was usually a mass of sprawling bodies and extended legs. So letter-writing was pretty much out of the question.

I was glad to hear that Isabel O'Shea was appointed to be principal of the Grammer School. She is steady and has had a lot of practical experience. It looks as though the School Board is due for a lot of work making replacements. It would be nice if it were as easy as the Infantry does it. They just pass down the order for more men and up they come from the various replacement centers.

Don't send any more money because I still have plenty even though I haven't been paid yet. There is little if anything on the beach head that you can buy anyhow.

No 23. Those white Sussex chickens sound good. How is the feed situation? I suppose that like a lot of other things, it will be hard to get this summer.

I will try to send you some cartoons which I will cut out of Stars and Stripes. No. 25. I hope that someday I will get the chance to visit Vincent Bedini's relatives. That would mean that Krauts would have hauled his ass back to the Po Valley or the Alps.

Maybe I can get you another powder jar like the one you got in Italy. In the cities the Italians seem to have a lot of things to catch American dollars. On the beach head life is reduced to essentials and the Army has taken over everything.

No. 26. I enjoyed your description of Tooki Scherf's contortions. The kids must be having a lot more fun and instruction under the present phys. ed. directors than they had before. Ray Eppolite certainly learned a lot about controlling himself and others while away from the gang he used to travel with.

It is faintly remembered but I think there was a Peter Jessup at the Ridge field school. I don't recall the years.

You spoke about the comfort and power of prayer in letter #26. I have always been bitter about theologians and creeds but I find great comfort and strength in silently confessing my belief in a Universal Power for Good and praying that the day will come soon when I will be with you again.

No. 35. John Nash ought to like working in the Q M Dept. He certainly got a break. He may even find that he will be somewhat happy in the work he is doing.

No. 38. Thanks for the snapshots. It did me worlds of good to see your dear face again. I certainly enjoyed the look of anticipation on Tippie's face. She's a smart little girl. Nobody is going to go off with her knowing it.

No. 41. If you were asleep when the chickens hatched out how could you have heard the mother hen tintinnabulate? How does a chicken do that anyhow?

No. 44. I hope that your arch supporters are giving you a little surcease from the pain. I know you must have suffered. Try to stay off your feet as much as possible after the day's work. I have found that massaging the feet stimulate the circulation and helps a lot.

I haven't received letters #39 or #40 yet with birthday greeting. A lot of our boys right near me have birthdays coming in May but non of them is seeing his 36th so I feel quite like the old man of the bunch.

You mentioned that Pa Cummings won't be using the hill patch this year. It would be best to have it plowed and seeded in with something that will hold the soil because that hill washes like the devil when it rains.

No. 45. Your luck at cards must have changed to get ahead of Grace in Rummy. I'd like to get into a hot contract game. I haven't played in so long I probably would mess up a one club bid.

No. 46. I was glad that you visited the Bryans. Helen's example of sex education reminds me of a very good article in May issue of Readers Digest published in abbreviated form for service men. The article is called "So Your Girl Thinks She's in Love."

No. 47. I received a letter from Ed Allan. The Scouts are having a tough time keeping scoutmasters. I hope they get someone who doesn't have to worry about being inducted.

I should have explained that business about eating breakfast in the afternoon. While up in the lines very often it is possible to move out of a foxhole only during the night. So sleeping is done in the morning and eating in the afternoon. Some system! What? Most of our lines are on flat land whereas the Germans are up in the hills looking down. Any unusual moving around is liable to bring an artillery barrage. Needless to say we confine most of our activities to the hours of darkness.

No 48. Thanks for more skyrite paper. However, the envelopes got stuck up with the dampness. Fortunately I have been able to get a pack of air-mail envelopes so will continue to use this means of writing as long as possible.

No. 49 Don't send cigarettes because we have plenty. The ration is enough for everyone. Even Camels.

No. 50. I have had letters from Levio and seems to think that his ear condition will prevent induction. I hope so because modern war is tough on ear drums.

Letter No. 53. When I read the last two pages of this letter the Devil arose and was ready for Anything. That canoe trip to Waccabuc would be like Paradise. I darn near tintinnabulated when I read it. Do you remember the rides we used to take up to Lovers' Leap? The ground didn't seem hard at all although something else was. You wore your buckskin coat as I remember and I had all sorts of fun exploring under it. Then we would come back to your house where we would lie together on the coach drowsily talking of our plans for the future.

Darling I miss you so and adore you. I long for the day when you and I can embrace and, with you on my lap snuggle down tight, talk over our plans for the future again. We'll go off by ourselves and it will be just like getting married all over again.

All my love
Chad

P.S. When I started addressing the envelope I just remembered that I was made a Pfc. May 1st.

Love, Chad

Sunday, May 14, 1944

My dearest little gal with the perky nose;

Well we have moved again to another area and things have been pretty busy since we arrived. I still have the same job as a runner attached to headquarters. I am in good health and except for my old knees and bum feet am doing O.K. We are dug in here in a pretty good foxhole although it is not as good as the last one we have when we were up. During the last few days I have received letters Nos. 9, 54, 55, 56, 57, a roll of clipping about volcanoes, a pkg. of candy with a cigar and Elsa's pkg. of candy.

Letter No. 9 rather gave me a bad time of it. You mention having terrible craps during the menstrual period. Don't you think that it would be wise to go see Don Soodford of if necessary some gynecologist to check up and wee what's the matter. I is possible that womb might be tipped. I have been told of several cases where an operation cleared up difficulties of this kind. Do you remember that, when we were having intercourse, it always felt better to you to have me straddle you legs after he got settle down? It seemed to me that when I cam between you legs that you felt that the angle was unnatural. Also you remember that you always liked it better when I put my hands down under and fanny and lifted up. Boy, just thinking about it makes the Devil itch for Hell. However, if Doc can help you out it would probably save you a a lot of pain and increase our joy in each other when we are together again.

Along this same line I'll bet that a lot of the Dixon's troubles stems from the possibility that Allie is going through sexual changes and being tired most of the time, gets irritable and takes it out on Jim. When you and I are in each others arms again I want our reunion to be perfect physically and mentally. Of course it will take a little time to get readjusted to each other. I have always believed that our readjustment will be more perfect if we both take a trip somewhere by ourselves even though we don't go very far away. But to be along together where no one knows us we can have a second honeymoon.

That idea of yours about sending some packs of steel wool hit the spot. It would help a lot in places where we have trouble keeping our mess kits clean. Wen mess kits get coated with a greasy film it causes anyone eating from it to get the G.I's or in common parlance, the diarrhea.

By the looks of Don Congdon's address I would say that he is getting additional training or has some rear echelon job. I hope it is the latter for his sake. As for getting home on rotation after 18 months, there are so many "old fellows" on the waiting list that non of the new fellows expect any change until the war is over.

I hope Lynne Anderson makes it into the Merchant Marine. Submarine sinkings are pretty well stopped by now and I doubt if Lynne could stand the Infantry with his trick knee.

I received the copy of times News Review with the Life clippings about volcanoes. I doubt that Mother saw a picture of me in Life Mag. The only possible time that I might have gotten into a picture was when I was in the honor platoon.

The occasion was a memorial service for boys in the 179th Regt. I am no longer in the honor platoon because of my job as a runner. The close order drill for the honor platoon was felt necessary so that a visiting brass hat might not be shocked by the sight of a platoon of combat soldiers with their torn pants and muddy shoes.

Souvenirs? Well, so far, I haven't seen any souvenirs I would want to send home. When I get home I don't want anything around to remind me of the "delightful" Anzio Beach head. As for trophies I have no desire to take any back home.

Every time I look at Ridgefield News it seems as though somebody is raised in rank or is going to school. By the time the war is over there ought to be quite a sizeable army of corporals and sergeants all set to march triumphantly down Fifth Ave.

You were wondering where I was Easter Sunday, as near as I can remember I was lying down in a foxhole on the left flank of the first platoon listening to Jerry send over Easter greetings which went swish-wham! As a runner, however, I am back a ways usually near our company head quarters. Jerry throws in plenty of stuff where ever you are on this beach head so no one is really out of the reach of enemy artillery. We have to keep a philosophical attitude about it (and you should to) or it begins to get you down. The good Lord is the only one who knows what's in the future. I wish I could see the end of this mess.

We had a big event up here this time. The news was flashed from platoon to platoon midst great jubilation. One of our lieutenants allowed a female cat to come into his C.P. with him. She liked the place so well that she settled down and gave birth to five kittens! The lieutenant immediately put in a request for five layettes but so far the supply sergeant hasn't been able to fill the order.

I received your first pkg. with the candy and cigar. I lighted up the cigar this P.M. and felt like a bloated plutocrat. I have plenty of socks but the candy idea is swell. I know it created a hardship at home because of the shortage of candy but it certainly is a treat. It is fairly simple to get air mail envelopes but, of course, the big problem is to get Sky-rite paper.

You letters are like oasis in a desert of madness. How I long to take you in my arms and cuddle you to me. I want to give you long lingering, quivery kisses and run my lips up and down your throat until I find the little throbbing hollow in your throat and the nice soft spot in your shoulder, then I would take you over the couch and lay you down gently and kiss you some more with a toast of sherry or port wine. Then I would lay you out straight and start between your feet and work my way up between your thighs until the Devil was knocking at the door of hell. Then if I could wait long enough I would pick you up in my arms and carry you upstairs where I would take off your clothes and lay you out on our big bed. Then, my dear, after kissing those two nice nubbins I would take you riding to Banbury Cross. Then over again to put the Devil in Hell until not even his hooves would be showing. Just to luxuriate with your body warm and throbbing against him until he would arouse from his lethargy and start moving between the gates of Hell. Then he would swell with fierce joy and pour out such a flood that he would engulf hell in a blurring embrace. Oh, my dear, I have so much to make up for. My dearest wish is to be able to tell you and show you how much I adore you.

All my love,

Chad

May 15, 1944

Dearest Bedie:

I am dashing off this flimsy excuse for a letter in between sorting mail, shaving and washing myself and mess kit. I sort of went off the deep end yesterday. I don't often do that but some times my longing for you chokes up inside of me and I have to let off steam. As a change from the physical side of our life here is a poem which a buddy showed me. It expresses a lot of the way we both feel about our being separated.

Anniversary in Absence - Louise Owen

Out of a lifetime, what's a year,
or a little more, or a little less?
Only 12 months without my dear;
12 months - like wearing the same dark dress.

Like watching a garden that's planted and sown
and never a single seed comes up
Like eating bread that tastes of the stone
Like tepid water left in the cup.

I hear the doors, they open and close.
The fire in the stove burns clear and steady.
Today it rains, or tomorrow it snows
Iron the clothes when the clothes are ready.

Time goes along. And what is a year
Out of a life of wind and weather?
And why are 12 months without my dear
longer than all of our years together?

Of course this is written from the feminine angle but if you substitute the daily round of life on the Anzio beachhead you still have the same sentiment.

I am O.K. and, except for a couple of layers of dirt, fairly comfortable. We have our food brought up in units of five men allotments. This a.m. we had canned orange juice, hot cereal, bread and canned Vienna sausages. This p.m. we'll have canned spaghetti and meat balls and rice with dried fruit.

I received letter #59 last night with the snapshots. It seemed natural to see Tippie up at her window. Tell Allie that Jim should have been holding the pruning clippers. Remember when Jim and I got started on Mommy Hartmann's rose bush?

I hear that the boys who are inducted now receive a gov't gift of $100.00 after they sign the necessary papers. What's the matter? Has Uncle Sammie taken to using sugar - coated pills again? Sounds like some more of the New Deal philosophy to me.

The news about Freddie Jackson was a terrific blow. Freddie has a lot of courage and I'm sure that he will overcome the handicap. I don't blame Marian Shaughnessy for the way she feels. Tom has had enough. Let some one else get on with the work.

That pkg. with pencils and candy sounds good. And how that cocoa will hit the spot. We don't get it near often enough to suit me. As I told you previously a well-intentioned but blundering cuss borrowed my scout knife and ruined it opening cans. Can you possible get some kind of a knife? Any kind as long as it has a strong blade. Keep the candy coming too. It's a good thing to keep up body heat when standing guard about 3 or 4 o'clock in the a.m.

Boy, right now, Peter could do a nice job of slapping only I think he would prefer a nice fur collar somewhere up around the hilt.

Give my love to mother and Dad, Mother B, and the R. Crouchleys. All my love and devotion to you.

Chad

May 16, 1944
Anzio Beach head

Dearest little girl with the kissable nose:

This afternoon seems fairly quiet so I am taking the opportunity while it is here. It is hot and muggy here and the damn flies certainly like the bald spot on top of my head.

Last night I received letter no. 39 (the birthday card with $5 and nice message.) letter no 40 and a second pkg. (with cigar, candy and candle) The candle and candy will certainly come in handy. Don't send any more money or tobacco because we can't use money and we get plenty of tobacco. If we ever get to some big city we will have chance to buy some souvenirs. Don't think that I don't appreciate everything you send my sweet. One thing I miss a lot is my knife. I hope you can send me one. Maybe Francis might have one in the store.

I received a V mail from Elsa telling about Spring and its effects on Catoonah St. I suppose the cats give you a serenade every night.

You must be quite a dirt farmer by now. You certainly were lucky with the potatoes last year, I hope your luck is as good this summer. Only don't overdo it please, sweetheart, you know how your back can bother you.

You have probably read about the big push on the Italian front. We are hoping that the grand invasion will get started so that Jerry can be put on the run. The where and when are of course, anybody's gun.

When I was back in a rest area last time our company was paid and I received #31.10 of which I sent thirty dollars home. My capital with me is $22.70 so you can see that I am practically a bloated bureaucrat. The captain asked me to write out the money orders for the fellows who wanted to send money home. Boy, that was the most money I had handled in a long time. I darn near forgot to make out my own money order. Let me know when you get the money.

Right now there is an airplane flying around overhead. It is one of our artillery observation planes. The Germans call it the "Hell-Raiser" because when it flies over their lines they usually catch hell from our artillery. The darn little things are light and can't go very fast but amazingly enough very few of them are shot down.

Well, day after tomorrow will be my birthday, I certainly would like a birthday present but the only ones who could give it to me are the Axis leaders. The end of this war. Every G.I. is dreaming of that happy day when the order will come down "Cease Firing."

The boat won't be able to go fast enough to suit me. Then to see old N.Y. harbor and get on that train and jump off into my sweetheart's arms and smother her with kisses. Then home to see the folks and that night to just sit and talk with plenty of intermissions for "lubbin." Then to bed with my snuggle bunny. I had a dream about it last night and boy, was it real! Just to start right down between you legs kissing your thighs and the soft spots where your little round tummy is. Then to travel up between to little nubbins and kiss them until each one had a nice little peak on it. Then to nuzzle into your soft throat and finally to give you a lingering kiss on your sweet lips. In the meantime Peter would be approaching his goal throbbing with pent-up passion. Then to come to rest with his head up against the gates of Paradise. He would be so impatient to get in where it is warm and cozy. Finally, with a little help, he would get started on his way until he came to a tight little ring through which he would gently push. Then he would slide upward and inward until he was thoroughly hidden in Paradise. But, like most males, he wouldn't be satisfied with that so he would keep backing off and pressing his head trying to get into some further Paradise. But to his fierce pleasure the confines of Paradise would expand until he had plenty of room. By that time the nerves of his head would be convulsing with a mixture of pain and pure delight and he would make one final thrust upward and rest in a delirious flood of fiery love. Then he would rest drowsily until the Keeper of Paradise would beg for him to rest outside for a while until he had recovered from the heat of his labors. After resting for a while he would return, stiff with pride in his first achievement only to find that this time the gates of Paradise would be open wide for him to enter. Knowing the joy that lay ahead he would enter Paradise in one thrust until in an agony of longing to gain his goal he increased the tempo of his thrusts. Finally he would come to rest pouring out his gift of love in the uppermost parts of paradise. Locked in each others' arms we would drowsily kiss each other good night and dream together of the days ahead together.

I don't care what the censor thinks of this, but it is such a release to just put it down on paper that it came out in a rush. I wrote the last two pages in about 3 minutes.

All my love, my sweet, from

Chad

May, 17, 1944

Dearest Petunia;

I don't know what you will think of me. This is the first time that I have been able to write you three days in a row. Yesterday and the day before I wrote some "snooky" passages because I had room to spread myself but on this V-mail I can just about get started.

Last night I received the package with the Dunhill lighter. It works O.K. after I got the wick charred enough. I can carry it in its cardboard box. Interruption of 3/4 of an hour to clean up garbage and old papers around our holes. Don't send hard candies because we get plenty of them with our rations. Any kind of chocolate or cocoa however is just the ticket. News continues to be pretty good from the front line. I hope they keep the krauts on the run. Then maybe they can be pried loose from the mountains here and pushed up the peninsula. Last night I also received letter no. 17! (18th March, 1944) It made me feel pretty ashamed about my not writing on the boat. I certainly have a lot to make up for when I hold my sweetheart in my arms again. All my love and take good care of yourself.

Your "Lubbin Hubber"
Chad

May 20, 1944

My dearest sweetheart:

We've been moving around again and are now in a little quieter place. We take showers this p.m. and this a.m. we received clean socks and underclothes. So I'll be pure again for a few days at any rate. Last night we got a canteen cup of beer. Although the beer was flat it still reminded me of home where we used to open up a quart bottle of Hoffman's and sit around gabbing. Yesterday a.m. we got PX rations of candy and three cigars. You'd probably split a gusset laughing at me with a big fat cigar in my mouth. It tastes good though to bite into and smoke good Havana leaf after smoking a lot of cigarettes. They send a lot of Fleetwoods, Ralieghs, Twenty Grands and Philip Morris over here so that when we get Camels, Luckies, or Chesterfields in our rations we prize them highly. However there certainly are plenty of smokes on the beach head. Fellows who used to smoke very moderately now find themselves using up one and two packs a day.

Last night (I should say evening) I got out my big fat envelope in which I have carefully kept your letters to me. I went through them carefully and made notes of things I should remember like names and places. I am afraid that I won't be able to keep so many papers so what I'll do is burn them. I don't want anyone to be pawing over letters from my sweetheart. When I was reading them I came to some parts (like no. 53 where you were describing a canoe trip to South Pond) which made the temperature in our foxhole rise considerably. The last letter I have is no. 59 and up to that number the only ones I haven't received yet are nos. 24, 42, 51, 58.

I was very much pleased to receive the name of the scouts. It's nice to be remembered like that. I haven't received the package yet but it will certainly come in handy.

When you mentioned meeting Mary and Betty did you mean a couple - (Interruption of 2 1/2 hours to go take a shower. I feel much better) - of queens who sometimes are seen in the vicinity of New York. The last time I saw either of those large ladies was from the west side elevated highway.

As I rest here on my blankets I wish I were back home stretched out on our big red Hudson Bay Blanket with you by my side. I would hold you so tight in my arms you would never be able to get away. I would kiss your throat and the nice soft skin just under your chin. In the meantime I would have two nice nubbins in my hands. Then I would press the Devil hard up against the gates of Hell where he could throb to his hearts' desire until Hell was so hot that the Devil would have to go in to put the fire out. After he had started in looking for the fire I would rest my head on your shoulder and put my hands under your hips until I could lift you up. By that time the Devil would be impatiently looking around for the fire going deeper and deeper with every thrust until finally he would find the fire and put it out. Oh, my dear, I'll never get enough of loving you. Each time I have embraced you it has been like a new phase of our love. And now that we have been apart so long it will seem just like that happy day in June ten years ago when we were at Cousin Bertha's camp tasting the first real joy of our marriage. Remember how impatient I was and yet afraid that I was going to hurt you. I guess it did hurt you plenty then but after a few times we learned more about pleasing each other. When we are together again and can drink a toast of port wine pledging each other our love we will have behind us ten happy years of living together. Still, because of this long separation, it will seem just like another honeymoon. I hope and pray it comes soon. Take care of yourself, sweetheart, and know that you are loved by your own,

Chad

May 22, 1944

My dearest Bedie;

Don't be startled by this two column affair because I'm writing on a long narrow cardboard box and thought this might work better. Also I borrowed some ink as I am using my old Waterman pen again.

Last night I received letters No. 58, 68, and 62 and the manila envelope with the flints and wicks for the lighter. The lighter works swell. So far none of your letters have been censored. Those rumors about the 50 tons of air mail in New York remind me of some of the rumors we get around here. Somebody walks up to somebody else with a mysterious air and says" Did you hear about the invasion? They've landed with so and so divisions" And so it goes.

I received the snapshots of you with tippie and Buzzie. I appreciated the remark about the "little girl with the coy can." I showed the picture of you to my foxhole buddy and he wanted to know right away where you got that sweater. I told him that you had designed it yourself and he said, "smart girl." I think so too. I'll try to get some foreign money to send home for a souvenir. You asked about my messenger job. I use tanks more. Only messengers of the larger units use motor cycles or bikes. That Malaria job was very short. About all I do now on that is to see that my platoon has an adequate supply of satabrine. Channels for the medical corps or foreign language are just about nil.

I don't blame Lyne for being distrustful. It's a wonder to me that anyone knows where he stands with the draft board.

I am glad you bought some new dresses. I know what that does to perk up your spirits.

Love Chad

My darling wife;

Don't think I'm crazy but I just happened to drag this V-mail out of my case and, as I proceeded I kept thinking of things to write about.

You don't like V-mail I know but we got a lot of it so it is always handy.

My dearest sweetheart;

I want you to save that piece of buckskin out in Mary's room but I don't care whether you throw away that small fir mat. I don't know what kind of animal it came from. Maybe it was from one of "Mrs. Buck's boys."

What you told me about Carl's getting an infected toe and Dorothy's lack of interest proves what I have always thought. That Dot is really self-centered and doesn't care about anyone but herself.

As long as we are issued new socks every two weeks at the most it doesn't seem wise to have you send any more. Just this P.M. I washed out five dirty pairs and they are hanging out on a bush now drying in the sun. I could use some more was candles though and of course I miss my knife. I hope you will be able to get me one.

(My buddy's wife want the recipe for Indian pudding.)

The old "Tater" patch ought to be pretty big by now and if you have the same luck as last year you will have a good supply for next winter. I hope I'm back by then to help you eat them. I know how you feel working way down in the back lot. I used to feel the same way.

It was too bad about Richard Brown. We have little chance to see anyone who is injured. They are often moved back to Naples. I was glad to hear about Mr. Tucker's new job. He is a good worker and should make a success as a headmaster.

Give my love to the folks. Tell Mother Bedient to take good care of herself. Remember me to the Dixons and Hartmans. Last but not least. Take good care of yourself, my darling and accept my loving thoughts.

Chad

May 24, 1944

Dearest little perky nose;

This is more like it. I don't blame you for cussing at V-mail. So here goes for some more things that I made notes on to write about. Just before I burn up old letters I re-read them and make notes of things I want to say.

You were saying that you would like to take some of the lead out of my pencil. My dear, that really would keep you busy for quite a while. I am afraid that before my pencil became soft you would be worn to a frazzle. When we are together again I don't intend to rush matters. There will plenty of time to cuddle up together and snuggle to our hearts content. I've no doubt that before we can put the Devil in Hell again I will have a good time loving you and preparing for the real thing. There are so many things I can do to make the temperature of Hell rise to the boiling point.

Rome is only twenty miles away as the crow flies but it seems a long way to us here on the beach head. I hope these attacks which you are reading about will jar the bastards loose so that they never stop running until they get to Berlin. Things are beginning to pop around here although I've had no part in it so far. When Rome is ours I hope I get the chance to visit the great buildings I often read about. I certainly will try to get you another powder jar like the one you bought on the square near St. Peters. Of course, the Vaticanate is a neutral state, so it will never be touched by our forces.

The news that Harry James has bought a place in Ridgefield certainly must have started a gale of ohs and ahs from the females. I'll bet the High School population is all agog.

Brownie must be a fighting fool. We could use him over here for patrol work. He would make short work of the krauts he met.

When I was back in the States at the last camp I was racking my brain to try to think of some way I could let you know. So I thought of the wall paint in Ralphs living room never realizing that there is a camp Perry in Williamsburg. As far as I can make out very few people know much about the camp where we were stationed before embarkation. Sorry I was off track.

I'm not the only one who gets off the beam though. You were talking about the apple tree in bloom, the last one down toward the garden. That's a Gravenstien, not a Baldwin. Which ever it is I'd like to looking at it right now. Of course the flowers here are very nice and much more vivid in their coloring that those in the States but right now a headache flower or a skunk cabbage would smell like a rose to me. This morning I was on guard just before dawn and heard the birds waking up but I would have exchanged them all for one robin or blue bird. This A.M. I saw a very peculiar cloud formation. It was a mass of two or three mare's tails over head but there were shadows running across them every which way like ripples. It was weird. Several of us saw it so it wasn't due to G.I. Water or food. As for vino I haven't had a drink of anything except 2 cups of beer since I left Africa.

I was glad to get a V-mail letter from Don Congdon. He is getting additional training but is still classified as 055 (clerk general). There is still a chance that he may be assigned to some rear area to do the kind of work he likes.

The other day my buddy and I were talking about various foods that made our teeth water and I happened to mention that I am very fond of Indian Pudding. He wants me ask you to send the recipe to his wife because I raved so about it. The address is: Mrs. William P. Stout, West Union, West Va. I am enclosing a snapshot of their little girl. Her name is Ann Huntington Stout and she is 11 mos. old. In her picture she look like a torch singer. I forgot to mention that I received letter No. 65 and was overwhelmed by the number of things you said you were sending me. Please don't send any more candy for a while because I've eaten so much candy lately that I skipped some meals. Also don't send any more underwear. Our division has a laundry going now so that we get clean underwear fairly often. I will pick out the knife I like the best and will sell the other two. There is a ready market for them here. Some candles would be just the thing if you could manage it. When those soft pencils arrive I will have a plentiful supply of writing materials. I suppose the Army never thought of powdered ink because there doesn't seem to be any that would work in fountain pens.

This morning, as I lay on my blankets after doing guard duty, I was dreaming of your sweet face and how I would like to kiss your lips until they got all quivery, soft, and warm. Then how I would love to run my lips down your neck until I could kiss the little hollow that throbs in your throat. Then I dreamed about carrying you in my arms to our great big bed where I would undress you and kiss your nubbins until you begged me to take hold of both your wrists and spread you out. Then to press the Devil against the gates of Hell until they opened wide to let him in. Then I woke up to hear the pounding of artillery. It was such a nice dream, my dear, and with the help of Divine Providence I hope to be back in your loving arms again where you can give kisses back to your loving husband,

Chad.

May 24, 1944

Well, we picked up our stuff and moved to another area. In the meantime I received a N.Y. Times and letters No. 42, 61, 63, and 64. You spoke of getting a letter dated March 31. That was just before I went up for the first time. At that time conditions were pretty static except for patrolling and artillery duels. I didn't go on any patrols so I haven't been within spitting distance from the Jerries the way Dave has. After that I was appointed a messenger and, of course haven't had any patrol work for which I am duly thankful. One time I did got out under artillery fire with the medics to bring in a wounded lieutenant and the body of one of our boys who was killed by a direct hit. On the way back with the officer we had to hit the ground about ten times because of enemy machine gun fire. That was about the most exhausting and nerve shaking night I have experienced. Please forgive me if I don't tell you about experiences at the front. Somehow or other we push them out of our minds and try to think of pleasant things like home and the folks we love. As for Nellie Bassett and her clucking she ought to be proud of her valiant son sitting on his fat ass in England. Oh well. Darn this V-mail any way I'm going to get out some air mail and write a letter that looks like one.

Chad

May 27, 1944

My dearest sweetheart;

It has been a couple of days since I have had a chance to write you. I know you hate this V-mail but it is the only thing I have handy since the air-mail paper is in my pack. I am writing this from the Italian front. You know from the papers why I am able to use that expression. Things have changed radically here and Jerry has put his engine in reverse. I am O.K. Although hot and dusty. It's pretty hard to find a nice cool spot when the sun is blazing down. From now on it will probably be difficult to keep in touch with home. I don't know what I will do when those pkgs. start coming in. I may have to get rid of some of the articles of clothing as we are now traveling as light as possible. I don't want to seem lacking in appreciation. It's just one of those things that happen. Remember me to Dad and Mom, Mother B, Ralph and Ruth and the rest of the folks. I love you , my dear, and pray for the day to come when I will be able to personally tell you how much.

Chad

June 4, 1944

Dearest Bedie;

I am writing this hurriedly on the top of a chest of drawers in an abandoned Italian house. As you can see by the papers we are all on the move and at last have forced Jerry to pull back up the peninsula. Although I have had some close calls my prayers and yours have availed. War seems so incongruous in the farming land of rippling wheat, barely, oats and bright red poppies. Although I am still dirty as two pigs we had a chance to wash up a bit today. It certainly felt good to wash my feet and put on clean socks. If I could wave these socks in Hitler's face he would surely surrender pronto. I haven't had any mail now for over a week and am looking forward to receiving a lot of back mail. The weather is getting pretty hot here now and we all sweat like the devil. That combined with a coating of gray dust makes a fellow look as though he were in a cement factory. All my love, sweetheart, don't worry.

Your loving husband,

Chad

June 7, 1944

My dearest sweetheart;

I am writing this sitting our blankets on a hillside at 7:30 a.m. The reason is that we have a few minutes before chow and I wanted to get a chance to write today. Yesterday I was within four miles of the place where you bought your blue glass powder jar. I doubt that we will get a chance to even see the place although some of the fellows took off last night and saw some of it. They say that the building are undamaged. Yesterday afternoon we were thrilled by the news coming from England. At last the Tedeschis are getting something to worry about from the west. Maybe they won't be able to send as much stuff down here now. We are all hoping that the Russians will take advantage of the opportunity. I had a letter of May 24 from Ralph yesterday, a copy of Delta and Colgate News, and 2 copies of the Press but no letters from you. The postman is moving quite a lot lately so maybe when he catches up I will get a bunch of letters from you. From now on my letters will have to written on the fly.

All my love sweetheart,

from Chad

June 8, 1944

My dearest sweetheart;

I am unlimbering the old faithful fountain pen to get off a few lines to let you know I am O.K.

It seems strange to be lying here on my blanket not listening to the sound of big guns. We have been passing through peaceful farm country with only occasional shell holes to remind us of the Jerries. The Italian peasants are all busy working in their fields trying to make up for lost time. Every where you go you see large fields of sheep or a herd of cattle, although according to the natives the Jerries got away with plenty. Yesterday I was one of about fifty in our outfit who was marched out to be congratulated by the colonel and presented with the Infantry Badge for Exemplary Conduct in Action.

- feel very humble about it because there are so many fellows who have gone through more than I have. God has been very merciful to me and I thank him every day in my prayers. We are on the move so much that we don't get our mail. I will be glad when we settle down in one spot for a while so your mail can catch up with me. I carry your pictures with me and look at your sweet face every day. How I wish I could be looking at the original and telling her how much I love her.

Chad

June 9, 1944

My dearest sweetheart;

Last night I received letter #68 with the birthday greetings and some more air-mail paper and envelopes. I still haven't received the boxes which you mentioned although I suppose they take quite a while to come over. Now that we are in one spot for a few days I think a lot of back mail will catch up.

We are resting up a bit and enjoy the warm Italian sunshine. The nights are still chilly and damp and a woolen blanket feels welcome. It was good to sleep under canvas again after many nights spent sleeping with a raincoat wrapped around the body.

Of course it is impossible now for military reasons for me to tell you about the last few weeks but it is heart warming to see the change in this war in Italy. Now that the Jerries have been forced northward and the invasion has hit France the spirit among our fellows has certainly become more cheerful.

On my last V-Mail letter I told you that I received the Infantry badge for exemplary conduct in action. It is a beautiful piece of workmanship made of silver. It has an oblong blue panel with a silver flint-lock rifle like those of Revolutionary war days. It is surrounded by a silver wreath of oak leaves. I feel very proud to be able to wear it.

Day before yesterday we got a ration of beer. One and a half quarts per man. My buddy drank only part of his so I had two quarts. I really felt it too. I was just thinking of that special blue bottle down in the cellar which Ralph brought back from Cuba. Boy! would that taste good. It will be a happy day when you and I can open that bottle together and toast the future.

Lately I have had quite a few chances to exercise my Italian. The nearer you get to the Eternal City the more easily the natives understand the lingua Romana which I learned in college. Today I picked up a small German-English dictionary and have started studying German. A few days ago I could have used it to good advantage. Another runner and I were taking some Jerry prisoners to the rear. It was necessary to make a stretcher for one of them who was wounded. A knowledge of German would have helped a lot but by using signs and a few words we knew we got them to search for some poles across which they could throw a blanket to make a stretcher.

According to your letters you ought to have quite a garden by now. Boy! What I wouldn't give to bite into a nice crisp head of lettuce or munch some young carrots.

Well, sweetheart, I have to clean my knife and shave off some whiskers because we are having an inspection this evening.

Take good care of yourself and know that I love you with all my heart and soul. I wish I could tell you how much I miss you on our anniversary month. You have given me ten years of love and understanding that serve to keep me grateful to you for always.

All my love

Chad

Give my love to Mother Bedient and the rest of the family.

Chad

June 12, 1944

My dearest little perky nose:

Well, I certainly have been catching up with by back mail. So far I have received letters # 67, 68, 71, 72, 80 and 81. a copy of Rotarian, a Press, and copy of the Sunday N.Y. Times. Besides that I received two packages one with tea, cocoa, steel wool and PENCILS and the other with chewing gum, socks, candy etc. Boy, that cocoa is bona stuff as we say here. As you have probably noticed am writing with one of the new pencils and what a difference it makes. Now I can really spread myself. First to answer you letters.

#67 Now that we are in a rest area of course it is possible to write more often than I did when at McClellan. There they were so busy making life uncomfortable for us dog faces that I for one didn't have much ambition or strength to write. Here, while resting, there is every encouragement to write home so that's the way it goes.

Being a runner under battle conditions is no picnic although of course we don't have to take part in patrols. But patching up broken wire and running messages can have its exciting moments. On one attack we runners carried boxes of machine gun ammunition. Boy was that a lot of work! The good Lord has been kind to us and as a result we haven't had casualties recently among our runners. All we can do is to work the best we know how and trust in Him.

It was quite a long time ago that I saw Bill Maver for a few minutes but that was back near Anzio. It seems likes ages. So much has happened since.

That "dear friend of the Finches" was Dave but the way I described it I couldn't give his name because as I remember I also mentioned the place and that would have connected his unit with that particular rest area. I must be getting childish and probably my letters would be comparable to those of a grammar school kid.

Thanks for Harvey Keeler's new address. I will write him and also Francis and Daisy.

I was sorry to hear about the death of Hubert Benedict. I know for a long time that he had a weak heart of course climbing stairs and sweeping up at the school probably aggravated his condition.

About our date in New York. I know for certain that you will be in no physical condition to stand a mad whirl of shows and night clubs but I know too that we would enjoy staying at a hotel and resting up together. Then later we could go off somewhere on a trip and really enjoy ourselves. I don't feel a bit worried about our getting readjusted to each other. We already love each other so much and have missed one another so much that it will be one of the happiest times of our lives.

You bowled me over with the amount of money you have saved. You're a regular banker. By the way, have you received my money order for $30.00 which I sent home early in May? I received your letter with $5.00 and also the very super birthday card which you sent.

During my birthday we were sweating out the approach of big doings and at the time, I felt as though I were 56 instead of 36.

I was surprised to hear that the Navy accepted Dick McGlynn. He is going to give some instructor a lot of very sad moments.

Mary Belle McGlynn has a lot of spunk. She will probably make a damn fine nurse. I only hope that she gets a chance to recover her equilibrium. She has the brains to do a good job.

I received a card from Readers Digest but haven't received any copies as yet. Probably they will be along soon.

#72 your description of that hat left me bewildered. Are you sure that it is a hat? It reminds me of a picture in Life Magazine of some of Heda Hoppers Hats.

I would like to help you apply your liquid stockings only I'm afraid that the paint job would have to wait until the legs had been spread apart for a while.

#80 You say you are down to 126 pounds. Don't forget, sweetheart, that weight isn't to terribly important. It's more important to feel in good health and get your rest.

#81 You say you were sick. What was the matter? It worries me when I think of how you get so tired and then some damn bug comes along and bang! You are in bed. I hope you are better now, my love, because I couldn't bear to think of you sick.

You were wondering what I was doing the day that C. Walker's house caught on fire. About that time I was going into an attack with my company. But the Lord was watching over me.

It is nearly dark and I can hardly see the paper so I will close! All my love sweetheart and soft kisses on your eyelids and a nice snuggle in that little pulsing hollow in your throat. I wish I could deliver them in person.

Love,

Chad

Somewhere in Italy
June 16, 1944

My dearest little perky nose:

Back to air mail again. I am accumulating quite a lot of air mail paper and envelopes now that I have received three packages. Last night I got my 3rd big package, the one with the knives. Thanks a lot. I've been lost without a pocket knife. I have so much candy now that you ought not to send any more for a while. Don't bother your curly head about packages anyway, sweetheart, because we draw PX rations and have plenty of candy and cigarettes. About the only thing I need is a small sturdily built notebook for taking down memos.

I have a new job for a while. I don't know how long it will last but I hope to be able to continue with it. We have an acting first sergeant and I am helping him as his field clerk. There is a lot of paper work because things were not kept up to date but once we catch up it won't be bad at all. At least I won't have to run out to my platoon for a while.

The other day I was in Rome. We got off at the Piazza S. Pietro and I immediately went looking for a powder jar for you but I'm sorry to say that I couldn't find one so I compromised by getting you some Italian Mosaic work. I bought some brooches and bracelets and a papal coin for Leve. We had to take our dinner with us because of the fact that it is almost impossible to buy food in the city. The people are dependent upon the authorities for their food. A package of cigarettes or a bar of candy will buy almost anything in Rome and I mean anything. My buddy and I were propositioned by a couple of girls about 18 or 19 but we weren't having any. I'm not trying to be a prude but I figure that if you love me enough to wait for me I certainly love you enough to wait until that happy day when we will be together again. During the P.M. we wandered out along the Corso Victor Emmanuel and saw the Italian monument of V. Emmanuel II and the tomb of the unknown soldier. Then to the old Roman Forum and the Colosseum. At the Colosseum we ate our lunches among the ruins and I struck up a conversation with an Italian guard. I made out O.K. until he got excited, then I only made out every third word or so. On the way back we wandered down the side streets stopping for wine or cognac. By the time we got back to the trucks we were very hot, tired and dusty and glad to be headed for the cooler countryside.

I forgot to mention that we spent a good part of the a.m. in St. Peters. It is magnificent but a bit gaudy with so much gilt and minute decoration. The mosaics behind the altars and the paintings in the domes are really wonderful. The colors are still so brilliant after all these years. I'm glad I got the chance to go.

Lately I have received letters #69, 79, 82, 85 and page 1 of #86. I received the birthday card and the $5 sometime ago. Have you received a special P.T.A. payment of $30.00 from me yet. I sent it about May 10. Please don't send any more clothing because it makes such a bundle when we have to move in a hurry.

I had a letter from Grace last night and will try to answer it very soon. I was glad to get the news of the school.

My chances of seeing either Ed Strait or Levio Conestrari are pretty slim. It is difficult even when a fellow is in the same battalion as you are.

I will have their addresses and write them. At least I can let them know I am in their neighborhood.

Sweetheart, this warm weather, seeing women again after months, and being separated from you is certainly doing things to my hormones. You say that you like my "lead pencil" letters and want "snooky" writing. I can assure you that a night doesn't pass that I don't dream about some of the experiences we have had together. I can just picture you in my arms as I climb those steep stairs with little Tippie paddling along behind. I can picture you as I used to take off your shoes and fumble with the fasteners on your girdle then slide your little silk pants down your legs. Then how I used to darn near burn up as I slid your dress and slip off over your head. Then to kneel before you and kiss your thighs and come up with the devil between your legs until he throbbed right against that nice soft spot. Then how I would pick you up and place you on our big wide bed to love you and kiss you until you were ready for the devil to enter hell. When I dream up to that point I wake up in a sweat and hope and pray that the day will come when we will actually be doing such things instead of dreaming about them.

Take good care of yourself and give my love to the folks.

All my love to you my sweet,

from Chad

June 22, 1944

My dearest gal with the perky nose:

When I get mail I don't do things half way. Last night I hit the jackpot and received 1 package (with pencil and pen set), 1 envelope of air mail paper, 1 pathfinder, 2 N.Y. Times, a letter from Sid Bedient, one from Dad, one from Readers' Digest and SIX from you. Their number of 73, 74, 75, 76, 78 and 88. Luckily we are in a place where we can keep a candle lit so I was busy reading until late. We have moved again to another rear area and saw some interesting sights. We are very hot here as the summer season approaches. The other day we were eating apricots, ox heart cherries and plums. Boy, it certainly was good to taste fresh fruit again.

According to your letter my letters must get pretty crossed up. The only way we will be able to keep things straight is to go by dates on my letters and number on yours.

About the last part of April my platoon lieutenant put my name in for Pfc. and about the first of May my appointment went through. A raise in rank is OK by me but all the raises, medals etc. don't mean a thing beside that trip home to my sweetheart.

When we were up the front the worst things we had to experience were the mortars and artillery. A runner has to be on the alert all the time when out in the open and watch for shell holes or fox holes into which to take cover if Jerry opens up with a barrage.

You made my mouth water with your account of that ginger bread with whipped cream. The other area we came from was in a farming area and we were able to have a canteen cup of milk nearly every morning. But now we have gone back to that well known armored cow which you don't like.

(time out for chow)

You mentioned the Thunder bird in your letter. It reminds me too of the times in Wisconsin Rapids when we saw the tribal dances of the Wennebegoes and the Sioux. I will send you a shoulder patch in another envelope.

We get the Stars and stripes and Yank O.K. but not in very large amounts. So when they come in most of them go to the platoons. We enjoy the cartoons by Bill Mauldin and of course "Lil Abner."

At the time I saw Dave back in the rest area his division was just moving in so I couldn't say anything about it. I saw him for only a few minutes before we pulled out.

By the way, I have plenty of air mail paper and envelopes now. The last time we moved I darn near filled a cardboard Butterfinger box with stationery and I carried it in my combat pack to be sure to deep it dry.

As I wrote you some time ago I have received letters #1, 2, 3, and 9. I haven't received the package from the Scouts yet. I have plenty of candy so far. I don't have the craving for sweets that I had while at McClellan. I suppose that is due to the change in weather. When it was raw, wet and cold I was anxious for candy, but now that it is hotter than the devil I don't care much about sweets.

As long as the cellar supply of canned fruits and vegetables seems to be holding out there isn't much sense in going to all the extra effort of keeping a garden. Your strength and health are more important. Certainly the potatoes are a tough enough job to carry through. Planting Timothy in the hill plot ought to hold the soil OK and can easily be plowed under if necessary.

I certainly was surprised to hear that F. Bassett was in the States although I wasn't surprised to hear that he had suffered a nervous breakdown. If he was working in a morgue it was a poor piece of personal placement work. Anyone with any sense just looking at him would have known that he wasn't suited for such a job.

It's peculiar that you asked about the conditions of my stomach. After the recent fracas south of Rome. I got a bad case of the G.I.'s or plain and fancy diarrhea. I have been feeling a little rocky ever since but am gradually recovering. That's why when I read about the Teacher's dinner I began to drool, slaver etc. Army food isn't conducive to raising an appetite. I'm afraid that there are going to be a lot of ruined stomachs among the G.I.'s coming out of this war.

I always knew I married a smart gal. You certainly knocked that guy for a loop. We are so spotty in our news that I am pretty low in my current events I.Q. That's why I devour the N.Y. Times News Section which you send.

Don't forget to write to Mrs. Stout and give here the recipe for Indian pudding and I am sure that she can probably tell you some things of interest.

June 23, 1944

Maybe I'll finish this letter after a while. My stomach acted up a bit so I didn't feel much like writing but after taking some more sulfadiazene pills I feel a bit better.

Tonight I received more letters Nos. 70, 84, 87 and 89 so I'll read and re-read them and start an answer tomorrow.

Take good care of yourself, my sweetheart and remember me to the folks.

All my love,

Chad

My Dearest Petunia:

Eight letters to answer! Boy, I'd better get on the ball and start writing if I want to keep getting mail. 8 to 1 isn't a fair score and I'll have to do better if I want to keep up my end of this bargain. The letters were Nos. 70, 83, 84, 87, 89, 90, 91, 92. So here goes. I can't guarantee to write on asbestos paper but if you like that kind of letter I'm the guy that can dish it out. I have wondered though whether or not it is advisable to write that kind of letter. It's tough enough just being separated without my stirring up your emotions by reminding you of the happiness we have had together. I don't know what do you think? However, I'll keep this letter on a strictly kosher level.

Your description of the garden effort and the generations of chickens coming on looks to me like a lot of work. Wouldn't it be a good idea to get one of the Boy Scouts to come in occasionally and help in the battle against the weeds? It would be worth it to you to save your strength and not get so tired out after already being busy all day at the bank. Jim Dixon hasn't recovered from his thyroid trouble and that is probably why is so pooped. His thyroid trouble may also have something to do with is marital problem.

That guy who advised the burning of all single and twin beds had the right idea. As for me, that great big bed of ours with its nice soft mattress is my idea of a No.1 article of furniture. I'd like to have a dollar for every time I have dreamed of that bed and what is in it. I'd be a millionaire. I agree with you that our second honeymoon should be spent somewhere far away from friends and relatives. Especially some place where there are nice cool nights so I can cuddle you in my arms and keep you warm. I have thought that it would be nice to re-trace the route we took 10 years ago, up through the Adirondacks and across the states of Vermont and New Hampshire, up into Maine and then down to Cape Cod. Or, if the season is such that the north is too cold, we could go out to California by the southern route and see a lot of the things we always have wanted to visit. The T.V.A., New Orleans with it's Latin Quarter, the American Desert, Yosemite Park, the Indian Reservations and the West Coast.

My buddy and I both appreciate the Pathfinder and N.Y. Times. It helps us a lot to get a general picture of the world news.

I am glad you got the $30.00 because when we're paid our back pay in May I accumulated more money that I needed. So as long as the government offered the chance to send money home with no risk to the individual soldier I took the chance.

So far your letters have not been censored. Over here if a fellow really ignores the censorship regulations repeatedly he is liable to find himself digging a new latrine or a garbage pit. Right at this time military security is very important and we are allowed to describe only our visit to Rome and the part our outfit took in breaking out of the Anzio Beachhead.

I doubt whether Levio Canestrari is anywhere me now. I certainly would be glad to see him. I'll bet he would get a kick of out getting a snappy salute from his old teacher.

You're getting to be a regular carpenter. The way some purple heart awards are made you ought to rate two or three with all your skinned knuckles and banged thumbs.

Tell the Scouts that as I remember it I made some poles and stakes for the tents out of strips of wood I got the from the Outpost Lumber Yard.

They were just homemade affairs. Let them use their ingenuity like we do over here. Wood is very scarce so when we pitch our pup tents we use fence posts or that bamboo - like cane which is fairly plentiful here.

I can't imagine John Nash standing the physical beating of commando training. He is the nervous type and that sort of thing would be too much for him!

Don't get too tired out working with the garden and the chickens. Working with a rake and hoe is strenuous and you use muscles that don't get much exercise in indoor work. Take care of yourself sweetheart and remember that I love you with all my heart.

Chad

To my sweetheart with the perky nose:

I certainly have fallen way behind in my letter writing. Lately I have been pretty busy typing and answering the phone. I am still working as a company field clerk although I don't know how long the job will last. The fellow who is acting as First Sergeant and I get along together O.K.. He comes from Georgia and has a regular Southern accent. When he gets a couple of drinks under his belt he is as funny as anyone I have ever seen.

Up to now I have received and haven't answered a whole slew of letters from you. Like Frankie to Johnny I been doing you wrong. I've received Nos. 83, 88, 90, 92-100, 103, 104. Forgive me if I wander all over the lot.

I'm glad you finally got the $30 I sent. I have been paid again so before long I will be sending some more money home. Only when a fellow gets into a city is there much chance to spend money. Then he really can spend the money. In some towns where the Red Cross has set up canteens a fellow can get ice cream. So far quite of a lot of the fellows have been able to get ice cream, but I have stayed pretty close to the typewriter. The main thing a fellow can spend his money on are food, drink and women. I haven't had enough drink in me to mention so the Italian women still look dirty to me. That sounds as though I was trying to appear as a goody goody boy but I know that there are too many risks both to health and self respect to get mixed up with any woman in this pitiful country. Oh nuts! You know what I mean.

You spoke of being waked up in a very nice manner. Nothing could give me more pleasure that to be able to reach over in the morning to pull you close into my arms and show you some real lovin! I am reminded of the story in De Cameron in which Boccaccio tells of a young Italian lover who got up onto the sleeping balcony of his sweetheart by telling her that he would teach her how to make the nightingales sing. She liked the procedure so much that he came every night to make her "face the music".

Boy: Doris DeForest certainly didn't waste any time getting hitched. She got a swell guy and I hope married life settles her jitters so that she will calm down a bit. Maybe that's just what she needs.

From the description of Francis Bassett's actions I would say that he is pretty clever. He may be able to convince the doctors that he isn't fit for duty. It's a trick as old as war itself. Generals in ancient times must have had trouble with neurotic soldiers and sailors. The only difference was that they blamed it on evil spirits.

Thanks for Jedge Eckerty's address. I'm going to write to him and also Don Condon this afternoon. Also thanks for the R.H.S. Graduation program. It doesn't seem possible that those kids are graduated. Tempers certainly does forget.

Tim Campbell's death was a great shock to me but somehow I feel different about people dying in warfare. I have seen dead and dying but somehow when you see them you don't have the same feeling as when one of your buddies gets hit. When you know the man and have gone through a lot of close calls with him you miss him more. That's why when replacements come into a company pretty soon you have a hard time keeping track of the fellows you know. Please remember, sweetheart, that I haven't been through a small fraction of what some of the "old men" have experienced, especially those who went through the early days of the Anzio Beachhead. That's why I feel very humble when a bunch of the "old boys" get together and start reminiscing.

I am so glad, my sweet, that my letter arrived on June 20th. I know from your letters that you are and have been under a great emotional stress for a long time. Remember dear, that over here in the midst of all this stupid killing and destruction that people who have been living in slavery and want are beginning to stir again and hope for something better. There is a spirit of confidence where there were some doubters before. I pray that this thing will end soon before the Nazis in a spirit of hate and frustration destroy more thousands of helpless people. The time that we have lost out our lives together will certainly make me appreciate you more than I ever did before and want to show you how much I really love you.

Your description of our honeymoon at Cousin Bertha's Camp gives me a big benefit of the doubt. As I remember it, I practically raped you. If I had known then what I know now after ten years of married life I can assure you that you would have wanted to stay at Lake Katrine for quite a while. I certainly do remember how shy you were but that made me love you all the more. Together I would say that we both have been eager students in the Art of Love. A man can be such a blundering, ignorant cuss when it comes to making love to a woman. I suppose she probably wonders what all the hurry is about and has pity on him. I know as time goes on you get to learn and enjoy all the thousand and one things that please your loved one. Don't boast too much about the beating you're going to give me because the way I feel you're going to be hard put to it to keep your end up.

Now that you have film, how about a picture of you in a nice snazzy evening dress just as though you were all set to go out for a good time. The more pictures of you the better. Speaking of pictures, Bill Stout gave me that picture of his little girl so he doesn't expect it back.

You were making my mouth water by talking about steak. We get steak once in a while. It is cut about 1/2 inch thick and is accompanied by a thick gravy which the boys call "Oklahoma Ice Cream". Last night to celebrate the 4th of July we had turkey and it tasted good even though it went through the Army system of cooking a turkey.

I haven't received letter #102 yet. It ought to be good if you were tight with a few drinks tucked away, you ought to be able to really tear loose and write a regular book. Remember that 23 page letter you sent me when I was at McClellan? How did you make out with that new dress you were making? I would like to be around to survey the handiwork and test the measurements.

Could you get me one of those folders which look like a pocket book but are used for snap shots. I would like to have one so that I can protect the pictures I have from wear and tear. If I don't put something over the pictures they won't stand much more handling. The other night I received 2 pkgs. containing cigarettes and one containing candy.

I will close this ramble though my thoughts are with the one that is always with me. Take good care of yourself, sweetheart, for you know I love you with all my heart.

Chad

July 12, 1944
Somewhere in Italy

Dearest Petunia:

I am trying out the new Parkette pen which I received some time ago. Lying on your stomach writing by candle light isn't conducive to good penmanship but here goes.

I really feel very guilty about my letter writing or lack of it, I should say, but that old bromide about being very busy is really true. By buddy has been very conscientious about keeping his wife informed so that I feel quite ashamed. I am OK and am watching my diet so as to avoid putting on weight. Typing and doing clerical work don't call for the husky meals I used to consume. I am getting now so that I can make pretty accurate copies with a fair rate of speed although I can't equal or approach your speed.

The other day my buddy and I were able to go on pass to a near-by town where I reveled in ice cream(!!) and cookies. We wandered about the streets window-shopping and drinking vino. The streets are quite narrow and the shops have heavy steel shutters which they roll down from the top when they close up for the day. I was very interested in the way cameos were made so much so that I hung around asking questions and using my limping Italian. In one little shop a salesman was trying to sell a whole box full of cameos. So we started haggling over prices and I finally bought one fine piece for ten dollars. I'm not much of a judge of cameo cutting but I think that you will like the piece I bought. If you decide to do something with it, take it to someone who knows the values and find out if it would be worth while having it made into a nice of jewelry. I also bought a coral necklace and a bracelet which I am enclosing in the same package. After buying the cameo and the coral pieces I got worried about finding a way of keeping them from being broken in transit so I went into another section of the same shop and bought a small wooden jewelry box made of walnut. The workmanship is pretty good and the size is just about right for shipping the jewelry.

Since it is the desire of the powers that be that every one who is interested get a chance to see the antiquities of Italy we have been visiting varous places where it is possible to see some of the old glories of the Roman Empire. One lieutenant, knowing my interest in history, put my name in to act as a guide so that will keep me busy for a while. Most of the GI's will be interested in the wall painting in the brothels. Over the door of each cubicle was placed a painting showing the particular specialty in the art of love at which that particular "fille de joie" was an expert. They carried out their oldest of professions on a stone couch! Ouch! On the same trip I was also able to get a souvenir made from hot lava and a glass tube containing the different sizes of ashes coming from the mountain. By observing the heavy coarser grains followed by finer ones you can trace the course of the eruption. Needless to say my damn feet and arches acted up again so I wasn't able to climb all the way but I did go out on the lava bed which was hardened and cool. It is very dusty and your shoes get full as you walk around. Tonight I received a letter from Elsa telling about her garden and library activities. Her accounts of the activities of N.A. and Tony and Mittens are really a treat.

Everyone is excited by the successes on the Russian front. The way they are going the Jerries will be fighting on their home ground. The sooner the better!

I forgot to include the letter from Mrs. Campbell which I promised to send back. She was right when she said that words are inadequate. She sounds like a very courageous woman. I am sorry I can't give her any information about Lin. As a matter of fact it came as a distinct shock to know that he was in Italy. When it came to handling the older fellows congress said one thing and the army went ahead and acted as it had planned all the while. By the way things are going now some of the older fellows are betting a break at last.

There is so much I can't talk about that I wasn't to tell you that I am afraid we will have many sessions of reminiscences. Once we have talked them over I want to gorget about this god-forsaken insect-infested, dirty bit of Europe the tourist guides call "Sunny Italy"

Remember me to Mother and Dad Ralph & Ruth, Mother Bedient and the rest of the family Take good care of yourself sweetheart and remember that I lubs ya.

With all my love
Chad

My dearest sweetheart:

This is the first time I have written you in a good stretch so please forgive the interval in letters. I can realize just how you feel about my letters coming in bunches but please don't worry.

For the time being I have a new job as assistant radio man. Not that I know very much about radio but I manage once in a while to make myself useful . Another man who has had a lot of experience handling files and records in now helping the first sergeant. He is able to do a lot better than I could because he has been in the army for about 15 years and knows the ropes. Also hie is a good typist and is able to take care of records and correspondence a lot more quickly than I can.

I spoke about an orientation program in my last letter. Recently I had a chance to run one of the orientation periods while the orientation officer was busy elsewhere. The class was right after lunch and it was hot and dusty so there were plenty of handicaps. Only two or three men dozed off on me so I felt that under the circumstances I didn't do so badly. I gave them a short resume' of conditions as I see them in the news coming from the eastern and western fronts. We get maps and circulars from service and supply (Special Service Branch) which help a lot. However you know how difficult it is to make sense out of the jumble of names of Russian and Polish town and rivers. The Russians seem to be moving so fast that it keeps you busy learning new names all the time.

Tonight I received a letter from you (No. 114) a Pathfinder, and a copy of the Press. I was embarrassed by the glowing terms of the item about my receiving the Infantryman's Badge. After all the award covers all kinds of cases from the fellow who may have killed many Jerries to the fellow who carries ammunition for the mortars or machine guns. A great many of our men saw a lot more actual combat than I. During the early phases of the attack I carried messages to and from the company commander to my platoon which was in a pretty hot spot for a while. Also it was necessary to lay down wire for the telephones so that there would be constant communication with my platoon. When we really began to push I carried machine gun ammunition until another fellow and I were picked to conduct some German prisoners back to the MP's After that I tried several times to get back to my company but the place was too hot so I waited until dark and joined the company at its resting place for that night. The following morning the company advanced on a little town and "took it". Fortunately the attach had already rolled beyond the town toward Rome so we met no resistance. By that time Jerry was pulling back fast and armored units were very near to Rome. From then on things were a lot easier and we were able to rest up a bit. I was able to see Rome although I was disappointed in lots of ways. By now, however, I have become inured to the dirt, squalor, and the pathetic sights of the average Italian city. Recently I have seen a lot of places which have had a chance to recover a bit from the effects of the war.

In this part of Italy there is a lot of fruit. I have eaten oranges, pears, olives, nuts, plums, apricots and nice peaches. There is one thing you have to give these paesanos credit for and that is their ability to get the most produce out of every square inch of land. Of course a lot of them are reaping a golden harvest from free-handed American boys. A meal of two fried eggs and a plate of fried potato chips costs one dollar and wine runs from sixty cents to two dollars and half a bottle.

I have been in Naples where I walked a lot and drank enough wine and champagne to feel pretty good. But I didn't see anything worth buying to send home. I have already sent you a package containing a cameo, and some coral. I don't think that it will get to you time for your birthday but when it does arrive I want you to know that with it goes all my love and the hope that you I will spend your next birthday in each other's arms.

It is now 10:45 p.m. and I can picture you returning from the bank and sitting down on the divan where I would like to be holding you in my arms the way I used to do. Only I wouldn't keep you on the divan very long. I'd be carrying you up stairs where I could really get down to the pleasurable business of showing you how much I really care for you.

The boys are returning from a movie show and I am getting drowsy so I will get off to my put tent and catch some sleep before I have to get up and go on guard duty.

Remember me to the folks and tell them I am OK. Give them my love and keep my best love for yourself. I love you so much. My heart is with you.

All my love sweetheart.

from your
Chad

My dearest heart:

Well, another job for a while. Our mail clerk is away for a few days so i am filling in for him. The work is very interesting although there is a great deal of sorting which takes some time to master. All the mail for the regiment comes into one place. There it is broken down by battalions then into companies. I take my company's mail and sort it into small groups. About supper time I take the mail down to the boys and distribute it. When I am through I pick up the censored out-going mail and bring it back to be stamped and sent off. It is a good job and I would like to be able to continue with it as the mail clerk's assistant but I guess that's too much to hope for.

I received letter no 120 last night in which you said you had been a bad girl for not having written. If you are a bad girl I must be a regular devil. When we were fighting on the Anzio front I wrote more letter home than I do now. But, of course, Anzio was a different proposition. There we were in a fairly stationary defensive position. Don't feel badly about not writing because I know what you have to put up with. Thanks for the photo folders. I got the snaps of the chicken picking bee out under the grape arbor. The feathers certainly must have flown. Pictures mean a lot to a fellow. They certainly help a lot to buck up your spirit.

I have visited Naples but only saw a lot of cheap souvenirs which weren't worth buying. The city is hot and dirty and full of paesanos hungry for American food and money. I had some fair wine and tried some champagne but found it to be of poor quality. Don't worry, dear, I didn't get "imbriacco" or "ziggy-zag" as the Italians say when they mean a fellow is plenty drunk. I haven't seen a city in Italy yet that really appeals to me. I suppose it is because I want so much to be back home. Where you can see clean streets and clean healthy people.

In my previous letters I told about eating cherries, plums, apricots, peaches etc, but I would give all the fruit in Italy just to be able to sink my teeth into a nice huckleberry or blueberry pie. Oh me! My teeth are watering just thinking of it.

You remember that I told you about visiting Pompei. Old Pompei must have had about the fornicatingist people in the world. One whole section of the city was devoted to brothels. I went into one and the guide showed us how the old Pompeians used to carry on their business. On the left of the vestibule is a painting of a man weighing his penis which resembled that of the King of France after the Noble Duke of Sussex got through with him. In the main part of the building there is a hall with little rooms on each side. Over the door of each room is a painting showing the particular specialty of the girl who lived there. One painting shows the girl astride with man who is lying on his back. This wall "stuttle la canelle" or snuffing the candle. Another shows the girl on her hands and knees being attacked from the rear (dog-fashion) This was called "fica espagnole" Another showed the man and girl resting on their sides with her right leg under his left and her left leg over his right. This was supposed to be very easy on both parties and allowed the woman to control the amount of the man's penis going into her. This was called "Greek style". Some of the other rooms were devoted to various forms of perversion. But the one I got a kick out of was one in the rear for old men. Here the man rested on his back on a couch. In the meantime a naked girl played with him while he fondled her breasts. The idea was that when he finally succeeded in getting Peter hard the girl would make him come with her hands. The Pompeians believed that this renewed a man's youth. The house also had a back entrance for married men. The girls must have had a tough time of it because their couches were made of stone.

When you go through the ancient streets you see in various sections a cock and balls carved right in the paving block pointing out the direction to the red-light district. Outside the ruins boys run around selling little metal good-luck charms. You guessed it. A cock with balls and a pair of wings!

After going through the brothel district you have a pretty low opinion of the Pompeians. Modern Italians are almost as bad.

Another interesting place is the house of Vetii which belonged to two bachelors who were rich merchants. The vestibule has an opening in the roof with a pool in the center of the floor to catch the rain water. The peristyle is beautiful with a garden and a fountain in the center. There are flowers and small shrubs and many stone benches. All around the peristyle are various dining and reception rooms. In the back are rooms for slaves and a kitchen. It is a fine example of Roman villa. I never thought that I would be seeing ancient Pompey in the days when I was teaching ancient history.

Well I'll sign off now. Take good care of yourself. All my love sweetheart.

Love
Chad

Dearest sweetheart with nice little nose:

I have received the two photo holders with the snap shots of you and the various shots of the chickens etc. When I saw that one of you with your dark dress and a flower in your hair my morale as well as my blood pressure went zooming upward. How I longed to be there to kiss your sweet lips and make you happy. The longer I sit here looking at the picture with more I wish I could make that roguish smile turn into one of ecstacy by picking up my sweetheart and taking her into the house. There I would lay you down on our favorite divan and cover you with kisses and tell you how much I have missed you and longed for you. I would hug you tight and cuddle you in my arms kissing your lips with long slow quivery kisses that would taste like sweet wine. I would kiss your eyelids and let my lips softly press against the little soft place under your ear. Then to travel down to your shoulders where I could plant kisses in the hollow there. I would follow the little valley around to the throbbing place in your throat which by this time would be beating like a drum urging me on.

When you were all warm and snuggly in my arms I would pick you up again and carry you up the stairs into our room where I would put you down on the bed for more kisses. Only those embraces would be more demanding and pleading than the first ones. Then I would roll down your nice stocking stopping to kiss the little hollows in your knees. I would take off your slippers and finish rolling the stocking off your feet. Then I would lift your dress up after pulling you up into my arms for another kiss. Then off with the dress, panties and girdle and into my arms again. By this time Peter would be throbbing and eager for some "lubbin." So off would come my clothes and I would kneel before you and kiss your thighs and nice round tummy.

Then I would come up into your arms and let Peter rest throbbing against Paradise while I kissed you with long deep kisses. Then I would pick up my sweetheart and lay her down on the bed where I could really caress her from ear to tummy to my heart's content. Then I would spread her legs and come up between them until my lips were on hers and Peter was laid right in the groove. Then you would close your legs tight and let him throb while you "winked" at him. After a while. Peter wouldn't be able to stand it any longer so he would begin to slide his head up and down in the groove. Then I would kiss my darling little nubbins and work my finger around inside Paradise until it would be soft, warm, moist and throbbing and eager for Peter's entrance. I would then come over between my sweetheart's thighs and put Peter's head right between the gates of paradise. Then slowly I would press him forward and upward and thrust accompanied by a nice quivery kiss. By this time Paradise would have expanded and started throbbing and quivering. Then I would catch my sweet by the writs and thrust until Peter was in up to the hilt. By this time each thrust would be more rapid until my sweet would quiver and struggle in my arms begging to be let free. At the last moment when we both had reached that peak of exquisite pain I would let go of her wrists and my sweetheart would twine her arms around my neck and kiss me fiercely. Then we would both sink back to rest on the bed lazily dreaming together and happy just to be together.

This, my dear is what your picture did to me. Some people would prudishly condemn me for day-dreaming this way about the one I really love. But every woman likes to be considered desirable by the man she loves. If you had any doubts before now maybe this outburst of passion on my part will help to change your mind.

All my love

Chad

August 3, 1944

Dearest Sweetheart:

this is a quickie as they say out in Hollywood because before very long I will be "traveling light" again. However there is one big difference this time. It is practically a certainty that I will get the job of assistant mail clerk. This will be a big break for me because I will be back where it is possible to get a hot meal occasionally and keep fairly clean. The thing isn't absolutely cinched yet but is pretty certain.

I sent you a rather "warm" letter last time I wrote. I don't know wether it is a good idea or not. Maybe it stirs up too many memories. What do you think?

Ill have to close, sweetheart to go to the company and pick up the mail. I have to stamp it, seal it and see that it gets off OK.

So a nice quivery kiss for you, my sweet, and a good strong hug with plenty of snugglin!

Give Mother Bedient my love and remember me to all the folks.

All my love to a sweet little girl with blue eyes, blond curls and a perky nose I like to nip.

Chad

August 23, 1944

My dearest sweetheart:

It has been a long time since I have been in one place long enough to even take my writing materials out of my pack Even this will have to be short because things are moving so fast that we may pull out and move at any moment. When I told you that I was traveling light again you probably surmised that something big was in the wind. Sure enough, off we went for the invasion of Southern France. I can't give you any details as yet but the progress of the campaign is truly amazing. The French people are such a pleasant surprise after what we saw in Italy. These people are really amazing to help and they have suffered terribly. It is impossible to describe the horrors they have had inflicted upon the. Every time they find someone who understand they pour out a torrent of words describing their experiences and their feeling toward the Germans. My French is coming back rapidly and of course that puts me in a favored position.

I am feeling fit as a fiddle although quite dirty but by now that is an old story. As long as I am with the mail section I will not be forced to March any long distances.

Well my dear I will have to close now in order to work over some mail which is going out soon. Remember me to Mother Bedient and Dad and Mon and the rest of the family.

All my love to you sweetheart with lots of nice quivery kisses on your sweet lips.

Southern France
September 1, 1944

My dearest little perky nose:

For a mail clerk I haven't been doing very well. I have received about eight letters from you since the invasion began but haven't written you more than a couple of times. That's a lot like the shoemaker's children. Our mail situation is gradually clearing up but for a while we were nearly snowed under. I received the little brown notebook and it will be very useful. It is a handy size to carry in a shirt pocket.

Probably by now you are better posted on the news from France than I am although we try to keep up with the radio reports. This campaign was quite a surprise to everyone who is familiar with the past in invasions in Sicily and Italy. Things move pretty fast.

I have met and talked to a lot of French people, some Italians and some Poles. Their accounts of the actions of the Germans are almost unbelievable. I have had many chances to use my French and have acted as an interpreter several times. The French are overjoyed when they find someone who can talk to them and they pour out their feelings in a flood. They have a tremendous admiration for the American troops, "bronze giants" they call them. They strain their resources to be hospitable and offer wine, fruit and vegetables. The Germans stole every thing they could lay their hands on and left the French with a starvation diet. The little children suffered especially because of the lack of milk. It is easy to understand the hatred these people have for the Germans. There are many things to tell you which will have to wait until I can tell them to you in person.

I like my job very much and, as you said, there is less danger of enemy fire when you are back aways from the front lines.

We have had rainy spells lately although each time we were lucky enough to be under shelter. You certainly must have sweltered back in the States. I can just picture you in my blue fatigues. I'll bet they are plenty hot.

You spoke of going for black berries Please don't over exert yourself. My darling, in the hot sun picking berries because the berries can't pay for the damage done by sun stroke or heat stroke. Save your strength as much as possible for that happy day when we will be together again. Your description of a berrying trip together sounded wonderful. Just be working together then resting together in each other's arms would be heaven.

Just as you have lain awake snuggling your pillow and thinking of me so have I lain on my blankets just savoring the phrases of your letters to me and dreaming of the time when I can gather you up in my arms and carry you to our own big wide soft bed. There to kiss your lips with nice soft quivery kisses then with deep hot demanding kisses which would be followed by thousands of caresses all over your white soft body. Then to come between your legs and go plowing until the time was ripe for planting the seed. Then to slowly push the planter in until it was firmly seated. By that time I would be able to hear your breathing increase until with a little moaning sound you would ask me to put my hands underneath you. After doing this the planter would increase the depth and tempo of its thrusts until you would pat me on the back as a signal to free my hands. Then I would spread out your arms and grasp your writs, rising a bit in order to make thrust of the planter nice and slow and deep. Then I would let your hands go free to hug me and the planter would pour forth its seed into the furrow. It makes me glow like a furnace inside when I think of it.

Since there isn't any mail this A.M. to sort over and get ready for the company I will take up from where I left off last night. When I wrote the last two pages I got in such a heat that Had to walk it off.

This A.M. I was reading again your recent letters, Nos. 127-135. I was so sorry to hear about little Buzzer. She was such a cute little cuss.

I noticed that you are storing away pieces of meat in our locker. Sweetheart please don't save those things for me because in these days when everyone is under stain it is so important to have the meat in your diet. It helps keep up your resistance and builds tissue. You need every bit os such things that you can get. So please enjoy them when you can get them and we will manage somehow when we are together again.

I'll sign off now in order to write to Ralph and Ruth, mother and Dad and some others I should write to.

Take good care of yourself sweetheart. Remember me to Mother Bedient and give her my move. All my love and devotion to you, my dearest, with thousands of kisses on your sweet lips delivered in my dreams by your

Chad

September 12, 1944

My dearest darling:

It is now quite late and I am writing this by candle light in a blacked
-out place where we won't give our position away. These days have been
plenty hectic with lots of moving around. Lately it has been rainy thus
making it very difficult to work with the mail. Today we were very busy
with lots of packages for the boys. Now that I am working along (my
boss is going home to the States) I am up to my neck in work. Maybe I'll
get an assistant soon. Every so often I have to leave my work to act as an
interpreter. I am beginning to get the swing of this French language now
pretty well. I have met mots of fine French people. You asked about the
Dunhill lighter - Unfortunately, in the scuffle, I lost it but never mind
I found another one although it operates with gasoline. The watch is
OK, though plenty dirty by now. I received tow more letters from you
today. It wrings my heart to know that you are worrying so much about
me. Please darling try to think of how much I love ;you and want you.
Know that I will take good care of myself and will love you more and
more each day. Try to be patient with my correspondence difficulties.
They are due to the conditions under which we are advancing. Give my
love to Mother Bedient and the rest of the family. All my dearest love
to my sweetheart from

Chad.

My dearest little perky nose about whom I have nice dreams:

This is about the umpteenth time I have tried to get a chance to write you. It seems that every time I reach for my writing materials somebody hollers that there is more mail either incoming or outgoing. Last night I stamped and sealed a whole big batch of outgoing mail so I have a little free time this morning.

It is quite cold now and it rains nearly every day. I sleep with my O.D.'s on and two blankets over me and I feel just warm enough to sleep. If it ever gets real wintery in this section I'll have to police up some more blankets. The other day I got a nice new field jacket which I needed terribly. For a while I was going around early in the morning and at night with a blanket thrown over my shoulders. It reminded me of the way I used to stand guard in my foxhole at Anzio. I also got a new pair of shoes, combat shoes, which I have been trying to get since March. With combat shoes it isn't necessary to wear leggins, thus saving time in getting dressed.

My job is a little better under control now that I have the swing of it. In our company there are a lot of "old fellows" in the hospital or in replacement camps. Their mail has to be redirected, a tiresome and painstaking job. Some days I sort and redirect as many as two sacks of letters, newspapers, and packages. (Time-Out) I just had to run out to act as an interpreter for a young Frenchman whose wife is expecting a baby. He wanted to take her to another village where she could have her baby in peace and quiet. That's just a sample of what happens about a dozen times a day.

Some Frenchman comes to our officers and starts ripping off French by the yard. They send out a hurry call for me. I leave my work, act as interpreter, and come back to my work. Sounds conceited perhaps, but I am very thankful for the hours I spent with my French books.

Speaking of letters I have received the following while in France. (Nos. 128, 133, 137, to 144, 146, to 148) I wrote you the first chance I got in France right after we landed and they picked up mail Dearest

I know these big gaps between letters from me play the very devil with your nerves but try to think, my dear, of the fact that I am in so much better a position now than I was carrying messages and laying wire. Of course there are gangers. There are dangers way back on the beach, but where I am chances are some much better of keeping out of trouble. I wish that we had a little boy or girl you could cuddle up in your arms when you are thinking of me. You would have someone to express your love and affection to. When I see little French children shrink away from soldiers because they have learned fear anyone in a soldier's uniform it makes me boil. Every village, no matter what its size is, has stories of brutality and inhuman acts. The French call the Germans "savages" and "saleaux" (savages and dirty ones). Everything is scarce and prices are sky high. A glass of wine (common red wind, "Pinard" they call it) costs 30 cents or 15 francs. Coffee is a gift from the gods. They haven't had any for two years and in many places longer than that. They make a kind of coffee by roasting oats or barley. What a smell when they are making it! Many of them wear sabots because of the shortage of leather. Few of them have enough clothes although in the cities you do see many well-dressed people. In the small towns the "Boches" burned many of the buildings because the people were helping the FFI. In some cases the "Collaborators" (French Nazis) burned houses and shot people. No wonder the Germans prefer to give themselves up as prisoners to the Americans. As an example of how they feel about it, I saw four German prisoners sitting on the curb of a little French side street waiting to be taken to the Prisoner-of-war stockade. Finally a truck came up and the Germans got on with their guard. When the truck pulled away the guard pulled out cigarettes, took one for himself and offered one to a German. The crowed of French who had been watching the Germans and taunting them cried out as though they couldn't believe it. One French woman said "Why do you Americans treat them that way. They should be made to march not ride to prison camp!" I'd better quit writing about conditions in France or I'll be boiling again.

I am enclosing a shoulder patch of our division which I promised. As you remarked some time ago it is a curious thing that I should land in a division that uses my favorite symbol. I am sorry that I don't have one of those nice silk embroidered patches to send you but I may be able to get one soon.

Your mention of Ralph's accident with the hay fever injection scared the pants of me. Tell him to be plenty careful with those damned things. I've had so many needles stuck in me since I've been in the army I feel like a pin cushion and I've seen guys pass out from the effects of a shot in the arm.

Last night, my sweet, I had the most wonderful dream. We had met in New York at the Grand Central Station and had taken a taxi to a nice hotel in the city. After the bell hop left us alone you came into my arms and gave me a nice hug and a quivery kiss. Then I picked you up in my arms and put you on my lap while we sat and cuddled together on a divan. I kept kissing your sweet lips and burrowing down into that little soft hollow in your throat. Then I put my hand on your knee and felt of the nice warm soft skin between your thighs then up until my hand rested on a lovely warm spot that was just throbbing. Then, unable to stand it any longer, I took you up in my arms again and carried you off to the big double bed where I laid you down and took off your shoes and stockings with appropriate pauses for kisses along your legs. Then I lifted you up and slipped off your dress and slip and removed your little "pants and girdle" Then I threw back the blanket and laid you out on the bed full length and got between your legs. I started kissing your thighs then your nice round belly then paused for a nice kissing session on two nice nubbins. Then up to your throat and shoulders and finally came to rest with my lips on yours and my Peter resting against the gates of Paradise then I got you "ready" by spreading wide those gates and moving Peter up and down plowing a furrow. In my dream I could feel you "wink" at him and finally that warm heavenly feeling when Peter's head just pushes past the gates of Paradise. Then half-awake I could feel the firm warm grasp of the walls of Paradise as they clasped him and throbbed against him. Then I awoke with a start and realized that it was only a dream but what a dream! Peter was throbbing like mad he had such a pressure of steam up. I had to smoke a cigarette and calm down before I could go back to sleep. Just writing this stirs me up. I'd better quit this.

I am glad you like the cameo. I am pretty certain that it is genuine and not faked the way some of them are. If you get the cameo mounted it should be very pretty. Those religious mementos I sent you can give out as you like Perhaps Grace would like the little chain and medal attached. Please give Levio the papal coin and the Hail Mary booklet.

Give my love to the family and know that I love you with all my heart and soul.

Chad

Somewhere in France
September 21, 1944

My sweet little perky nose:

I received your letter number 150 the other day and promptly proceeded to get up a head of steam while reading the last part. We have moved so much lately that I haven't had a chance until this P.M. to start a letter to you.

This A.M. I went with the first sergeant to see whether I could get the watch -maker to fix some watches. While there I had him make some adjustments on my wrist watch. The stem had slipped loose so that I couldn't set the time. He fixed it all right and now it works O.K.

This P.M. while on another errand I saw the French marching a girl through the streets. Evidently she had collaborated with the Germans a swastika on her blouse and cut off her hair. In several French towns I have seen the "poules" but that's what happens when feeling are made bitter by several years of inhuman treatment.

We have had some pretty good places to stay considering everything. One place we had wooden cots with straw mattresses. Several times I have slept in hay or straw and have been nice and warm. Other places I have slept on the ground, which, of course, is an old story by now. The other day I got another blanket from the supply sergeant so I keep warm.

The other day we received a lot of packages from Naples. Wow! Some of them were certainly beaten up. Even some that were packed in fairly strong boxes were so damp and crushed that they weren't much use to the fellows who received them. All of which brings me to the question which Ruth Crouchley asked me in her recent letter. The way things are going and the condition of the packages leads me to believe that it would not be advisable to send any more packages. Also there will be plenty of packages going through the mail for Xmas and they will probably arrive in January or February. The best gifts I can receive are the letters which tell me that you and the family are all well.

You asked me if I saw that great big moon. Although we have had many cloudy and rainy nights there was one night I did see that moon and it made me think of the same thing that you described. Of that night up at Look Out and also over at Devil's Den. I hope that soon I will be able to besiege that same sweet body of yours and we can again enjoy the life together that was meant to be.

Another fellow in the postal section has just asked me to go with him to see some French. I am getting along pretty well with my vocabulary but when the French get excited, Oo, la la!

So, au voir, my sweet. Take good care of yourself. A nice quivery kiss on your sweet lips.

All my love,
Chad

Dearest Petunia:

Another rainy day with very little mail except packages and newspapers. The same old story of wet cardboard boxes which fall apart if you handle them very much.

Two little French girls are hovering around the door way of the barn grinning at me and chattering away at each other. Many of the French girls wear felt slippers and when the ground is muddy and slippery they put on wooden shoes and go clip-clopping over the cobble stones. These people are good farm folks who are happy to be once more able to reconstruct their lives. They have not suffered perhaps as much as those in the cities but they now feel That they can breath free air again. Of course the first few days of their new freedom find them celebrating the arrival of the French or Americans as the case may be. They also celebrate the funerals of the men and women who have lost their lives fighting The Boches. In the ranks of the French there were many losses due to the spiteful spirit of the Germans. Every village has stories about the acts of the Germans which make the atrocity stories from Belgium in the last war seem pale in comparison. Every day I spend at this job with the Mail Section makes me feel more and more thankful that I am not up in the midst of the mud and artillery dodging Jerry shells and trying to keep reasonably dry. France must be a truly wonderful place in peace time. But now everyone and every place has been marked by this war. But enough of that. The mind always likes to turn to more pleasant subjects. Such as the one that is uppermost in my mind, my sweetheart.

On a rainy day like this I would like to be with you in New York where we could call a taxi and go to a nice place to eat, chat and dance. Then to a show where we would sit in the dark and hold hands. After the theater we would go to a cafe for a few drinks and some more dancing. Then back to the quiet of our hotel room where we could toast each other with wine in our own special way of kissing with wine. Then I would take you in my arms to our bed where I would undress you and cuddle you in my arms until you were nice and warm and tingley all over. Then I would start caressing you where you really like it. On those two nubbins which stand up like points when I take them between my lips and roll my tongue around those little pink circles just around your nubbins. I would put you on top of me so that every once in a while I could draw down on your nubbins and make you start panting for more. While you were astride me I would thrust Peter up between the gates of Paradise where he could plow a nice furrow. Then I would stretch you out on top of me with Peter snuggled in tight between your legs. By that time both of us would be at white heat and ready for a nice roll over and that heavenly feeling that comes when Peter just catches his head firmly inside the gates of Paradise. Slowly but surely he would thrust his way in until he was throbbing in the innermost parts of Paradise. Then I would rest my head besides yours and put my hands under your hips so that I could lift you up and let you swing your hips around a bit. One or two such thrusts by Peter and he would fairly explode leaving us both throbbing and dreaming together in each other's arms. I may seem to be a very physically-minded husband but I can't help it. I guess that is the way I am built.

Take care of yourself sweetheart. I'll try to write again soon.

With all my love.

Chad

October 1, 1944

My Dearest Petunia:

I've been sneezing and coughing for several days but am feeling much better now. We had so much rain and cold weather that I finally caught cold. The main reason was that I couldn't keep my feet dry for three days in a row.

The mail situation has been poor for two weeks now. No first class mail to speak of. We have been busy redirecting a lot of packages and newspapers. We expect a lot of air-mail soon and I hope I will have some letters from you.

There isn't much to write about here. We don't see a lot of civilians unless we go out into a town. The French are very hospitable and are crazy about American cigarettes. The kids are all anxious to get chewing gum or chocolate.

I'll sign off now. A big truck load of mail just came in. Here's hoping.

All my love,

Chad

October 8, 1944

Dearest sweetheart:

Just a few lines in between handling damaged packages and sorting newspapers to let you know I am O.K. My cold is much better since the weather has improved. For a while things were certainly plenty miserable. From the news accounts the Atlantic coast must have had some pretty tough weather. Day before yesterday I received the package containing deviled ham, peanut butter, cocoa, etc. I have also received letter of Sept. 2,6, and 12. I can understand how you feel my sweet about the mail situation. We feel the same way. Of course it is a question of transportation now. I know that it sounds peculiar to tell you not to worry but please believe me sweetheart when I tell you that it hurts me to know that you worry so much. I am O.K. and pray that you are in good health. Give my love to the family and know that I love you and think of you always.

Love

Chad

October 13, 1944
Somewhere in France

Dearest sweetheart:

I am writing this at 8:30 p.m. just about the time when you are typing out those long pages of foreigns. The boys are playing hearts and laughing over their strategy in trying to avoid getting the Queen of Spades. They call the "Black Bitch."

The mail situation continues to be pretty spotty with lots of newspapers and packages. I received the funny papers, N.Y. Times and Pathfinder. We still haven't had much first class mail. I haven't had any from you now for about 12 or 13 days.

The weather reminds me a lot of New England in the late fall, cold and wet. I have already put on my "long johns" and still feel the cold. At night, however, I have a nice warm bed on some crates with a soft sack of fiber for a mattress. Some nights I talk for a while with the French and have a drink which is a mixture of very weak beer and "lemonade" and is called "melangee." A lot of the fellows drink "eau de vie" made from Mirabelles. It should be called "eau de feu" it's such hot stuff. I can't take it. It's too strong for me.

The other day I bought a small pair of sabots for a souvenir. I am sending them to you in a ration box. If you don't want them give them away to one of the kids.

The people of this part of France are very reserved and it takes them quite a while to warm up and become friendly. I had a great compliment the other day. One of the French kids called me "gentil" which is about the same as the Italian word "simpatico."

When I see the boys who are on their way home after many months of combat it reminds me of what you said about rotation. My dear, my chances for rotation are practically nil compared with the fellows who went through the Sicilian campaign, the Salerno landing, the crossing of the Volturns, the Anzio beach head, the Rome push and now the drive across France. As long as I am mail clerk of Co. G. I am going to be plenty thankful that I was able to get the job. If I had remained as a runner or an asst. radio man in headquarters platoon I probably would be in a hospital right now. My dear I long with all my heart to return to your arms again. Never fear that modesty or anything else will keep me from trying to get back home to you as fast as possible.

It's getting late for me. I'm pretty sleepy now. I'll go to bed now and dream of my sweetheart.

All my love to you, my sweet, Take good care of yourself.

Love

Chad

Dearest Petunia:

It is now 7:30 p.m. and the boys are kidding me about calling you Petunia. I had to explain that the name is my pet name for you. Tonight is quite peaceful because most of the fellows have gone to see a movie nearby. Most of the pictures are class B and somehow or other I'm not much in the mood for a movie tonight.

In today's mail I received letter #167 with the three photos of you which I promptly trimmed and put in my wallet. What do mean talking about your "mug." It's the sweetest "mug" in all the world to me. How I would like to be kissing it right now! When I wrote some time ago that I thought that I would be laying siege to your body soon I was talking in the full flush of optimism which struck every one right about the time of the race across France.

The Krauts were running so fast that it seemed as though they would never stop. But they did and are just as fanatical as they were in Italy. Now it seems that they will have to get the devil knocked out of them before they will quit. Tant pis pour eux! Even if it means that every city and village in Germany has to be levelled.

The radio is now playing "L'amour" which is supposed to be No. 1 on the Hit parade. It's quite a song. Better than a lot of the hill-billy music we get. "L'amour" over here means a lot of things including that word you don't like. A lot of the soldiers have sampled French amour but so far I've abstained although I saw some pretty nice dishes in Grenoble. Fortunately, while in Grenoble, I was pretty busy with mail and acting as a translator so the only people I got to know very well were business or military people. One of them, an engineer, wrote me in Sept and I just received his letter. (It had to go through base censor.) He had invited me to come to breakfast or "brunch" but Malheaureusement we all moved on farther up the line. He says that there is snow now in the mountains around the city. It is beautiful. If we ever come to France I want you to see Grenoble. The people are truly wonderful. Their spirit of patriotism and loyalty for France is remarkable. Even hardened veterans of the

Italian and Sicily campaigns who were used to walking up to a girl and saying "Fica, Fica?, you speak how much? Were thoroughly chastened and began to remember a little of their manners.

Here the people are very reserved although they have thawed out considerably now that they have seen for themselves the difference between the German soldier and the G.I. The French kids of 6 to 16 flock around to see the Americans eat. They and their parents have a tremendous respect for American material. Some of our G.I's have formed alliances purely for purposes of pleasure but they are very quiet about it.

Recently a buddy and I visited a family for Sunday dinner or "la soupe." First came the soup made with potatoes and other vegetables. Them came a delectable dish (for which I obtained the recipe) I can't tell you the name of it now. Next came rabbit with gravy and a well-seasoned salad. Then a dish of browned potatoes and macaroni (mistake that came before the meat course). Then a pie made with mirabelles (a kind of cross between a cherry and a plum). Then coffee and brandy or eau de vie. Here the recipe for the delectable dish:

Recette

1 - Faire une pate brisee (comme de la pate a tarte que l' on met dans un plateau. In other words make a pie crust and put it in a pie tin.
2- Parsemer dessus une vingtaine de petits morceaux de lard coupes fins. Scatter over the pie crust about twenty or so little pieces of port cut up fine.
3- Mettre dans un receipeient deux oeufs entiers debattre avec un demi litre de creme fraiche. (a defaut avec un demi litre de lait)
Salar legenement, verser le tout sur la pate disperser dessus une dijaine de petits morceaux de beaurre et mettre au feur jusqu a complete cuisson. Put in a receptable two whole eggs. Beat them with 1/2 litre (wouldn't that be a little more than a pint?) of fresh cream. Lacking cream use 1/2 litre of milk. Salt lightly turn it out into the pie crust. Scatter over the mixture about ten little pieces of butter. Put it in the oven until it is cooked. It look like a thin custard pie and boy! oh boy! Is it good! Whenever I can I'll collect recipes if you like the idea.

Time is marching on and soon it will be lights out. (that sounds like McClellan doesn't it?) Then to bed where I will dream of my sweetheart.

As I curl up in my blankets I think of how I used to give you a tail while I took tow nice handfuls of nubbins. Presently I would feel two little points ruse up on those nubbins and I would pull you over on top of me where I could give them a nice warm massage by running the tip of my tongue around the two little points. By that time you would be breathing fast and ready for the "frontal assault". Then I would lay you on your back with Peter firmly in the groove. Then Peter would slide up and down with his head just inside the throbbing gates of Paradise. Then you would guide him into Paradise until he was well started on his way. By that time Peter would be thrusting his way home until he was up to the hilt. Then I would put my hands under you and bring up your hips to the proper angle for the final thrust. With sweet deep kisses we would savor the joy of perfect union. Oh, my darling, that would be heaven. I love you so and miss you more and more each day. When we are together again I'll never be able to tell you how much. Words are too weak to describe it. Goodnight, my sweet, with all my love and thousands of kisses on your sweet lips.

Chad

Somewhere in France
November 2, 1944

My dearest sweetheart:

I am dashing this letter off after another hectic day wrestling with the mail. However every time I think of what it is like up at the front I thank the good Lord above and realize how lucky I am. Right then and there I stop any complaining that I might have started.

I have received a lot of letter from you recently Nos. 160-166, 169-172, 175-181 and 183. We call letters from our one and only our "sugar reports". No. 178 certainly was a "honey" report because it certainly raised my blood pressure. Peter started throbbing like mad while I was reading it. Baby how I loved it!

I received several small packages of cigarettes and a large package containing mixed nuts, candies, cigarettes, lighter wicks etc. I now have three lighters. So I am all set. Thanks a lot sweet for the packages. That part about the sweater sounded good because this part of France is colder than the proverbial witch's teat! Also it is plenty damp so those of us who are lucky to be stationed in buildings make out better than fellows on the front lines.

I am afraid that I'll never get a chance to write to or visit the cousin in Lyons. First because we are not allowed to write to French civilians (although they can write to us through the base censor we can't reply) Second the Xmas rush keeps us going from breakfast until 8 or 9 o'clock at night. The packages that are coming through directly for xmas are in good condition. Thank the Lord. They are sacked up by regiment in the U.S. and the sacks are not unsealed until they reach us. Some different from the way things were handled back in Italy.

As far as an early home-coming is concerned we are reconciled to another winter over here. I feel humble when I talk with fellows who have gone through two Xmases away from home. However that can't keep me from hoping and praying for some fluke or circumstance that will make Germany crumple and fall apart. This xmas will be terribly lonely apart but we will try to make up for it when we are together again.

Dave may have the fungus disease which has caused a lot of trouble over here. Doctors don't seem to be able to do much for those damned skin diseases. I hope his trouble is cleared up quickly. The water over here is dangerous unless chlorinated or boiled so I hope he takes precautions if he washes his hands in it.

I wasn't too surprised about May's suspicions concerning the Denton Fortune. J.D. has been working his way around that particular pile of cash for quite a while. I remember your first impression of Joe. However, as you say he has been very helpful to us both.

Speaking of impressions of people, it's going to be come job for me to get up to date on a lot of the local happening. Karl & Dot and Joe and a lot of other things. However my principal job will be in getting acquainted with my sweetheart. After living among men for so long I'll probably have to batten down my hatches because in the course of events one's language is bound to become pretty rough. It will take a lot of understanding and patience on your part before I get used to mixed company. The most delightful part of our getting acquainted again will be the lazy dreaming together in each others arms. When I can cuddle you in my arms with both of us settled down nicely on the divan. Then I can let my lips wander softly over your face pausing every so often to stop and taste the sweetness of your lips. To run my lips lightly over the soft part just under your ear then around your neck until my lips rest in that little hollow which shows your pulse then around to the larger soft hollow near your collar. Just to dream together, talking when we felt like it but snuggling together just for joy over being in each other's arms. Then when your lips were all soft and hot to run my hands over other parts of your sweet body until you were ready to go to bed and let me make you even warmer. What heaven to wake up in the morning and look over to see your blue eyes greeting me. Then to turn over and kiss the sleepiness from them and arouse your warm body by pressing mine against yours. Then to kiss you from head to toe until your breath was coming in quick gasps. Then to take you in my arms and make a gentle insertion until Peter was resting snugly within his nice warm love-nest. Just to let him throb against the walls of his prison while I kissed you and fondled your two sweet little nubbins. By that time we would be blissfully wrapped in each other's arms and drifting off in a sweet delirium. I get such a thrill out of just writing about it. I hope I don't upset your physical equilibrium by doing it. May I have a masochistic tendency that makes me like to torment myself by longing so hard for you in a physical way.

My eyes are beginning to burn so I had better quit before I have a headache. I have been using my eyes all day in pretty poor light.

Remember me to the folks and give the family my love

All my love to you my sweet from

Chad

Somewhere in France
November 5, 1944

My Dearest sweetheart:

Well, the day's work is over as far as I am concerned until 4 o'clock tomorrow A.M. when I go on guard duty so I will seize the opportunity by the tail and write a few lines. It's colder than the proverbial _____ here so I am making the pen fly.

We have winter clothing now so we bundle up when we stand guard or go out on the trucks. I have an extra jacket which is really quite windproof. I also have my "long johns" or long-handle drawers as we call them. Topped off with an overcoat it isn't so bad.

I forgot to tell you that my assistant is no longer with me so I, like the rest, face the Xmas wish of packages with some trepidation. It makes a long day but being a mail clerk is helluva lot better than being upon the front lines.

The other day I sent off a package of booklets dealing with languages and historic spots in Italy that I would like to keep as souvenirs. I don't have any of the pornographic souvenirs that some of the boys collected. You remember I told you about the brothel section of ancient Pompeii. Some of the fellows bought pictures of the murals in one of the brothels showing the different positions. However I didn't get any. They also bought little metal good-luck charms in the form of a winged penis with balls attached. The Pompeians regarded it as a sign of great potency. I imaged that a winged penis would be very potent! You asked me about why they call the position of intercourse dog-fashion "fica espagnole." I suppose that it is due to the same reason why the Italian called syphilis the "Spanish Disease." Always blaming something like that on another nation. Anyway the picture showed a woman kneeling on a divan and the man making the insertion from the rear between her open legs. Give me the good old-fashioned way!

Here in France, especially where we are now, we have very little to do with civilians. Those of us in the mail section particularly we are pretty busy from morning until dark.

Dave Moore was in a position to see a lot more things of interest than I am. Another thing is that, being a mail clerk, I have to watch my statements about people, places and units or I might find myself paying a fine and toting a rifle again in the bargain. You were right in your statement about the handwriting of Lt.Peterson. Once in a while a base censor will sample a letter and it just might happen to be my letter so "I ain't taken no chances."

Well I see election day fast draws near I have a confession to make. In the rush and bustle of moving around I didn't get to vote. Isn't that just like me? After all the trouble you went to and my making application I just plumb didn't vote. I hope you aren't too provoked at me.

Boy my hands are about frizzled. I'd better quit soon.

I had a thrill in reading the letter in which you described our being together on our big broad work-bench. I could see how you started off with nice broad flourishes of your pen then as you really got heated thing about it I could see how your pen went faster and faster and the strokes of the pen went sort of quivery like your tummy must have been at the moment. Oh my dear I love you so much and I have lots of nice dreams like that about us two. The other night I dreamed we were out camping together ad we had a nice soft air mattress and lots of nice fluffy wool blankets over us. We were cuddled together under the blankets watching out through the head opening at the moon as it shone down through the pine trees. Then as we got more interested in each other I took you in my arms as tight as could be and you put hour heels in the hollows in back of my knees and pushed up hard against me as I thrust Peter deep into Paradise. Then as our love flowed together within your sweet body we lazily dreamed together and snuggled down to sleep the night through in our little nest. So many times I have dreamed of being together like that. But no matter what the time or place you need have no fear about our getting readjusted to each other physically. Remember my dear we have a wealth of happy memories behind us and we both are eager to take up the threads where we left off. I remember how you felt that first time at Cousin Bertha's camp on our honeymoon. I was so afraid I was going to hurt you terribly and you were afraid that I wouldn't be satisfied. Now we both know the joys of loving and caressing and getting "ready" so that the experience of getting readjusted shouldn't be disappointing at all but really a new way of showing our love for one another.

My lines are getting all scribbly so I'd better stop now.

My love to all the folks and lots of quivery kisses on your sweet lips, my darling. I love you so much.

Chad

Somewhere in France
November 15, 1944

My dearest heart:

Things are fairly well under control tonight so here I am after a heavy day at the company. The mail situation here isn't too good as far as in coming mail is concerned. There is a lot of directory work for fellows who have joined the unit. Some of them haven't had mail for about a month. The last letter I have is no. 188 of Nov. 4th. I received it on the 13th Also some letters from Elsa containing Xmas messages and little booklets of leaf soap. I had heard about that kind of soap but had never used it before. For someone situated as I am they are OK because I can keep them dry but it would be hard for a font-line soldier to keep them.

In my preceding V-mail letter I spoke of my receiving a promotion to T/5. The rating is really a corporal technician. The stipes that go with it are like this

It was a lucky break for me that I was made assistant mail clerk back near Naples. Then the mail clerk was sent home and I became mail clerk. The lucky thing about it is that recently all the assistant mail clerks were sent back to their companies. So but for that I would be back right where I was about the time of the Rome push. I am not what you would call a religious person but I have a firm belief that some great power has been very kind to me. I thank God for it and pray each day that He will continue to watch over me just as I pray every day that I will soon be able to return to my true love. Perhaps, when put down in black and white, my expressions may seem mawkish or stilted but I have seen enough heart-break and suffering to make me have deep feelings on the subject of human relations.

The news continues to be good and, though the fighting will undoubtedly continue through the winter, the Germans can't last much longer. The Russians are going great guns in Hungary and Now Germany is surrounded by a ring of steel.

Just now the radio news mentioned a big fire in Hartford. Conn. It said that people were forced out into the rain-drenched streets. Conn.. must be getting plenty of rain this fall. So are we here, although occasionally we have snow squalls. Also the stories the boys of 1914-18 used to tell about French mud are certainly true.

The native in this section are real farm folks. Each house has the stable and hay mow built together and out in front is the usual pile of manure for the gardens. They grow a lot of cabbage, potatoes, turnips and Brussel sprouts. They have a few chickens and a cow or two which makes them much better off than the city people. Lately the only contact I have had with the French is in getting laundry done. Where we are now there are two middle-aged French women who do the wash. You can imagine the mix-up in clothes with 8 or 10 fellows looking for their laundry. It is necessary to sew a little mark on your clothes to be sure of getting them back.

I can't seem to write tonight dearest because I am worried about you. When you said that each night you take a drink in order to take the edge off your thoughts of our separation, I worry that you may undermine your health. Please be careful my sweet, I love you so much, I don't want you to hurt yourself. When we are back together again I have so much to make up to you. I can't imagine every being able to adequately express my devotion. When I see fellows who have been over here a year and a half I wonder how they stand it.

My eyes are burning again so I'd better sop writing for now. Several times I have been tempted to tear up this letter. I know that is isn't a very good expression of my thoughts.

Goodnight my sweet. I'll try to write a more cheerful letter tomorrow. Give my love to the family and remember me to the neighbors. Just about now you are sitting down to supper. Bon appetit ma cherie. J'espere que je pourrais etre tite a tite avec vous. Enfin Je purrais explique conime je vous aime et vous desire. Milles embrances sur vos douces levres.

Chad

November 15, 1944

My dearest sweetheart:

I am in the red-faced department for sure. Here I am. A mail clerk, and I haven't written you in Lord knows how long. "Been busy as the devil with Xmas packages and many orders. Took in over 37 hundred dollars in the last two days. You probably notice by the address above that I am now a corporal again. Remember the day I was inducted and walked into the house with the news that I was an acting corporal? Certainly has taken a long time to get up the real thing. Not that I am not satisfied with my job. I think its the best one in the infantry. Yesterday, I received my Good Conduct Ribbon for being a good boy for a year. What makes me mad is that, some son of a so and so stole my Combat Infantryman's Badge - Received big package from you with candles and another with the wool sweater. Thanks sweetheart. Also package from Rotary Club with lots of useful articles. In my previous letters, my sweet, I didn't mean to imply that I love being tempted by les Fransaises. In the first place I love you more than I will ever be able to tell you and secondly, I am too busy to worry about women. I received your loving Xmas card and am sending you a special card which we have received. Had a letter from Ralph with pictures of the hurricane damage at Atlantic City. It must have been a rip snorter of a storm. I carry the photos of you with me always. They give me a mental lift when I look at them.

All my love, sweet,
from Chad

Dearest sweetheart:

Another busy day at the company taking in money for money orders. The boys are certainly sending a lot of money home. That's a lot better than just "pissing" away their money on schnapps and other diversions. Also had lots of letter to re-direct.

Received my issue of a pair of arctics. Also a pair of shoe packs with heavy wool socks. The light sweater you sent me is just the thing for night.

November 20th

Been busy as the devil with Xmas packages. I sure am glad that the boys are receiving them now, instead of months after Xmas as they did last year. I received three letters today and a package (from Ralph). Letters from you are nos. 192, 193, 194. Damned quick service I call it. Letters and packages have been coming through much better lately. I received the money you sent. I thought that I had mentioned it before. My brain must be getting woozy. I can't keep track of all the things you write me. But such things as letter No. 193 in which you describe a bicycle trip out in the woods certainly raised my steam pressure. It was wonderful. Don't be worried, my dearest, about what will happen when we get back together again. After all we have been separated a long time and I realize that it wouldn't be the same as when we were first married. I would like to court you again until you feel ready for us to come together physically. After all there is so much to tell you and so much I want to do with you such as seeing our country together, dancing together, going to some good shows together. When we have become reacquainted then we will enjoy more the physical side of our life together. I'd rather imagine that it wouldn't be too long before your sweet body would glow with love and your whole being would throb with he same desire that I feel for you. Then my mind would be easy about taking you into my arms and showing you how much I really love you. Just the thought of it makes me glow inside as the rough wintery winds blow outside our windows.

It's late now and I should be trotting off to bed to snuggle down in my blankets and dream of your smile and hundreds of little ways of being the sweetest woman in the world.

Love

Chad

November 28, 1944

Dearest sweetheart:

Just a short one to let you know that I am OK. Yesterday we had three truck loads of mail and I just finished re-directing the last of my letter for the hospitals. I had two letters from you (No's 190-191) and two packages from the teachers with Leve's name as sponsor. I've had lots of packages lately and have accumulated quite a store of stuff. However please don't send cigarettes because we get plenty of them here and of course we know about the terrible shortage. Things like handkerchiefs or candles are highly prized. Recently I had a chance to visit the company every day and renew a lot of friendships. I have seen Bill Stout several times. He has a good job now in the rear at Personnel. I am glad that he got the chance to go back after being up with the company. In my job we move around a lot although I would be glad to move twice a day if it would finish up this damned war any more quickly. I have managed to acquire two bottle of perfume which I am sending to you. Take the one you like and the other one to Mother Bedient. I didn't mean that the way it sounds but I do want you get the one you like best. More tomorrow.

Love,
Chad

December 6, 1944

Dearest sweetheart:

Another V-mail after a long, hard day battling with packages and the Xmas rush. After finishing my regular work I polished up my Carbine in preparation for inspection. I am writing this by candle light for the damned electric lights are so weak that they aren't much good to us. The people here are good farm folks although they have a different slant on the war then the folks down toward the southern part of France. Lately we have been moving around like a hen on a hot gridle. We moved these this time in four days and certainly were pooped out by the time we finally did settle down for a while, the last town I was in had a good store where I was able to get a large bottle of perfume which I will pack carefully and send off to you. From now on, however, I guess there won't be much buying of French luxuries. I received a package the other day from Dad and Mom but recently I haven't had many letters. The mail situation is pretty well jammed up. Give my love to the folks. I am OK and feeling fine. All my love sweetheart. Take good care of yourself.

Love
Chad

My Darlin -

This is gonna be short because I'm dead. I left the bank at 1 today and Mom & I went Xmas shopping in Danbury. My feet have been bothering me anyhow & we walked all over the damn place and came home without much. You can't get anything decent any more, & prices are sky high, & you have to wait hours to get waited on because they're all short of help. We had supper in the cafeteria of the Green, arriving home at 6:00 At 6:30 I had to go down to the theatre to make out bonds for the Truth or Consequences show next week. And I just got home.! I'm so pooped.

Sam Denton died this noon at 12:30. I told you yesterday that he was very weak.

Am enclosing another picture. I hope you like 'em. I got my proofs today of those I had taken with my old 4 or 5 year old hat & they're much better. It'll take a week or 10 days to get them printed so I won't be able to get them to you in time for Xmas.

Let me know when you get them because if you don't I've another copy of each & Ill send them in that case.

Well good night sweetheart with all my love & kisses.

Bedie

December 7, 1944
Somewhere in France

My dearest little perky nose:

I am dashing this little note off by the light of a German candle. The two grease spots resulted from my moving it around so I will have to detour. We see a lot of captured Jerry stuff now. Your statement in letter #201 which I received today about my probable locality wasn't very far off. The day's work seems longer than ever now with lots of packages being re-directed and keeping track of fellows going in and out of the company.

That must have been quite a gig ride you had. I would like to have been right along side you. Just to take an old-fashioned ride through the country side in the fall. That's one of the many things we will have to do together when I come home.

We are in a typical little French town of this area. The people have seen a lot of war. Many of them have or had sons or brothers in the German Army. The area has been under French control for only a short time in recent history when you come right down to it. From 1870-1718 was German control and also from 1940-1944. Many of the people can't understand or speak French. They speak a sort of dialect which resembles German. When it comes to speaking the language I am out of luck although we are fortunate in having several fellows who can speak German. I'll be damned glad when the only thing I can hear will be good old American. The news continues to be pretty good although it looks like a long tough winter.

When the cold wintery winds are blowing I would like to be snuggled down under our Hudson Bay blanket with you spooned up tight against my tummy and Peter firmly catched making a nice tail. Then when my sweetheart was nice and warm I would roll you over on your back and caress you until you were ready for plenty of lovins. Then I would press Peter firmly between the gates of Paradise until he was engulfed. Then he would slide deeper and deeper until he poured his love into Paradise. It would be easy to forget winter and everything else in my sweetheart's arms. I love you with all my heart and want you to know that I am thinking of you always.

Love,
Chad

Somewhere in France
December 25, 1944
Christmas Day

My dearest darling:

Since I wrote you last a lot has happened to make an ideal Xmas present. As long as I have to be way from your side I know that you will be happy to know that I have received an opportunity to put my experience in education to some good use.

There is a lot of reading to be done in order to become familiar with the educational program. But after a few days of studying the manuals I will be able to get into the swing of things. Today I used a typewriter for the first time in several months. My fingers are still pretty stiff and clumsy but after practicing for a while I'll be more accurate and have better speed.

It was quite a wrench to leave the old job. I was lucky enough to make many good friends among the boys in the mail section and it felt funny leaving them and starting off learning new names and faces. The boys in the section where I am working all seem to be regular guys. They work well together.

I hope you get my two packages soon. I hope they come through the mails in good condition.

One bottle of perfume was packed in a small cardboard box with newspapers packed around the small box containing the perfume. The other box had one bottle of perfume inside a tin can packed with newspaper and another bottle inside a small cardboard box. I tried to pack them solidly so that they wouldn't rattle around inside. At any rate I hope you like them.

The Navy certainly is plenty busy in the Pacific. I hope Everett Roberts is OK. If anything has happened to him his folks would know by now.

Received the money order for $15.00. I think I mentioned it before but repeat just in case letters get crossed on the way home. I am going to drop a line to Francis and Daisy thanking them. Thanks a lot sweetheart but it isn't necessary to send my money. I haven't anything to use money on. I don't care for cards or dice and only once in a while take a glass of wine or schnapps. Must be my Scotch blood.

I received the piece of sheet music entitled "I walk alone". I had heard the song on the radio program from the States but when I read the chorus I know what you meant in your letter.

I also received several boxes containing cigarettes. We hear a lot over here about the shortage of tobacco so please don't send cigarettes because we get plenty of them in our rations. I have heard of cases where GI's have sold them to natives but those we see around here are little boys and girls who are hungry for chocolate or chewing gum. Many of the small kids have never had much chocolate and now they can't seem to get enough. We receive small bars of candy each day. They are called the tropical chocolate bar. So we give them to the kids.

You spoke of requests in letter #200. There is one thing I would like to request . Hauling mail sacks around and working in cold rooms a lot I have worn out several pairs of gloves. So if you can get some brown work gloves I would appreciate it very much.

Did you say hot buttered rum in front of the fire place? How well I remember the passages in "Hervey Allen's Roger's Rangers." That's one thing I would like to experience plus those delightful paragraphs you wrote just following that description.

It's getting late and time for me to go to my sack so good night, my sweetheart, with the hope that another Xmas will see us enjoying the fact that peace rests in every part of the earth.

Your Chad

P.S. When you write don't forget the change in address.

December 26, 1944
Somewhere in France

Dearest sweetheart:

I thought I would sit me "dune" and write a short one to my Petunia. I am OK and am recovering from turkey and stuffing. We had a big meal yesterday with lots of turkey meat, stuffing with onions in it, mashed potatoes with giblet gravy, cranberry sauce and mince pie! I enjoyed the meal very much but a dish of Daisy's Indian Pudding would have been much better.

I spent most of the day reading pamphlets and circulars describing the educational program which will go into effect when hostilities cease. There are two of us working together and, as I see it now, we will act as a sort of clearing house of information for the men who are going to set up programs for their units. I am gradually getting the cob webs swept out of my brain and am beginning to see light.

Tonight I say my old buddie with whose wife you have been corresponding. He looks fine and now has a good job. How did she like the recipe for Indian Pudding? Damn it, I can't spell anymore.

Almost time to lie myself to bed so good night sweetheart with all my love and the hope that the New year will bring us both lots of good things.

My dearest sweetheart:

I am using this machine in order to practice a bit on a machine which is different from the usual run of machines where I work. Yesterday I was cutting stencils again and am now able to get one cut with only one or two mistakes to a long legal-size stencil. Not too bad after having been away from a typewriter for such a long time.

Last night I wrote to Leve and to Aunt Carrie so, by the time I was finished, I had about run out of inspiration for letter writing. Boy! I wasn't wrong then I said that this machine different. Our company mail clerk is now sending my mail on to my new address so I received an accumulation of several days' mail. I had a letter reading orgy. Your letters were among the early two hundreds. As I remember them the most recent one was number 217. When I read about how Jim has been acting, I'll admit I was burned up but I understand how it is with him. Drinking is probably the only way he can express his disgust with life in general. He thinks that by numbing his brain with alcohol he can get a little rest from the thoughts that must be worrying him. It's different with us because we are both in our thirties and have a lot of wonderful memories of perfect moments spent together and hope of lots more to come.

Karl must have gone through some hellish times in the last year or so. I can see where he would be relieved to have some decision reached. The one my heart really bleeds for his mother who brought up her own family and now has to take care of grandchildren too.

You spoke of standing in the snow looking eastward; Many times, in Italy as well as France, I have stood the same way breathing in the beauty of the night and, with each breath, sending out my prayers and my love to you. Sometimes you wish so had that you seem to ache all over and a lump comes up in your throat. Then you come to with a start and realize that you are knocking yourself out. Whenever that does happen, I have the feeling that, way off to the west, you are receiving my thoughts and are feeling the same way.

That clipping that Mary Zandri showed you was incomplete. I thought that everyone in the States had read that information by now. The only thing is that the names of many of the leaders have not been mentioned. Don't be frightened by the fact that I am getting plenty of cigarettes. It doesn't mean what you think it does. The candles will still come in very handy because, though I work now under good electric light there are many times when candles are very handy; such as those five or ten minutes just before crawling in the old sleeping bag. I received the dark glasses OK and put the leather case in a box with the perfume, I think which I sent some time ago.

It was a shock to hear about the death of Bee Tator. For a moment I thought that you meant that Lil Tator had died. But when I the part about pregnancy I realized my mistake.

The chicken business certainly must be thriving at 22 Catoonah Street! You must have humdingers of chickens when a fellow will pay $4.00 for one and not even murmur.

About the souvenirs of money: I can get you different examples of currency and maybe a swastika but nix on the helmets or such stuff. When I get home, I want as little as possible to remind me of this damned war. Not that any of us are going to gorget what fascism has done to innocent people everywhere. If we ever fall asleep again wrapped up in smug dreams of strength in isolation, we deserve to have a dictator push us around.

I am afraid that I haven't impressed you with my ability as a typist and I know that typing is a cold form of expression but I know that you will overlook this once. If I were with you now I could use a much warmer method of expression.

Give my love to Mother Bedient, Francis & Daisy, and all the Crouchley family. Good night, sweetheart, with all my love,

Chad

January 3, 1945
Somewhere in France

Dearest sweetheart:

Not much to write about tonight except that I am well and a hell of a lot cleaner than I have been in a long time. When I was with the Mail section there were a lot of times when personal cleanliness was something to be desired but difficult to obtain.

Spent almost all day going through personnel cards getting information for our files. I see Bill nearly every day. He looks fine.

Haven't received mail in several days but that may be caused by the moving around of the different mail units. Just found out last night that I hadn't sent your glasses cases as I thought. I will make up a package and send it.

Well sign off now as the lights are gong on and off.

Love,

Chad

Dearest sweetheart:

Oh happy day! As Lil'Abner would say. Three letters from you (#218, #219, #222) Xmas cards from Grace and Cliff and three packages (Peter Punkin Lyme & Ruth and Rev. Lusk) It was a great treat to have mail dated as late as Dec. 26th. For a few days now I haven't been receiving mail so I really devoured your letters.

As I told you previously Xmas day was pretty quiet. We had turkey with all the fixings. It's hard to explain your feelings about a day spent so far away from home when you know that it should be spent with those you love. Except for the fact that we ate more than usual and didn't get much work done it was just another day. You think that after you have been overseas for a while the ache and emptiness will wear off but it doesn't.

I added the colored picture of you (wearing your pirate hat) to my collection. It makes you look very devilish (which is what I like). I have quite a collection by now and I carry it with me all the time.

When you mention different fellows in the service heading toward San Francisco. I really think I have been lucky. Now that I have this wonderful opportunity working in the I & E. Section I know darn well I have been lucky. I wouldn't want to feel that I were heading that way (toward the Pacific) although naturally there will be some personnel shifts after the end of hostilities in Europe.

That black and gold braid you saw is used by all officers in the Infantry. The blue braid is worn by enlisted men. I am glad that Lou got his commission. I know he will make a "good officer". By "good" I mean he will have plenty of consideration for his men and will treat them fairly.

Don't think that you are acting nuts when you talk about Xmas. I know how you feel but right now the only ones who can do much about it are the Nazi leaders. This time it's going to be Germany that will be drained of man power. Germany's leaders are trying to prolong their own evil lives by sacrificing their men and boys. It seems as though they are like a drowning man grasping at straws just to keep up a little longer.

Please don't send me any money. As a matter of fact I am going to send you a PTA which will reach you in the form of a government check. I think that I will have it made out for $240. That will leave me with $20. (Nope! Beg pardon,) $50.00 which will be plenty. I just don't have the chance to spend money over here. Since I have been moving around a lot I haven't been paid for Nov. or Dec. yet. So, you see, I have a lot more coming to me. By the end of the month my pay will be all straightened out. I hope.

I hope that all the folks are well. Give my love to Mother Bedient and Dad and Mother Crouchley and all my love to you.

Chad

January 6, 1945
Somewhere in France

Dearest petunia:

Another short note to let you know that everything is OK. I am sitting in a nice warm room writing at a desk and enjoying good clear electric for a change (some different from the mail clerk days of working by candlelight.) It all makes me feel that I am a very lucky guy.

Today I did a lot more typing and I reached the resolve that even though I have been using a type writer ever since 1921 and have had everything from a Blickensderfer to an Underwood or a Royal to work with, I am going to do my derndest to learn the touch system. I'll probably get all tangled up and try to hit the q with my wrist watch but I'm going to try it.

There isn't much to write about tonight except that I am busy and using what little gray matter I have quite frequently.

All my love sweetheart, take good care of yourself.

Chad

Dearest sweetheart:

I forgot to tell you I had a xmas V-mail from Don Congdon. It was just the drawing showing a country scene with a church and a peasant seated in his wagon drawn by oxen. I am going to drop him a line tonight.

And I received your very professional looking job of xmas V-mail drawing entitled "a V-mail message for My Husband". Except for the fact that I know your distinctive style of printing I thought that the drawings were commercially printed. On the upper left hand corner you showed the husband reading a newspaper and sprinkling ashes on the carpet. What the heck is a carpet? I haven't seen one in so long I have almost forgotten. And the one showing the husband tracking mud all over the clean floor. Isn't his nose a little to dark for me? You know I wouldn't come home with my nose glowing like W.C. Fields' but you can bet that when I get home I am going to have at least one good toot. Not that I want to get roaring drunk but just a nice mellow glow so that everything looks rosy. Thanks a lot sweetheart for the message I enjoyed it very much!

We are working away at our survey of possible instructors for the post-war educational program. We are getting so that we can go through a stack of personnel cards pretty rapidly. When we get our information about the man's educational background and vocational experience we type up our own cards for our files. This particular job is my assignment (I mean making the survey) so you can see that we manage to keep busy.

Tonight we had a special treat at supper time. The band played some real sweet dance music. The boys all appreciated it a lot and most of them are going to a special show tonight which the band is putting on.

Last night and the night before I saw movie shows, the first I have seen in a couple of months. The first was "Christmas Holiday" which was hard to appreciate because the sound apparatus was so weak that it was almost like the old days of silent films. Last night though, I saw

"Guildersleive's Ghost" and the sound machine was working O.K. I hadn't seen a movie in so long that I laughed my head off at the simplest things. It's certainly a treat to see a movie again. I know what you mean when you say that love scenes have a peculiar effect on you. It gives me "butterflies in the stomach" too. After being married ten years it's difficult to think of yourself being separated from the one you love for ten months. Those ten months seem like centuries.

Mail has been spotty lately and comes in bunches. I haven't had mail now for several days but here's hoping a lot of it catches up with me real soon.

Take good care of yourself, sweetheart, remember me to the family and all my love to you from

Chad

Dearest sweetheart:

My outgoing mail to you may get jammed up a bit so that it reaches you in bunches because lately we have been sending out our mail in bunches through the mail box. Sometimes we forget about getting it our right away after it has been censored so two days mail may go out at the same time.

This afternoon one of the boys brought in a Hq.Co. order stating that were raised in grade. I was raised from T/5 to T/4. The stripes that are worn to indicate T/4 look like this:

This will mean that I can increase my allotment to you which I will do as soon as I have a chance to talk to our company clerk. I also haven't sent you the $240. which I wrote about but will do so soon. I am going to send it by a P.T.A. form and the money will come to you in the form of a government check. I will have a receipt for my money so as soon as I hear from you that you received it O.K. I will be able to destroy the receipt.

Today was another busy day looking over personnel cards and getting ready for the setting up of our file system of men who have had teaching experience or good vocational background. While searching through the cards you certainly learn some peculiar names of trades. They run all the way from "truck swamper" to a "steel pickeler". A truck swamper is evidently a man who loads trucks and acts as an assistant driver while a steel pickeler is one who dips steel poles in an acid bath to remove the scale of impurities. You find men who are illiterate and those with two or three degrees after their names. A great institution, the infantry. Nowadays the "Queen of Battles" embraces all types.

Will close now. All my love, sweetheart, and take good care of yourself.

Chad

January 10, 1945
Somewhere in France

Dearest sweetheart:

Just a quickie to let you know that I am OK and in good health. I found out that it was permitted to write Mme Jasquementton so I did and sent the letter off today. I will let you know if I get an answer. It's possible that she may have moved but the chances are pretty good that the letter will get through OK because of the fact that she has been an inhabitant Lyons for a long time. We are beginning to see light in our survey work but still manage to do a lot of typing each day. Incoming mail is till very poor and I haven't had any since the days I received three packages and four letter. I suppose by now the oil burner is really working overtime keeping the house warm. Are you sleeping on the feather bed? I'll bet that Hudson Bay blanket feels good. Saw a movie tonight getting to be a regular movie goer. I've seen more movies in the last week that during all the rest of the time I have been overseas. Will close now with all my love to my sweetheart.

from
Chad

Dearest sweetheart:

The working day is over and before I go off to my sack I want to write you to let you know that I am OK.

I have been pretty busy today working on our survey which has reached the point now of gathering statistics for large groups. The actual searching for information is about over and soon we will have our survey complete.

I just read this evening an article called "The Army in Europe" by Walter Lippmann. It is very good and since it probably has appeared in the papers back home I wondered whether you had seen it. It is well written and shows a sober but down-to earth picture of the war in Europe.

By the way, if you come across anything of special interest in the field of vocational guidance or special work that is being done in the States for the VOC guidance of troops try to send it to me and it will be of great help. Ask Elsa to be on the look out for anything along that line which she thinks may be of interest. Soon I may have the opportunity to write little descriptions or give short talks on things like that for the troops so I would like to be prepared.

The mail situation continues to be slow but I have had that happen before. When I was a mail clerk I got a pretty good picture of the ways and wherefores of mail distribution and can understand the difficulties better. Just the same I would get a big thrill out of receiving some letters from my sweetheart.

Well, tis time to lie myself off to bed so good night my darling with all my love.

Chad.

Dearest sweetheart:

Just been to the movies again. You must think I'm nuts the way I keep saying, last night I saw this show or tonight we have music. I've seen more movies in the last few weeks than all the rest of my time overseas. Perhaps it would be more accurate to say that I have seen more movies that I would have seen in a comparable period of civilian life. But you can bet that when I return home and you want to go somewhere to a show or a dance, by gorry, we'll go. And if you get that fed-up feeling which comes on you about once a year when you want to pull up stakes and travel and have some fun, darling, I'll be right by your side. Of course for a while we will want to be by ourselves enjoying our reunion.

You mentioned in letter #193 which still makes me tingle that you were lonesome. And then you described a bicycle trip during which we rested by a nice cool brook. I still keep that part with me as long as I am not in any immediate danger and carry it along with the pictures you sent me. But back to being lonesome. I will not take the Scoutmaster job back when I return because in order to do a good job without the help of other you have to devote too much personal time. I want our weekends to ourselves. (Of course during the week it may not be possible to get away much, but our weekends belong entirely to us and, my dear, I'm going to do everything within my power to use them for our mutual relaxation and happiness.

I received letters #224 and 225 yesterday and enjoyed the xmas poem about the gift to papa. I like the picture of you with the pirates hat and our eyes looking up. I will admit I like the one numbered 2D23942 - 3 the best. It shows my sweetheart's fluffy, curly, top-knot and there's a look in your eyes that makes my heart go galloping like the Lone Ranger's Silver when he hollers "Away!"

When mother B took the picture of you holding the hornets nest I'll bet you both were pretty jittery. If I remember white faced hornets, the only guy deserving such treatment as they hand out is a Nazi or a Jap.

Back in Italy we used to have yellow jackets swarming all over our mess kits whenever we had pudding, jam or anything sweet. We just batted them with our spoons and kept on eating but I think I would stop and consider thing a bit before I smacked a white-faced hornet on any part of his anatomy. Come to think of it, you know there is an interesting analogy. Italian bees (striped honey bees) are fairly even-tempered and easy to get along with but the Black German honey bee is a son of a b------. Ouch!

The package mailed November 4th contains a book entitled "How to Say it in Spanish" by Lt. Col. Harry M Gwynn. The point is that the book belonged to a man who took an interest in me and shortly afterward gave me my first real break in the Army. I would like to have you save it and the other things (oh, yes, the agates Harvey sent too) until we both have a chance to look them over.

When I read about the blues you had New Year's Eve I feel pretty low. Here we stayed around the office working until late and finally I couldn't stand it any longer so I went to bed. As I lay in my sleeping bag I kept track of time until midnight. Of course it was just evening back home but I sent my New Year's wish to you with all my love. Here's a poem which was written for our Stars and Stripes by O.Y.S.

The Letter

Swiftly, swiftly, gentle East Wind
I am bound and you are free;
Take these words and tenderly
Take them where I may not be.

Gently, gently, when here eyelids
Close to drive a tear before,
Brush your sleeve across here lashes
And sigh, "I cannot love you more."

Lightly, lightly, where her hair falls
In enchanting disarray,
Dance on abandoned bacchanal
and whisper, "I am yours for aye."

Softly, softly, say "I love you."
Now carefully remember this,
When she turns and seeks to find you
Place upon her lips a kiss.

Good night, my sweet,

Love,
Chad

Dearest sweetheart:

Just a few lines to let you know that I am OK though somewhat pooped. We have been looking over more personnel cards and they are very tough on the eyes.

Tonight Mac and I opened up a can of chicken for supper and made sandwiches. Very tasty. I received a big box of candy from Lois Bennet and the box is about half gone by now. I am gradually getting my packages cut down so that if I have to move I won't be so encumbered.

After supper Mac and I sat down with the serious intent of writing some letters but we both got started talking shop and comparing experiences. Two hours rolled by and we were still going strong talking about teaching problems and courses we had taken. We hadn't know each other very long before it developed that Mac and I were both at M------for basic training. He knows Dave and was in the same barracks with him. It's certainly a coincidence that I should wind up working with a fellow who trained right next door to me.

Last night we enjoyed a concert given by the band. The first part of the program was very long-hair but the last part was interspersed with some good bits of sweet music. The band has a swell brass section.

Well it's getting late so I will say good night, my sweet, with all my love.

Chad

Somewhere in France
January 16, 1945

Dearest sweetheart:

I spent some time this evening after going to another movie reading some your letters for the umpteenth time after which I destroyed them. I had quite a group of 190's and early 200's although I still keep No. 193 in which you described a certain bicycle trip. When my morale needs a particular lift I read that letter over again and feel much better.

It is pretty cold in these parts although we have had quite a few nice bright days. We have an oil heater in our office so we keep the room plenty warm while, at night, I retire to the warmth of my G.I. sleeping bag.

The only mail tonight was a copy of Newsweek Magazine. Very little first class mail seems to be coming through right now. Perhaps it will pick up soon. I hope so. I haven't heard yet from Kathryn Smith Jacquemetton although it is still a little too soon to be getting any news from her. Their letters have to come through the base censor so it takes a little longer.

Sometime ago you said you saw Freddie Jackson wearing a badge looking like this a Revolutionary War Musket in silver on a blue background. That is the Expert Infantryman's Badge. The Combat Infantryman's Badge looks like this the same panel with silver musket on a blue background but with a wreath of what looks like oak leaves. Although, as I said before, someone made off with my badge I still have in my wallet a copy of the original order signed by the colonel awarding me the Combat badge. They were awarded to a whole big group of us right after the push to Rome. At that time I was a runner for the first platoon and had the job of checking communications, carrying verbal messages, and helping distribute rations of food and water to the men. Once in a while we would have to act as litter bearers for the wounded. One day during the push I even acted as an ammo carrier for the light machine guns and one afternoon I was lucky enough to get the job of herding some Jerry prisoners back to the battalion. While back with the prisoners we were shelled but at the same time the fellows up the road were going through a tough mortar barrage. I guess all the protecting saints were watching over me those days. So you see that the badge isn't awarded for any act of heroism or anything like that but just the day by day performance of assigned duties while in combat, not only the gruelling days of the push but the sweating-out of Jerry shelling when we were maintaining defensive positions on Anzio. Personally I hadn't then and I haven't now any ambitions of being heroic. I think that's the way nearly all the fellows feel about it no matter how they may have felt or expressed themselves when they were safe back in the States.

Glancing at the old reliable wrist watch which, by the way, is still ticking em off without any trouble, I see that it's time to get off to bed. So my sweet, good night and a thousand kisses on your sweet lips.

From Chad

Somewhere in France
January 18, 1945

Dearest sweetheart:

Hooray! Two letters today after a general drought of about a week. The mail situation hasn't been very good. I was talking to one of the mail clerks and he says there's lots of Xmas cards and newspapers coming. Through but very little air-mail. But I was surprised to receive your letter No. 227 mailed Jan. 6th because that's pretty good service. I also had a letter from Ruth Anderson in which she mentioned how happy you were to get the news about my new job. I don't blame you for blowing off steam and getting tight. You can't keep your emotions bottled up inside you. It's too much wear and tear on the human machinery. I'm glad that you feel better now. Better watch that "code id d doze" though because being in a tired condition for so long, your resistance isn't so good and a cold can so easily put you in bed sick for a long stretch.

I appreciated the picture of Miss muffet snoozing under the xmas tree. I can just see her opening up one eye to make sure everything is all right. As for the clippings from the Sat. Eve. Post, what I wouldn't give to be able to perch my hat on a hall table lamp or go to a movie and reach out and twine my fingers in yours.

Lots of typing today cutting stencils and keeping up with personnel cards. The three of us manage to keep pretty busy from 8:30 a.m. until we go off to bed about 9 or 10 o'clock at night.

News looks good from the Russian front. I hope they really keep going this winter and bust right through to Berlin.

I wasn't really complaining about the mail situation. After all men and material come before mail. So right now, when every little bit helps a helluva lot, let them get the stuff over here and we can wait for mail. It's a big thrill to get a letter from home but it's a bigger thrill to know that we are building the power to bring this mess to an end. Then we will have something to be really happy about. This program to which I am assigned in no way interferes with a G.I's returning home so don't be worried on that score.

It's getting late so off to bed. I just noticed that the coast had a big snow storm. I hope that it didn't hit Ridgefield had. Well, good night, my sweetheart, with all my love.

Chad

Somewhere in France
January 20, 1945

Dearest sweetheart:

Wow! I almost fell out of my chair when I read in Letter #228 that I had pulled the prize boner of sitting down, writing a 2 page letter to you, putting your letter in my envelope then tearing up my letter. I must be really getting absent minded although if the letter was written about xmas time and still had the Co. G. 179th address on it I probably wasn't accountable because it was about then that I was going around and around trying to get my mail job cleaned up before coming to work in the I.& E. Section.

The latest letter from you is No. 230 dated Jan. 10th so that's not bad at all. I hope you receive the two packages containing perfume which I sent you. If they don't come through the mails O.K. I doubt if I'll be able to get more. Most of the boys bought up all the perfume they could and, before long, the supply had disappeared. The small bottles of perfume are supposed to be pre-war stuff which a coiffures had in stock. Maybe she was giving us the run-around but we opened one bottle and it smelled really oo-la-la. Every one of us agreed that it was good stuff although I sometimes think that we have gone so long without smelling perfume that anything would smell good.

Just finished that last paragraph and in came the mail clerk with Letter #229 and a letter from Elsa. So I had to take time out read the two letters.

I have received a new pair of gloves so the glove situation has eased off for a while. It's really cold and snowy here so gloves are very important. Those work socks sound good. My feet perspire a lot and wearing a pair of socks for more that two or three days makes my feet get cold pretty easy. When I was a mail clerk I really used up gloves pretty fast but now I don't believe I'll have as much need for them as I did. If you can get some magazines especially ones you think might be useful in my work please send them. Also if you come across any really good pictures or maps covering topics in which the fellows might have interest please send them along. As for candy, you know I don't have a real sweet tooth, so save the candy for Mother B. I am quite a way ahead on my supply of cigarettes. I get them every day still have a reserve carton of Chesterfields. So don't worry about smokes for me. I can just imagine what they are up against in the stores with jealous customers keeping an eagle eye on the other fellow to make sure that he doesn't get away with anything.

We were just talking about butter and how you get so you don't miss it after a while. We get lots of spreads, peanut butter, jam, and marmalade and occasionally butter so when the butter comes along with appreciate it but have come to not caring much whether we have it or not. I know how you feel about the black market situation. Our fellows who were in Italy and in some parts of France ran into it and cussed at the so-and so's who were making big profits from other people's wants.

I was staggered by the amount of work you're doing on the S.S. Denton Estate. It really must be a gigantic task. Old Sam collected real estate the way an antique man collects antiques. No matter how battered and beaten up they were he could always see some way of getting a profit out of them.

When you said that June told you more news about me than I do myself, as Mr. Peavey would say, "Well, now I don't know about that, Guildersleeve." As a matter of fact you are nearer right than she was. Right now seeing Arnold Brewer would be too much of a trip. Since I have been put in charge of the office I wouldn't have much chance to get away anyhow. I see Bill every day and once in a while we get a chance to talk together. Bill is a very quiet fellow but I manage to get him talking about how his wife is and about things back home. He shows me his snapshots of June and I show him my pictures of you. By the way a line from the movie "Mission Tokyo" impress me. Cary Grant said, "it isn't what a woman looks like that you remember the most but the things she is, the way she laughs, here sense of good sportsmanship and her zest for life." I wouldn't part with the pictures you sent me for anything except a chance to come back and hold the real Bedie in my arms and tell her how much I have missed her and how I love her

I haven't looked real close for Northern Lights although, when I step out to plod my way to bed I can look up and see Orion and the three Kings gleaming in the sky.

Yes, I got your package containing the paper. It came in very handy at the time although now we have a good supply.

I'll never forget what you said about Tippie. I am glad she is peppy and full of ginger. I'll bet when she has had a BATH, she is very snooty and proud of her fine feathers.

My gosh I hope you aren't saving the entire Sunday Edition of the N.Y. Times. Just the Magazine Section and the News Review of the Week if you can. Even at that I don't know. Some morning you're liable to look out and see a deep hole where Mary's Room has fallen through.

Thanks for renewing my Rotary dues and tell Woody that I will try to send him a French postal card. I can't remember his full name and the address Ridgefield would probably be all right. The only thing is that the card will show a little French girl up in a tree. As a matter of fact, the only things that might be classed a pornographic postal cards were the ones I saw a Pompei.

I hadn't heard about Joe Bascknoichi but it is not surprising considering the way they were several years ago.

Having rambled all over the lot I ought to close now. Good night my sweet with all my love.

Chad

Somewhere in France
January 23, 1945

Dearest sweetheart:

Just a quickie to let you know that I am OK and thinking of you - Lots of snowy weather and pretty cold here. The hold "long johns" feel good and I appreciate the extra warmth afforded by the wool sweater you sent. Received a funny paper, a Press, a News Review of the Week, two Rotary bulletins from Cliff and two copies of Newsweek, so have been doing a lot of reading. Hope you seen the New National Geographic Map called "Germany and It's approaches? Very complete and now the Russians are really moving it gives you a good picture of the European fronts with the exception of Italy. Don't forget to send any maps or educational material you think may be of value. According to the paper I see that they want people to keep house temperatures down. How are you making out with the oil situation now that old man January has really turned off the heat?

Good night, sweetheart, all my love to you.

Chad

Somewhere in France
January 25, 1945

Dearest sweetheart:

Received your letter No. 231 yesterday (it was written Jan. 11th) and today I received three long envelopes with Pathfinder, a snap-shot folder and a funny paper.

I was sorry to hear that your cold got worse but was glad that you made up your mind to stay in bed for a few days. After all your health is the most important thing.

I was amazed to hear that Tommy Lazor got in the Navy. I didn't think that he could pass the physical after what Allie had said about his eyes and kidneys.

Gussie must be quite a puppy. How does Tippie like the idea of a young puppy receiving attention from you?

Thanks for sending the socks etc. I hope I don't have to use the regulation ear muffs very much. So far I have done much riding around but when we get caught up on some of our office work we may be on the road visiting various units.

From all I can make out about the New draft regulations. They really must mean business. I hope they don't get the idea that the I & E. Section can be dispensed with. I don't see how they can do very much to Ralph after all he's 39 and is over the combat age limit. Can they force him to give up his job with the boys and make him take a defense job? When you told me about Tommy and I read in the Press about kids whom I taught in school entering the service it makes me feel like a real old man.

Not much to report about my activities. The usual typing and writing today. I saw "Buffalo Bill" last night. You know how I like western pictures with lots of Indians. Maybe I am not so old after all.

Good night, my sweet, take good care of yourself and give my love to the family. All my love to you. Get better quick sweet but don't take chances with that cold.

Chad

My dearest Petunia:

Dr. Edwards certainly hit the nail right on the head. For my money, he's a good weather prophet. Old man winter has really been working over time as far as we are concerned.

Yesterday I received letter #235 which mentioned him and I can't seem to remember him although it's almost 15 years since I left the classic halls of Colgate.

I was sorry to hear that the Shorehaven Club burned down. Remember the teachers' dinner down there? I makes my mouth water to think of the sea food Dorlon's put out. That reminds me of Lobster Newburg and Chablis and clams on the half-shell.

I received a xmas V-mail form from Don Congdon and wrote him but, as yet, haven't heard from him again. Personnel work is right up Don's alley because it has a lot of details concerning insurance allotments and payrolls. As I remember his job was insurance before he went into the army. Right now he must have a swell setup with women doing the laundry and working around the place.

You asked about a paper vouching for the fact that I earned the Combat badge. I have one which is a regular form and is signed by the regimental commander. However, where we're located, it isn't possible to replace the one which was stolen.

I'm glad you like Ernie Pyle's way of writing. He has the reputation of being a keen sympathizer with the G.I. and since he took the trouble to actually see how conditions are in the front lines, he really has an understanding of the way a front-line soldier thinks and acts. Bill Mauldin and his cartoons give us a great kick. One cartoon I remember particularly shows a kitchen scene with open boxes standing around a big can labeled "Orange Marmelade" placed on the floor. A blanket hangs across the door and a couple of mess kits hand from the nails on the walls. Two typical bearded G.I's are sitting on boxes. One of them has a warped and nicked bayonet which he is fitting on the end of a rifle. He remarks, "Jeez, Joe , this can-opener fits on the end of a rifle!" It is hard to describe the humor of Mauldin's cartoons but he has a touch which very few cartoonists have been able to attain. If I see another good one in the Stars and Stripes I'll send you the whole issue. We are not allowed to make clippings any more.

Thanks for the little curl from your top knot. I put it inside one of the snapshot containers which you sent me. If you are crazy then I am too because receiving that little reminder of you gave me a terrific lift.

You are probably getting lengthy radio reports on the progress of the Russians. From what we read here they must be putting plenty of pressure on the Jerries. I hope they knock out Silesia because that's where the krauts moved their big factories when the bombings in the wester part of Germany reached alarming proportions. It also contains lots of coal and minerals needed for their war machine. Then if the Russians get over into Austria they can nullify the Italian front and old von Kesselbring will have to pull in his horns. I suppose by this time they have taken everything moveable out of Northern Italy. A lot of wishful thinking, I suppose, but it's in the minds of all of us. The sooner it does happen the sooner this mess will be finished.

I can just picture you curled up in the corner of the divan writing away furiously and damning and dabbing at "your dabbed dose." Take good care of that cold, sweetheart, and I hope you get rested up. Don't make the mistake of going back to work before you feel well again.

Give my love to the folks and good night my sweet with all my love,

Chad

Somewhere in France
January 30, 1945

My dearest sweetheart:

I have a feeling that westbound mail is all jammed up somewhere along the line. The latest letters I have from you are Nos. 232, 233, 234 which is pretty good but my letters to you must be wandering around plenty. I suppose those boxes containing the perfume which I sent before xmas will probably reach you in time for Easter.

I am glad to hear that your cold is getting better. Even if you didn't sleep just resting during the early hours of the evening do a lot to restore your strength. Gosh, I hope you don't have any more polyps in your nose. It's bad enough having sinus trouble without having your "doze stubbed dub." When you have Doc Woodford look at your nose why don't you ask him about the cramps which bother you so much or have they stopped? If the Russians keep up the good work I will be able to supply my own remedy for those cramps sooner than any of us realized or thought possible. Last September there was a real wave of rosy optimism everywhere you went but that was followed by the sobering events of December and early January. Now everyone asks "What's the latest news about the Russians?" You can see the old rose-colored glasses being polished up again. In other words, I have seen enough of the Germans Military organization and strategy to know that whatever is taken from them has to be fought for. If they have ten places to defend and only enough troops to defend eight of them they run like hell and give up the two least valuable places then fight like the devil for the eight they mean to defend. The optimist thinks that this time they have really hit the position where everything just has to fall apart but the realist knows that this mess won't be over until the German Army is really helpless. That is something that no one can predict. The sooner the better. As far as afterward is concerned it's hard to tell what they will do with the old 45th.

You must be having a lot of snow. The newspapers all say that the eastern coast has had a real cold time of it so far. Soon February will be with us and we will begin to see the end of old man winter. We have snow flurries every day and it is quite cold.

Lots of typing today so my muscles are rather stiff. Goodnight, sweetheart, all my love to you from,

Chad.

Somewhere in France
February 2, 1945

Dearest sweetheart:

As happens so many times with the mixed-up mail situation, I received letter #238 before getting #237 (which I received this P.M.) I was nonplussed at first about your comments in No. 238 but everything was cleared up by the time I had gotten into No. 237. I wouldn't feel sorry if I were you about your desire to go away somewhere far from the cut-throat competition of business and settle down somewhere in the country on a nice farm. So many fellows in the Army feel the same way about it. One fellow may have worked in a steel mill and he vows up and down that he'll never return to that type of work. He wants to try raising poultry. Fellows who have been going along in a job they chose (often without very much thought or planning) were suddenly jerked out of their rut by going into the army. Now they have a chance to mull over in their minds a lot of things, and wonder whether they might not be better off and a lot happier in another type of work. I have to confess that I have been tempted lots of times to reconsider the teaching field. But of course, everything now is vague and unsettled. A fellow realizes that this thing over here may last quite a while in spite of the Russians. Nobody is predicting any more after the severe jolt our military peers received as a result of Von Runstedt's offensive. Then they were predicting the end of the war by Nov. 15th but now they must be keeping very quiet. All this sudden hustle and bustle over arms production and changes in the draft seem to show that a lot of the complacency which existed last fall has disappeared.

Going to the movies will do you a lot of good sweetheart because they will help you to relax and when you come home you will be able to sleep better. I know that seeing movies here helps to perk me up and gets my mind of personal problems.

I wasn't surprised by Jo Jo's discharge from the Army. I remember that, while in school, he had trouble seeing the blackboard. That, plus his chip-on-the-shoulder attitude, made him a poor prospect for the armed services.

I appreciated the jokes you told and am sorry I haven't picked up any good ones. We get Yank magazine and Stars and Stripes but lately Bill Mauldin's cartoons have been replaced by others that aren't very good. Mauldin has the real touch that makes a good cartoonist.

Well, I finally was paid Thursday and sent the PTA for $240 which I promised. I have the receipt for it so in about a month you will be getting a government check for that amount. Don't feel that you should put it away but, if it happens that you see a hat or hats or dresses which suit your fancy, spend the money. In another month I'll send more money home. I don't need money here so you might as well have it to use as you see fit.

I'll be looking forward to receiving that snooky letter you promised. Goodnight, Petunia, and forget about such subjects as divorces. You'll never get away from me unless you want to.

All my love,

Chad.

Dearest sweetheart:

This P.M. I received letters 236 and 240 and a swell "Valentine" with a poem and everything. I got a kick out of the OPA bulletin and the comments about the weather and feeding the chickens. We must have gotten the same snow storms you did because, for a while, it certainly "snew" here too. Fortunately it thawed and the ground is fairly clear now. I imagine you must feel like a regular farmer with your lantern and pail of water going down to the barn to tend the chickens. It doesn't seem possible that those cute little rascals we got through the mail could be old hens now.

I would like to have seen Jim's face when Mother Bedient said good morning to him. I'll bet he was really "confused." I can't quite picture Dick F as one of twelve possible candidate for Annapoles. The Navy must have done wonders with him to get him really pepped up enough to make the exertion. The move I see of Army and Navy methods of education the more thoroughly convinced I am that we are going to need a tremendous amount of guidance work in our educational system. Teaching methods have been revolutionized especially in languages and the sciences. Teachers are going to have the benefits of some fine training materials which have been prepared by gov't experts.

I forgot to say that I received the Rotary card O.K. Thanks. I haven't written to the Rotary members in quite a while so I think that I'll do that before many more days slip by.

I enjoyed (that's a poor word) the V-mail Valentine. Maybe I'll be able to design one for my Petunia. I hope to be able to pick up some cards soon. While I am at it I may be able to get one that would please Woody.

The job continues with beaucoup typing and composing. Each A.M. we take down the 9:00 o'clock news given at dictation speed. We type it up and post it on our bulletin board then we bring our war map of Germany and its approaches up to date. The rest of the day is spent typing letters, cutting stencils, making maps, mounting clippings and working on our survey.

Will end now. As with you, goodnight seems to be the appropriate remark. Give my love to the folks.

All my love,

Chad

Somewhere in France
February 7, 1945

My dearest sweetheart:

I slipped up on letter writing the last couple of days. I have been doing a lot of reading in the evening and also have been catching up on Newsweek "Battle Baby", N.Y. Times News Review of the week and Readers Digest. I have certainly received some swell letters from you. I enjoyed the jokes in them a lot and appreciated your remark about the "Battle of the Bulge" Maybe I could help out considerably in the reduction of the bulge. Either that or create a larger one! You must have had writer's cramp after finishing Nos. 239, 242, and 243. I can never hope to reach that record. --Today I received a letter from your second cousin in Lyons, Mrs. J. L. Jacquemetton. She mentioned the fact that Bob Crane had written to Ella reassuring the family that she was OK. She says she got her first letter from her sister on xmas day nearly 2 1/2 years since the last one. Her family is all together they are not too hungry or too cold. The general conditions there aren't too good as far as I can make out. Fortunately her husband has lots of clients in the country so they are able to get food enough for all. They live on beans and potatoes as a basic diet with frequent additions of poultry. She is quite curious about me and my civilian background so I am going to write her again. Of course a visit is out of the question right now because of the distance. I am also going to write Eleanor (Mrs. Walters) in Ocean Grove and give her a list of things that they need.

I am relieved to learn that one of the two boxes containing perfume came through the mail OK. The other one is probably on its way unless some curious so-and-so decided he wanted a souvenir of la belle France. I can't guarantee the fine discrimination of my smellers. After all it's like a question of painting or music. You don't know why, but you know what you like! Remember how I used to brush my nose through your hair and bring it around behind your ear. Oh my! Just the thought of it makes me, like the wolf in the Army cartoons, want to woo-woo-woo!

About my address, I am really assigned to Headquarters Co, 45th Infantry Division but lots of times I neglect to put the Co. in. It really doesn't make a hell of a lot of difference. Just so long as those sugar reports come along regularly.

I am glad you got the Reichsmark. I am enclosing in this one a Bank of Algeria note for 100 francs. When I was mail clerk I had a lot of "paper" to handle and some times it wasn't all good stuff. Some was torn or lacked serial nos. So you had to watch pretty closely. The note is, as far as I can make out, not worth much anywhere, except of course as a souvenir.

About that PTA which is on its way to you. It represents money earned over a period of two months by doing special favors for fellows. I wish I were good enough or lucky enough to be able to get that much by cards or dice. But you see I never was or will be because I was really lucky in love (and , God willing, will stay that way)

I was bowled over by the size of our savings account. My golly how did you dood it? Don't worry about my taking a trip to England although maybe some day I'll get to see the city you saw in 1925. If I do go I'll try to keep up my letter writing but, of course, I don't know yet about censoring and mailing facilities. Don't worry about my having money, right now I have 11000 francs or about $220, plenty until next pay day. I think I'll wait until then and see how things are and will probably send home another PTA for you. Here's one case where PTA is doing a lot more good than it did most of the time in school.

I am going to write to Arnold Brewer. I can see where he would be really a big help over here with his fine knowledge of the language.

Speaking of knowledge here's an address I want you to save for me (the Recording Division, N.Y. Univ. Film Library, Washington Square, N.Y. 3, N.Y. Free catalog of selected educational recordings). I am storing up and taking note of all the material I can on visual and special educational practices.

I ought to quit now because it is getting late. I am glad you are sleeping better now. Goodnight, sweetheart,

All my love,
Chad.

Dearest sweetheart:

You described the Ridgefield folks digging out from under the snow drifts. Well I had to literally dig my way out from under the big pile of mail that was waiting for me when I returned to my job. But how I love that kind of digging.

As I intimated in an earlier letter I did get a chance to go to Paris to take the I & E course. It lasted a week and kept us going each day from 8:30 a.m. until 5:20 p.m. except for Thursday afternoon off. The course was very interesting but I must confess I am worried by the problem of getting enough materials to carry out the task which will eventually confront us. Personally however I think our division program is equal to any and better than most divisional I & E programs.

As for Paris itself I made a vow that someday, somehow you and I are going to visit the city and spend sometime there after France has had a chance to recover from the shock of the war. Of course she never will completely recover from her terrible losses. The Germans deliberately planned it that way. When I think of the two million prisoners the Germans took and kept away from their families I can see why the Germans believed that they could survive the war and come out with a larger population than any other European country. There are hundreds of women, thousands of them who haven't had news of their husbands for 4 1/2 years. What a loathsome thing the German mind is. I was window-shopping on the Champs Elysies Thursday afternoon and was looking for perfume when two French women stopped and started talking about different kinds of perfume. I finally went in and bought two small bottles of a secondary brand (not Patou or Molyneux) (I can't remember both the brand names but one was Redfern). After I came out of the shop the two women walked along with me toward the Etoile where I wanted to take the Metro to get to Madeleine. When I got on the subway care one of the women got out with me and she told me about herself. She said that she hadn't seen her husband since May 1940 and that as far as she knew he was a prisoner of the Germans. I have heard many French women say that and those that aren't looking for a soft touch are so bitter and frustrated. You can see the pain in their eyes. But they are too proud, fiercly proud to admit defeat. The Germans have stolen from them the protection and love of their husbands and women who should be enjoying the brining up of a family are frustrated. As I changed stations and left her she wished me good luck. Such things stir up my mind so I wish the whole country of Germany were under the North Sea.

I managed to see Notre Dame on two separate occasions and you can tell Elsa that although I received no degree I went through the Science Department of the Sorboune. Nortre Dame is wonderful even in war time. It is cold and damp and badly in need of cleaning. The Rose windows have been safely stored away for the duration. But when you stand inside and look toward the altar the whole design seems to lift your eyes up toward the sky. When you are on the bridge over the Seine looking at the maze of buttresses in the rear of the cathedral you certainly admire the architects who planned it. There is a serious lack of coal. Electric power and lights and gas for cooking are rationed. Food is scarce and clothing is very difficult to get. I was talking with a French Red Cross worker and she said she was wearing one of her brothers muslin shirts. The women wear fantastic hats which rise roll on roll and swirl on swirl building up an immense turreted structure on the forward part of the head like this.

The hair is worn long and is caught up in the back with a netted pouch (snood). I suppose they couldn't satisfy their desire for new clothes so they went overboard on hats and hair styles.

I met a Sgt. from Marseilles at the school and he and I went around to a lot of the interesting places. We saw the Casino de Paris and the Folies-Bergere. We had good seats at the Casino where I could hear very well and catch the French patter but at the Folies we couldn't get tickets for anything but the second balcony where it was very hard to hear but of course, it isn't always necessary to hear at the Folies. Seeing is plenty and I must say those French gals are really well constructed.

We spent a lot of time at the Red Cross where I met some fellows from the 179th and I even met one fellow from G Co. He is now on limited assignment.

I am going to have to quit- my eyes are starting to burn. I'm sorry sweetheart that I haven't kept up my end of the correspondence lately but I'll be doing better now that I am settled down again from my travels.

Goodnight, my sweet, I'll write more tomorrow and try to answer some of the questions you asked in your recent letters. Remember me to the family and save all my love for you.

from Chad.

Dearest sweetheart:

It will probably take me several letters to catch up on things you wrote about in letter #244-255 which I now have. As I told you, when I returned from Paris, I had a big stack of letters and a package. I was busy reading for several hours. The package was the one with the gloves, socks, and handkerchiefs all of which will come in mighty handy. Spring hasn't come to France yet by a long shot and the gloves really fill the bill.

I can imagine that Tippy enjoyed hopping up on that feather bed during the real cold weather. My sleeping bag has been just the thing to keep in the body heat.

So far I haven't seen a place where it would be possible to get another combat badge. The only badge I'm really interested in is that gold one the ex-service men are wearing in the States.

I am certainly relieved that you had Doc Woodford check up. As for the cure. I am ready and anxious to be the doctor. I think I know what you mean about the sensations you experienced while lying awake. I read a description that went something like this "Her insides burned. She seemed to be shaking although she was not. Some invisible part of here, then was shaking. She knew sudden physical craving - not for a special person, but just for men in general; a yearning of the invisible, unreal part of her which seemed to shiver constantly" Does that sound like cheap sensationalism or do you think that it described the situation. I thing you are right about the effects of reading or writing things like the description of the bike trip up to Turtle Pond. I can also picture something like the Annie Neth situation happening. There is a chapter in "Save Sex Life and Sex Living" that deals with that very subject.

With regard to that 3 shiploads of mail being lost. We hear a lot of rumors over here and now we've reached a point where we go pretty easy on believing any talk which may affect morale. So many screwy things have happened as a result of false statements that we are very skeptical to say the least.

About going home. Nobody knows what will happen to the division after hostilities cease except the very highest officials. Such information is a closely guarded secret. But I do feel sure that the fellows in the division who have been overseas a long time will get a break. Naturally there will be an interim during which personnel will be shuffled around. I do know that this Information and Education Program will in no way affect any body's chances of going home. As I said before we have a lot of veterans and after all our outfit has more actual combat days than any other overseas in this theater.

Yes I received the poem "A Christmas Present" and like the idea of that kind of present. However I like collars better than caps.

My speed in typing has reached a "plateau of learning" as the psychologists would put it. I reach a certain speed then seem to level off. I suppose I'll have a devil of a time unlearning my "pick and poke" system. Your V-mail lesson in typing hits the nail on the head. My job is to apply and get plenty of practice.

Now that you have received the 3 bottles of perfume I feel a little easier in my mind about sending stuff. I didn't send the wooden shoes after all. They are resting in my duffle bag along with several other souvenirs which I must get around to sending home.

I received several News Reviews of the Week and 2 Pathfinders yesterday. If you see any more good clippings which would make good bulletin board material please send them along.

I now have all the wallet size photos which I carry with me. I still like No. 4 the best. I guess it's because it shows your nice curly top to advantage.

What a mess Karl has run into. If he doesn't snap out of it he's going to be a regular neurotic. I can remember when we were going to grammar school together he always insisted that the was going to have a large family. It's a shame a fellow with his desire for a family like had to take such a jolt under the chin.

From all I can make out the cigarette situation must be really bad. I see that the manufacturers claim that there will be enough for 15 cigarettes per person per day. The trouble is there's the damned black market and the favoritism shown by the wholesalers who give larger quotas to retailers who can get 20 cents a pack.

That Spanish-English book I sent home did belong to a fine officer. As I probably told you he gave me my first break when he got me into company headquarters. He was a swell guy with more courage than I'll ever be able to muster.

The Stars & Stripes has a lot of poems which in a stumbly sort of way express what is in every GI's heart. They have a column call Pup Tent Poets which occasionally has a poem that is well written. You know that old saying about there being no atheist in fox holes.

The "Mac" I mentioned in letter of Jan. 15th is Donald MacDonald of Quincy Mass. who was in D Co. of the 25th Bat. at McClellan. The same bunch as Dave Moore. He and I have had a lot of talks about Baines Gap and the rest of our basic training. He's a former high school teacher also and, of course, every so often we get to talking shop.

I'll have to quit here sweetheart,

All my love,

Chad

My dearest sweetheart:

Your letter telling about Bill Maver certainly stirred up old memories of the many nights when I should have told Spike Ward to take his passes and put them where they would do the most good. Later I found out that a lot of the boys in B comapny just went ahead and saw their wives. I guess I have a law-abiding steak in me somewhere. I'd never make a clever confidence man. But back to Bill. Before I went to Paris to take the ITE course Mac (Donald Mac Donald) and I were talking about a nespaper clipping that Mrs. MacDonald had sent Mac telling about the welcome Quincey gave to Bill. The list of guests at the welcoming dinner looked like a roster of Quincey's Who's Who. I'm glad Bill seems to be in good spirits. It must be a terrific mental as well as physical adjustment for a fellow to have to make.

Just a few minutes ago I received a telephone call. The connection was very poor so I just about heard what the other fellow was saying. It was Ed Brundage and he mentioned Ridgefield. he is going to try to see me some Sunday soon. I can't tell you where he is of course but it isn't too far from here and he will probably be able to catch a ride in here to see me. I certainly was glad to hear the name Ridgefield over the phone.

Alice's deductions concerning the armbands was correct. Dave's division has been cited by Gen. De Gaulle for it's splendid work with the French. That means that Dave can wear the fouragere a special colored braid which is looped over the shoulder and hangs down across the chest. i can picture the furore that would be caused over here if a Frenchman saw an FFI armband in the same display as a German helmet.

The last movie I saw was in an English Servicemen's theater on the Champs Elysies. I haven't seen any more since and probably won't for quite a while because I am alone at our Main office. Mac is taking the course in paris and the others are at our other office. I haven't seen the D-day film yet. Maybe it will get around to us some one of these days.

If I saw your face on the screen I would probably go wandering around in a blissful daze for the next month.

I'm not worried about the theft of my combat badge. I have the order which awards it to me. The only time I might want to really have it would be if I were back in the States where some of the USO commando might start complaining about the terrible hardships they have endured.

My watch is ticking along like an old seasoned veteran. I had it fixed by a watch maker back in Xertiguys and it has performed very well ever since. Now it loses about 30 seconds in a week which is darned good when you consider the beating it has taken from the delightful climate of Alabama, N. Africa, Anzio, the push to Rome and the invasion of S. France.

According to the mileage on the Buick it is just about broken in. When I get back home I'll feel funny getting behind the wheel of a car. I haven't driven a car in a year now. You can just bet there will be no high speed stuff for me. I've had some wild and woolly rides on army trucks and I have no desire to copy the procedure in civilian life. I must be getting old.

If you can get any vocational guidance material on aviation, auto-mechanics, air-conditioning, diesel engines, livestock production, poultry management, crop management and soil conservation, radio or electrical engineering. I would appreciate it very much. Elsa may know of some materials that are recent and available. You see the fellows over here are thinking pretty seriously about what kind of work they would like to do when they return to civilian life so anything in the way of information we can furnish from our office will be of great help.

Here are some of the topics we deal with in our displays of materials:

1. Why we fight, 2. The military situation; 3. The nature of the enemy; 4. Combat tips; 5. What the home front and the gov't are doing; 6. Knowing our allies; and 7. World news. Probably no. 5 is the one on which you may be able to find some material.

With regard to vocations the men are interested in: "What is going on in the States?" Whether the field is over crowded or not." "What sort of preparation does a fellow have to get to enter the field?"

Please see if you can get the Vocational Guidance Journal, 20th and Northampton Sts. Easton, Penn. I don't know how much it costs but I think it would be a valuable thing to have. According to a fellow I heard speak at Paris the Nov. 1943 copy of Fortune Magazine has a lot of interesting material on the nature of Fascism. I don't know whether you could get a copy of it or not but, if you can, try to send it.

I have received the packages of Dec. 9th and Jan. 9th and appreciate the contents very much. As for the Nat. Geographic Maps don't send me the ones you have saved because we are continually getting maps through our regular channels. We have plenty of copies of "Germany and its approaches" which is the chief map we use now.

That booklet "Insignia of the Armed Forces of the U.S." sounds darn good. I certainly would like to have a copy.

The weather man wasn't kidding when he prophesied snow. The picture you sent of the snow drifts in front of Dixon's & Cummings reminds me of a certain night in Feb. 1934 when you reminded me that there was a blizzard howling outside and I got in my car and just barely made it up East Ridge and pulled into the yard through hub-deep snow. I was having such a good time there on the couch snuggled down close to you oblivious to the weather outside. I don't remember whether we were drinking port wine that night but in my condition I didn't need port wine to keep my attention centered on something other than the weather. I still feel the same way only more so.

Eddie Dowling probably missed me because we did move and, I might say, in a hurry. If you remember the situation at the time you will know why. All the time that I have been in France I haven't met anyone from Ridgefield. It would be a pleasant experience just to see someone from the home town.

Mac and I had a big laugh over that 3.1416. I was made a T/4 on Jan 1st and shortly after ward wrote you about it. The stripes look like this: Yes, there is such a thing as a T/3. The stripes for that rank look like, that is it's the same as a staff sergeant except for the "T" meaning technician.

It was a lucky thing you had that coal in the bin. I should think that a lot of people would get caught without fuel and would have their water pipes frozen. I was sorry to hear about the pipes in the barn. When it starts to really thaw out you will have to watch out for leaks in other parts of the barn.

I hope Ed Robin, Allen Toby and Larry Aldrich are enjoying themselves. The b.............s are going to be embarrassed if some returned veteran hangs a left hook on their nice fat double chins. Just as we have AWOL's and other unsavory specimens in the Armed forces so civilian life has its share of prime skunks.

I was interested to read that Nate Perry has left the finca and gone into the wholesale meat business. By now he ought be a pretty prosperous guy. I'll bet he never leaves Guatamala for any length of time, unless, of course, the political situation changes a lot.

Eyes are getting tired my sweet so good-night. Will write more tomorrow.

All my love.

Chad

My dearest Petunia:

I am still bogged down in the mountain of letters I received when I returned from Paris. #253 that single spaced typed letter 7 pages long just about floored me. I can never equal that record.

I just finished writing Mrs. Herbert Walters telling her about the things her sister Kathryn would like to have sent to Bob Crane. I also wrote Kathryn because she was curious about me (my civilian job, my age, etc.) and also to tell her that I had relayed her message.

In letter #253 you wrote that I might want another type of job. To be perfectly frank I don't know what I want exactly but I do like teaching, I do like to work with young people and I don't think I would like the political entanglements of the administrative side of educational work. The work I am doing now is beginning to get me back into the swing of dealing with people in an educational way but I know that I certainly will have to take some kind of course to brush up if I go back to teaching. I'm sorry, sweetheart, but my mind isn't made up. Maybe there is some other type of work in which I would be happier. I don't know. All I do know is that I want to get back to the one I love and make sure that she doesn't get lonesome.

When I read about the kind of winter you have been experiencing back in New England I realize how lucky we have been. For a while we did have a lot of snow and very cold weather but now everything is beginning to stir. On the way to Paris I say any number of swampy places where the pussy willows were coming out. It must be that the Gulf Stream has a powerful effect even this far inland.

Today I received 2 Herald Tribunes, one Pathfinder, 1 Press and 2 Funny sheets. The Herald Tribune has a lot of pictures and maps which are valuable. I can use them for bulletin board material. Also we have decided to keep a file on Britain, France, Russia, China and Germany so the articles in the H.T. are good. Those clippings from Life Magazine sound good too.

I have seen pictures of June and she looks like a very sweet woman. The period during which she didn't receive letters was the one I mentioned that caused us to move. As for me going up to the front, that's something that no man can predict. All I know is that my boss is very well pleased with the way our work has been going. I think I told you that he put me in charge of the office. I have been very fortunate in working for such a fine officer and with two swell fellow workers. Mac, whom I mentioned before, is the type who doesn't get upset easily. He takes things in his stride and puffs on his pipe then comes out with a practical suggestion that just fits the need. He's the type who makes a good advisor. Fellows coming into the office for information and guidance really open up and spill their problems when Mac gets to work on them. Charley Bucknaur, the third member of our section, is a very clever and likeable fellow with a very sensitive nature. He's a musician and has done a lot of work with psychological tests and placement problems. All together we enjoy each others' company and have managed to cook up some pretty good ideas so far.

I am surprised at you making me older by ten days than I am. You said my birthday is May 8th. Those 16 pages of foreigns were too much I guess.

You needn't boast about your eating steak. I ate a real home-cooked French meal three nights ago. Charley and I visited some friends of his and we were invited for a "petit dinner". We had an hors d'oeuvres and some good vermouth wine. Then we had beef pot roasted with some kind of wine sauce that was delicious. We also had peas and mushrooms. I'm drooling now just thinking about it. We finished with some kind of brandy. (I've forgotten the name). French brandies and schnapps are really powerful. You mentioned our boat rides at Wisconsin Dells and at Ausable Chasm. Some day, sweet we're going to take a boat ride on Lake Mead and we're going to see the Yosemite and the Pacific Coast. That will really be a trip.

I'm glad you got the $240 PTA I sent you. I still have a lot of money left because I spent very little while in Paris so, when I get my next pay I am going to send another PTA to you. Please use it for yourself because, although I know you are a better manager of Money than I am and did a wise thing in getting those shares of AT & T, I want you to use money I send you so that you can get some pleasure out of it.

I haven't noticed that your writing was messy. The only think I have noticed is that when you get mad or excited you write with flourishes and

I can just picture your hand flying over the paper. Also when you are tired or sleepy or maybe have had a snort or two there is a difference. Then when you write about something like our plans for a bicycle trip up to Turtle Pond and all the pleasant things that go with it your hand gets sort of wobbly and I know that you are emotionally stirred up. I devour such literature but I also know the effect that it has on you because I feel the same way. I won't mind your getting in my hair. What little I have left. If anybody so much as looks cross-eyed at you I'll be tempted to let go at him. I never thought that I might be a jealous husband but I can feel the potentialities with me.

About Kathryn Jacuementton again. I imagine that soap would be OK. The things she mentioned in her letter were tea, sugar, pepper, rice, any kind of stockings for her and 9 year old boys shoes for her boys who evidently wear out shoes pretty fast since they walk 5 miles to school. I don't know which would be better probably sending it direct would be better because I would have to do a lot of explaining in order to re-direct the package.

I have two more bottles of "stinkum" but they are not as good as the ones I got in a small city in December. All the better brands in Paris are sky-high and practically unobtainable. For a long time Paris was the Paradise for German soldiers and officers who came loaded down with French money. So perfume, stockings, dresses etc found their way into the hands of the Master Race.

The meat situation is mentioned quite often in the papers now. I'm glad you were able to get that quarter of beef put away in the locker. By the way how's the chicken situation or does the mention of a chicken bring back unpleasant memories of spreading litter and plucking them? Chickens and rabbits are about the only types of meat left for the French farmers over here. Meat is very scarce in the cities and those Frenchmen who have friends out in the country are lucky. They go many miles on their bicycles to do their shopping for extras to bolster their diet.

I am glad that Lou Price has been able to be with his wife. Maybe he will be lucky enough to stay in the States for the duration.

Do I remember those apple fritters? You make my teeth water just thinking about them. Just for that I am going to eat a chocolate bar.

Goodnight, sweetheart, remember me to the folks. All my love to you.

from Chad.

Dearest sweetheart:

Just a short letter tonight to let you know that everything is O.K. Not much doing except for working on the files and typing. I was paid this afternoon because the last few days I have been moving around from one office to the other so wasn't around when the rest were paid. I am going to send you another P.T.A. Only this time it will be for $100. I figure that doing that will leave me plenty for anything that may come up although the only thing I can think of would be a nice powder jar. When I was in Paris I had my eyes peeled for one but didn't see any. I wasn't able to shop very long on the Camps Elysees because I had to go take care of some business at the ITE Field Service Office.

After we were through at 5:30 we ate our supper (by we I mean the staff Sgt. I mentioned previously, the one from Marseilles) then washed up and shaved. By the time we arrived at the Etoile or the Madeleine depending on where we were going it was 7:00 p.m. Since the last train back was at 11:00 p.m. We didn't have much time to go very far.

One night we saw the Casino de Paris and another night the Folies but most of the time we were at the Red Cross Club. I did manage to see one fellow I know from G Co. The staff Sgt. met a french Red Cross worker and several evenings we sat and talked to her. She wrote down a French sentence which is really a stickler. It's as bad as our "She sells sea shells etc" This is it: "Un chasseur, sachant chasser, chassoit sans son chien dans des brunchages deseches" I gave her Karl's favorite about Theophilus Thistle and she had some time with that.

My trip to Paris was just one of those lucky things but it made me determined that someday, somehow you and I are going to see Paris together!

Ton amant

Chad

March 7, 1945
Somewhere in France

Dearest Bedie:

I am writing this dehydrated note for two reasons: 1 I think this will reach you more quickly than air mail and 2. Because there isn't much new today. I finally got around to applying for the PTA for $100 which I mentioned previously. Don't worry about my having enough money because I am well helled. I am the only one at the office and tonight I got so lonesome I had to come ever and visit with some of the boys I know in the 174th. I am getting now so that I go around talking to myself. Today I checked more personnel cards and did some more typing. The news in the papers looks pretty good and Churchill's comment when he visited the front sounded good. "One more good heave and the worst can be over." Those boys up on the 1st, 3rd and 9th Army fronts certainly deserve a lot of credit. I hope they push a hole somewhere soon. I must have been wal-gathering when I said that Ralph was 39 when I know that he was born in 1904. I hope that he won't have to decide on the Navy because it seems to me there ought to be enough younger fellows available. However, if he has to make a choice, he would be wise in choosing the Navy. His chances of getting a job more suited to his abilities would be greater. Goodnight, sweetheart, take good care of yourself.

Love,
Chad

Dearest sweetheart:

I am writing this while seated on the edge of a typical French bed in the front bedroom of a farmhouse. Since we are in the process of moving about agian we have nothing to do but walk around the little village and deep warm. The nights and morning are very cold. However the last few days have been sunny so by noontime the frost melts and the fog burns off. During the afternnon the fellows bask in the sun or play volley ball. Having shaved and cleaned up a bit I feel better and thought of writing you to let you know everything is O.K. I wish I had been possible to ease your mind as often in those days of waiting and anxiety you went through in August and September when we invaded Southern France. We landed on the afternnon of D day and finally caught up with the regiment that evening. I didn't see the company agian until we were well above Grenofle. Many days we made big jumps of 80 or 90 kilometers and some days we made short jumps but moving at least twice in the same day not bothering to upack until evening. Since we were in the mail section it meant many days went by when it was impossible to get mail out let along write even a note. Our present move reminds me a little of that same period except for the fact that here it is possible to dash off some letters and get them mailed later.

There is the real bucolic atmosphere in this little village. They have seen several different groups of American troops stay here for a while then pass on. They know all the miseries and terrors that do with occupation by the Germans and unfortunately, they came to know some of our rougher side too. When they were in hiding because of the shelling the American troops occupied their houses and in many took everything that they could lay their hands on. It's a hard thing to explain each man knows that it is stealing, but he is probably so hit by the mania for picking up souveniers that he takes such trifling things a s a French peasant's knive and forks, articles which are no where near as good as the ones obtainable back home. It makes it difficult for the French to like us when our artillery knocks their homes down or our troops come in and act like petty theives. If american blood were not purchasing their freedom from the Germans they could easily come to hate Americans.

The French peasant's life has been colored by the days when they were under the Nazi heel. To illustrate the thoroughness of Nazi methods I'll describe the system they used to get farm produce. Every French Farmer had to turn in a list of the number of animals he had, the amount of grain, the number of farm machines etc. Then when the peasants weren't expecting it the Germans sent inspectors around to check-up. If they found a farmer had five horses when he had only two listed they would tell him that the three extra didn't belong to him so they would take them. During the fruit picking season they had inspectors around to note down how much fruit had been picked. However most of the time the French managed to fool the Germans by sending warning on ahead so that the farmers would have a chance to hide their extra animals and produce. Any remarks against the nazis were punishable by imprisonment in a concentration camp. A man made a remark about Germany one day while buying some groceries in store. A Nazi sympathizer overheard him, reported the incident and the man was sent away to Germany. Another family had a son who was hidden away to escape the German draft for the Army. The Germans came and, being unable to locate the young man, took his sister and sent her to Germany in his place. There are so many instances like this told by so many different people that you feel that it is a true picture of the German way of doing things. It has the stamp of Teutonic Thoroughness and callousness to human suffering about it that makes realize that the whole business must be wiped out once and for all. I don't know how long it will take. We have tricked ourselves too many times with wishful thinking But I do know that we are going to have to stay over here until all Germans know that they are a beaten nation and know the cost of trying to enslave other people. If we are satisfied with a soft-hearted policy of cotnrolling German affairs it won't be long before we will be making another crossing of the Atlantic to try to set things right

I don't know what set me off on this track unless it was the renewed contact with peopole who have seen the Nazis for just what they are. It is always nice to hope for a quick ending and the news coming in tempts one to be very optimistic. But we have seen enough to become very cautious about predictions of any early end. Hope springs eternal however and we all hope and pray that the end will come soon.

Mac is returned from Paris where he had a busy and interesting time. He managed to see some of the more important places and met some fine people. He is the type who would get along with people wherever he goes and I am glad he had the chance to take the trip.

I am trying to pick up a little knowledge of German because so many people in these parts speak it. However, when we get into Germany the non-fraternization policy will prevent any contacts with the people except in the line of duty.

I applied for the PTA for $100 and hope that it reaches you soon. Do what you want with it because I am sure you will put it to good use. Over here it is impossible to spend money wisely. The only things we can spend money on are an occasional souvenier or having laundry done.

Well I will quit now and write more tomorrow. Remember me to the folks.

All my love
Chad

Somewhere in France
March 20, 1945

Dearest sweetheart:

Last night I tried to compose a letter to you but I gave up in disgust and tore it up because I couldn't concentrate or get my thoughts onto paper. Somehow or other, perhaps because of the changeableness of the weather or because I took a bath en ran around getting heated up, I caught the sniffles and felt miserable. I went to the medics got some pills and by this afternoon felt a little more like a human being again. Yesterday my sinuses ached and that darned cold settled in my eyes so I couldn't do much but sneeze, sniffle and snort. Charley Bucknam says I have a very peculiar type of snore when I have a cold because ever so often I let out a disgusted snort.

Mail has started to pick up again after a lull. I received your v-mail which came in the new style without an envelope but sealed with glue in a thin line down both sides of the letter. Shortages of envelopes I understand caused the change. I also received air mail letter #267- and #271.

My gosh, sweetheart, please take care of yourself and don't get chilled through like you did packaging that meat. You might catch a cold and have more trouble with your sinuses. I can imagine that you wouldn't feel very much like writing one of those real snooky letters feeling the way you did. Speaking of letters though, Mac had a pretty good record today. He heard from his wife today and she mentioned a letter of his sent March 5th which she received the 9th!

You certainly were lucky to get that quarter of beef. From the papers here the meat situation back home is getting tighter all the time. I think it said there would be a 12% cut in the supply. One headline in the stars and Stripes said that housewives were even turning in desperation to cooking spam than which there is nothing wickeder especially if you have had spam shoved at you enough times.

We shouldn't kick though, when you think of the unfortunates in Europe who have been existing on starchy diets for so long.

I will write Kathryn Smith and tell her about the packages also about Vail Smith. I understand the "Katoonah St." address OK.

Petunia, you don't need to send me the Herald Tribune. First it's a helluva job cutting it up to get in mailable size or weight and second, we get a good coverage of news from our 7th Army radio programs and the Stars and Stripes. Every A.M. at 9:00 we hear the news read at dictation speed so we often type it up and put it on our bulletin board. Just send me whatever clippings you think would be of interest on any of the post-war plans or on vocational guidance. I received the two long envelopes of map list from the Gov't Bureau of Documents. If you come across any maps of German cities or articles giving the economic, social or historical background of regions in Germany, I would appreciate them very much.

Mac told me today that he had news of Bill Mavers' discharge so evidently Bill is well enough adjusted physically so that he can get around OK.

News sound good every day. I hope they really retire a bunch of Krauts from the war this time.

Goodnight, my sweet, I'll trot off to bed now with my "code id by node". Give my love to the folks.

Ton amant

Chad

Somewhere in France
March 23, 1945

Dearest sweetheart:

Not much doing here today except the usual typing and personnel file card work. No mail to make a spring-like day much brighter. Sometimes I get so darn mad at myself for not being able to compose interesting and well written letters I could haul off and kick myself.

This afternoon I sweated out a line of twelve guys in order to get my ears set out because my few remaining hairs were beginning to get very noticeably shaggy. On this shop, as is true of many shops all over France, there was a girl apprentice barber. Fortunately I was waited on by the boss! The girl was doing pretty well though. She gave one fellow a very good shave with no blood shed.

This evening Mac and I went for a walk and stopped to watch a softball game. I guess I'm not athletic enough to get into those games because I can't move fast enough. You've got an old man for a husband. At least his feet feel old. But I have young ideas as you will some day find out for yourself. We get out into the fresh air as often as we can because the weather has taken a turn for the better and the buds are beginning to burst open. Spring really comes with a rush here. People are busy getting their gardens ready and the other day one of the boys picked some violets near the walls of a church.

You mentioned seeing the Fighting Lady. I saw a review of it in a magazine and it received a big build-up. There is theater not far from us but I haven't gone to any of the shows yet. I guess I'm not really a movie enthusiast. Of course I understand how you feel about going to the movies with Jim. That doesn't keep me from being a bit jealous however. I wish I were with you so that we could go to a show and I could feel your hand in mine as we enjoyed the show together. Then to saunter home and raid the refrigerator talking over the day's events and making plans together for the future. Then to sip some wine while we snuggled together on the couch until you were all warm and drowsy, then to pick you up and carry you up to bed where I would show you how hungry I have become for my lubbins.

Goodnight, sweetheart, with all my love,
Chad.

Somewhere in France
March 25, 1945

Dearest sweetheart:

Lately I have had a devil of a time thinking of things to write about because all of us here are in a back-wash of the tremendous surge toward Germany and the days pass by so evenly with the usual routine of office work. I can see what you must be up against working each day at the bank and not getting a chance to go away from the routine. It's funny (peculiar) that when I was in a rifle company plenty of things were happening every day but there was only occasionally an opportunity to really write about we were doing. Now that I am in a relatively robs me of writing subjects (although it may be because I am not very imaginative).

Speaking of mail Bill just came in with a letter from June saying that she had an 8 page letter from you in which you said you were very worried about me. That made me disgusted with the darn mail situation because my letters certainly aren't coming through to you very well. I haven't had mail either in several days now and I am thoroughly "browned off" with the mail distribution. When you come to think of it though it is really a question of transportation. Our forces have very important needs for trucks now. Anyway my dearest please don't worry about me because my job does not call for me to be in the area of actual combat. I want to impress on you that there is no need for you to be worried.

I received the maps of Japan and Maps of Europe you sent. They make swell display material. We need display material now because we haven't been getting much new stuff lately. This afternoon I received 2 copies of Newsweek which I will read from cover to cover.

We saw a softball game this evening in which some of our fellows played a team made up of Negroes. It was riot with plenty of laughs from the antics of the colored boys.

Just heard Bob Hope and Betty Grabble. It was very good with a scene from the Princess and the Pirate. Our radio goes by fits and starts and sometimes just when you want to hear a news broadcast the darn thing starts acting up. The news has been very good over here but back home old New England seems to be having a tough time with more snow and lots of cold and rain. Here the days are balmy and the trees are beginning to leaf out. It seems so good to see green fresh foliage after a winter in the Vosges.

Spring makes me miss you more and more each day. I take out your picture and look at your sweet face and long to kiss your perky nose the way I used to do. To plant deep quivery kisses on your lips and hear you sigh and whisper, "Hold me tight" and "I get in my own way." I love you, my sweet, so deeply that you are like a part of my heart left far off there across the sea. This war may keep us apart many more months because there is still a tough job to be done but keep your courage and know that I love you with all my heart.

Ton amant

Chad

My dearest sweetheart:

!**:?%ueca""!++e is a mild expression of the way I have been feeling about my ability to get a letter written. For the last few nights I have been striving manfully but unsuccessfully to write you and tell you how things are mit mire. Every time I got settled down to write in would come two or three crazy coots pliantly illuminated and that would be the end of the letter writing for the night. You are probably wondering what kind of a cement mixer I'm using to write this with but it is really quite a versatile machine. It has a few disadvantages such as the inter-position of "W" and "Z" and "m" and ";". The period is upper case and the figures are all upper case. You also have such delightful things as "e", "e" "^". "c", "a", "o", "=", "+", "i", etc. Oh, yes, and "u", and "o"; as a matter of fact, it was quite a feat just writing that last sentence without turning inside out. The machine is of Italian make and can do lots of tricks such as half spacing like this. It reminds me somewhat of the old Blickensderfer I used to have. You were never sure whether you write or add or subtract. This machine is mere infant compared with the behemoth one of the boys brought back from a little trip over into Krautland. It was an electronically-operated typewriter which must have weighed about thirty or forty pounds. It stands about a foot and a half high and is about two feet deep. The numbers are in two separate banks down below the letters and attached to the bar in from of the platen is an adding machine. On the platen itself is a weird attachment for working with special size ledger sheets. In order to turn the sheet up for the next line you find off on the right a large dial about five inches in diameter with about a dozen holes containing numbers. These evidently have to be worked just the same way you would dial a telephone number. The whole thing is so awe-inspiring that you just stand for a minute looking at it with your mouth hanging wide open. I think it even rivals the famous cement mixer you told me about in the bank.

Day before yesterday we has a mail call, the first in about a week! Things have been moving so fast that mail has had to take a back seat.

I had a letter from you (No. 277), a V-mail from Ella Avery, four newspapers, nine National Geographic maps and two packages from 22 Katoonah St. for Mme. Jacquemetton. I am going to see if they will go through the postal authorities OK. We know have a swell library of maps, thanks to you. Oh, I forget to mention the two Dept of Agriculture booklets, one on cotton and the other on poultry diseases.

The account of making bacon was very interesting. I had read somewhere that they injected hams in order to cure them but had never heard of making bacon by using smoke-salt. Bacon and eggs cooked by you with toast and coffee would be like manna and ambrosia. Just to have a midnight snack like that followed by a lazy conversation with you snuggled in my arms on the divan. We would drink some port wine in our special way and I would taste the wine on your lips until I became so hungry for you that I would let my lips wander across your cheeks until I kissed your sleepy eyelids and felt you snuggle down deeper in my arms. Then I would gently lay you down on the pillows and, holding you firmly in my arms; would kiss your pulsating throat and burrow deep with my lips into the warm hollow at its base. By that time my hand would have found two nice nubbins which would begin to rise to firm points under the caresses which I gave them. I would feel your body tremble under my touch and hear your breath come faster as my hand felt its way up to the little hill above the fates of Paradise. Them my finger would part the fates and slowly and gently push deeper and deeper until the walls of Paradise were throbbing with pent-up desire. You would throw your arms tight around my neck and I would lift you up and carry you up to our bed where I would lay you down and with lingering kisses and soft caresses of my hands. Off would come each part of your clothing warm with the perfume of your body. After tucking you under the covers I would quickly throw off my clothes and kneeling between your legs would lay down full length on you with both your legs locked firmly around my thighs; a shudder through your body and a tightening of your arms would tell me that you were experiencing the delights which you so longed for. While you were still quivering with ecstacy I would press my throbbing key into the gate of Paradise and, in one steady thrust, would reach its fullest extent and unlock the gate. By that time we both would know the very peak of that physical union which is so necessary for a complete life together. Oh, darling, I don't know how you feel right now but I'm burning up. Forgive me if I have done wrong in writing to you like this, because you have told me that you are affected the same way. Sooner or later my thoughts come swirling back to some of the happy times we had together. I know that only a small percentage of them were purely physical. There have been so many other times when we have been so happy together without the physical side of it but this long separation makes my longing for you stronger and stronger with each passing day. I love you so much, my darling, and, now that there is some hope of an ending, I let myself think things that tear me apart inside. The fellows call it, "knocking yourself out" and each day's news makes it more difficult to keep from letting the disciplined gates of the mind down and letting fancy run free. You know that you will be emotionally racked by the experience but you go ahead and disregard the effects. Writing it somehow acts as a release for a while but it has the disadvantage of the one who receives it. Damn it! I didn't mean to rationalize.

Take good care of yourself, my sweetheart, and all my love to you.

Somewhere in Germany
April 12, 1945

Dearest sweetheart:

I hate to repay the kindness of the eight or ten letters I have received recently from you by using this damned V-mail but things are moving fast. Now I am leaving the heart of Germany to ravel to Paris again for another conference. I have a bunch of souvenirs to send if I ever light in one place long enough to make up a strong package. I have been enjoying good health and have seen some beautiful country, but some cities that have ceased to exist. Its almost impossible to conceive of such destruction. Have to quit now. All my love sweetheart. I'll write from Paris.

Chad

Paris France
April 16, 1945

Dearest sweetheart:

After moving shadily eastward across Germany, I proceeded to town right around and come back again. I had time for only one hurried V-Mail just before I left. We were moving and getting the office set up. By the time we teturn our office wil probably be moved on still deeper into Hitler's backyard. Also my mail will have piled up and I really will have a feast of letter reading and writing. Paris is a beautiful sight but of course there is a great lack of everything. Prices are skyhigh. I got a Medallion with the Paris city coat of arms for your bracelet. Spring has really hit Paris. Lilacs are in bloom and this last Sunday thousands went out into the country and returned with armloads of blooms. The last couple of days. I have been catching up on things I missed seeing the first time. I have the loan of a camera and have to send pictures. I am OK my darling.

All my love,

Chad

Somewhere in Germany
April 25, 1945

My dearest sweetheart:

When I saw the mountain of mail waiting for me I darn near keeled over. I sat me down and devoured it for about two solid hours. I won't try to answer all the news you mentioned in your letter but will try to bring myself up to date with this short letter tonight then tomorrow, after I'm rested up a bit I'll write my sweetheart a longer letter.

As I told you in the hurried V-mail I wrote just before leaving for Paris, we have been moving around a lot and letter writing has been quite a problem. We left for Paris in a little captured vehicle called an Opel which goes like hell down hill and on the level but has a tough time of it on the hills. The weather was very warm for this time of the year and the trees were fairly bursting with the business of getting their flowers and leaves out on display in a hurry as though in apology for the rough and bleak winter we have had. The Rhine Valley was really beautiful with fruit trees in bloom and the carefully cultivated fields showing just a green tinge of grain. The cities which have undergone a terrific pounding from the air for so long have been still further hammered in rubble by our artillery. I remember when I was a kid being awed by the destruction caused by big fires but this makes that seem like something insignificant. When you see city after city with only a few undamaged building left you wonder how in hell they stood up under it for such a long time. I suppose it was like the old Chinese story of the man who had the tiger by the tail and didn't dare let go.

We crossed France to Paris in less than a day and as we went saw how much more advance the trees and gardens were as we went westward. Right near Paris it became more noticeable because flowers seemed to be everywhere. I noticed the lilacs specially. The air was heavy with the fragrance of them. The French are very fond of them because on Monday I saw great crowds returning from a weekend in the country just loaded down with armfuls of lilac branches. Every block in Paris seemed to have a flower stand of some kind and in one section we drove past a whole market place where only flowers were sold. All the main parks and boulevards have lots of horse chestnut trees which were in full bloom.

I attended a lot of the classes at the university and had a chance to talk with several of the officers there about the plans we are working on. The week just about flew by before I realized it the course was over and it was time to heard back to the unit. However, this time, I did manage to see many of the places which I missed in March. I took an interesting tour of the main points of interest and saw the Eifel tower, The Tomb of Napleon, the Bois de Boulogne, the Basilique de Sacree Coeur, and the Monmartre Section. I did miss the trip out to Versailles and the inside of the Louvre. Most of the works of art in the Louvre have been taken elsewhere for safe keeping. Several nights we went touring in a jeep just watching the sights. During the day driving in Paris is no pleasure because of the Pedestrians and the bicyclists. They swarm all over the streets and you have to have eyes in the back of your head to keep from running them down. Added to the distractions are the sights of young Parisiennes cycling along merrily with their skits billowing in the breeze thus exposing some rather exciting attractions of Paris.

Two outstanding features of your letter are really on my mind. It was a terrible shock to read about Dave. I don't know what to make of it. I hope that if he is as the telegram reported him he will soon be recovered by our advancing troops. As for myself my dearest, don't worry about my traveling around because we very seldom get near advance units.

I was really pleased to read that your visit to New York was productive of some real comfort after all the misery and nervous strain your feet have caused you. I hope that the treatments give you lasting relief.

I will have to stop now because I am really tired out from the long trip. Good night, my darling, with all my love.

Chad

April 30, 1945
Somewhere in Germany

Dearest sweetheart:

After getting back from Paris I was busier than the proverbial paperhanger. I am now in the throes of finishing up the Standing Operating Procedure which will lay down the rules and regulations for setting up the post hostilities educational program. It has been a tough job but a helluva lot better than toting a rifle and chasing Krauts. As we listen to the news broadcasts each hour we begin to see the end of the actual fighting coming nearer and nearer. Yesterday we heard about the short shift that was handed out to Mussolini., his mistress and several others of the inner ring of Italian gangsters. In Germany Hitler seems to be the only one left to make negotiations. He and his precious killers will do everything possible to avoid the fate they know is coming. The sudden collapse of the Italian front south of Bologna was surprising. We know what fighting in the mountains of Italy is like and we all pictured northern Italy as being about the last place where the Germans would be pried loose. Of course everybody over here is wondering about what is going to happen after hostilities. Except for the very few who will probably be sent home the best hope us old duffers have is to be used for occupation troops. That certainly would be a lot better than taking the long trek to the Pacific theater. We'll just have to sweat it out.

As you said recently the mail situation is really all balled up. After I came back I had a mountain of mail which had accumulated but since then the guys just roll by with an occasional newspaper or magazine. Very little first class mail is coming thorough. By the way, my curly topped darling, please don't tire yourself out nights going through the papers clipping out the ads and getting them ready to send because it takes too much of your time and the situation that often I get about ten or fifteen papers at he same time. If you see some article on the GI Bill of Rights or something extra special you think I should have please sent it, but sending a whole bunch of papers is not only though on the pocket book but takes too much of your time to prepare. I would much rather have you go the movies and get a little relaxation or perch your feet up on the divan and rest up. That reminds me of the black pants, slip, stocking and nightgown you mentioned in your letter. I would need asbestos paper to write on if I were to get started on the thoughts that such items arouse. I'm sure thoughts of them will be in my dreams tonight. All my love, darling, and take good care of yourself.

Chad

Somewhere in Germany
May 8, 1945

Dearest sweetheart:

Celebrated V-E Day by keeping the old nose to the grindstone. Still working like a beaver on our S.O.P. Received lots of newspapers and when I begin to total up the postage I nearly faint. Don't bother, sweetheart, with the Herald Tribune. It isn't worth all that work and expense. Thanks for the Dept. of Agric. pamphlets. Our vocational guidance library is swelling daily. Lots of our fellows celebrated today. Beaucoups of cognac and appropriately enough Lowenbrau beer. Everybody is speculating about his future as for me, I have no illusions, with only 15 months overseas, my best chances are to get an occupation assignment over here. At any rate, I doubt very much whether I'll get home soon. Have seen lots of interesting sights including Hitler's old stomping grounds. As usual the big places are badly damaged by bombing and artillery. We all thank God that it is finished over here. It was thrilling to hear the English celebration on the radio. I'll try to write an air mail soon. Take good car of yourself.

Love,
Chad

Somewhere in Germany
May 10, 1945

Dearest sweetheart:

Busy times for information and Education now that V-E day has come and gone. A lot of the boys celebrated but in general the boys were pretty quiet. Everybody has just one thought uppermost in his mind and that is When? Oh, When There is a lot of figuring going on of course, totaling up number of years in the Army, overseas, etc. It makes my head ache when some of them start talking about 3 and 4 years in the army. That would be like a lifetime. Tonight we got our 45th division histories in from Paris and I will send you one. It only carries the story up to the Seigfrid Line. After many days of wind cold, rain and even snow Spring has finally come with a rush. The other day I looked to the south and saw a great chain of very cold looking mountains. Good night my sweetheart, with all my love.

Chad

Somewhere in Germany
May 11, 1945

Dearest sweetheart:

This is the first evening in quite a while I have had a chance to collect what few thoughts I do have to write you and tell what's going on.

As I told you previously we are in Hitler's back yard and I have seen some cities that were really messed up. My boss and I drove around the "city" of Nurnberg several times before we could find our way out. The place had already been blasted by Allied air power and when our artillery gave it a going over there wasn't much left. Our outfit may have been "stopped cold" as the papers say for a short time but when they got through with the place it was a ghost city. The same thing happened in another German city but I'll have to tell you about that later.

The weather here is so warm now that it almost uncomfortable. Spring evidently comes with a rusk in this part of Krautland.

Just before starting this I was going through some of your letters before burning them although I saved #275 in which you raised my blood pressure by describing our lying on blankets under the pines looking at the moon. That plus the perfume that still clung to the writing paper really started my hormones responding. Well here goes with a few comments and questions about thing you have written. The latest letter from you is #303.

I have been snowed under with newspapers but the only trouble is that the mail backs up and I get about 15 at a time. I think that it would be easier on you and not so tough on the pocket book just to send a clipping here and there that you think might be especially interesting. The postage cost must be up somewhere near the national war debt by now. But all kidding aside, sweetheart we are getting radio news casts and the Stars and Stripes (By the way how did you like Bill Mauldin's Pulitzer Prize Winner?)

Since V-E day we have been as busy as beavers and so I have resorted to V-mail. Also there have been times when I have been on guard duty or we have been on the move so quicky letters are about all I can manage.

I finally had to get rid of the powdered ink because it was causing complications. When we travel things get jolted and jostled around a lot so some of the powder got distributed around with interesting results!

The other day I passed but did not enter an ex-German concentration camp (it is very much off limits) I did see the pictures of the interior and all I need say is that the interior of the camp was so bad that hardened veteran's who had seen plenty went completely off their nuts. When it was over and the guards were captured. Many of our boys heaved up at the sight of what was in the camp. I was interested to read in Newsweek that movie audiences in N.Y. were stunned into silence except for an occasional gasp when they saw the picture of Buchenwald. This time the story of German atrocities is down in black and white and in actual pictures. Any German who starts boasting about German honor, decency or culture only needs to hear the names of some of these horrible places to shut him up forever. No body knows how many millions of innocent victims were starved, beaten, tortured or gasses to rid the world of what the Nazis called "scum". I know I'll never forget it. But to more pleasant topics.

Such as the bottle of Liebfraumilch which we had tonight. I had a glass and thought of the much happier days when you and I drank some then when it was time for you to go to bed and some rest. I kept you up and pestered you by laying you down on your couch and kissing you. How I'd like to be pestering you now with us sharing our wine in our own special way. The boys here have lots to drink. Cognac, Benedictine, Lowenbrau, and various other kinds of wine. The special drink at present seems to be to take a glass about 2/3rds full of Benedictine and add 1/3rd of cognac. This delightfully potent mixture is called a "B and B". Guaranteed to make you stiff. The thing that makes me mad is to see young fellows who I know in civilian life stuck to beer or milder drinks getting ossified with liqueurs and brandies. That were never meant to be swilled down like water. Speaking of drinks that mixture of gin and hot water must have been hard to take. Not particularly strong but hard to get down. I guess I never was a gin drinker.

Thanks for the V-mail birthday card. By golly I'm getting to be an old cuss. But age doesn't seem to have much to do with getting home. Unless you are 42 and I'm not quite that far along yet.

Last night all the boys had their ears glued to the radio to hear the point system. Figuring 1 point for every month in the army, 1 point for every month overseas and 5 points for each battle star I have now 50 points whereas I would need a critical score of 85 to qualify for a discharge from the army. My combat badge is not considered, only such awards as the D.S.C., the Legion of Merit, Silver Star, Soldier's Medal, Bronze Star, and Purple Heart. Not being of the heroic mold, I have no medals for heroic or distinguished action. However I do have hopes that I will have enough points to avoid taking the trip home by way of the Pacific. Here's hoping anyway.

Will quit now to write Mother and Dad. I hope your feet are improving. Be sure to follow the doctor's advice and rest them every chance you get. Remember me to Mother Bedient and tell her I remember her especially for Mother's Day.

All my love, my darling,

from Chad

Munich Germany
May 15, 1945

Dearest sweetheart:

It seems so strange after many long months of writing somewhere in Italy, France or Germany to be able to come right out and say where I am. Of course I was able to mention cities which I had visited but never anything which would give the exact location of the 45th. Yesterday we received a new postal regulation saying that we could mention places and send home pictures of places. Many of the fellows have already visited Oberammergau of Passion Play fame. I don't know whether I'll get a chance to go but I do want to the see the Bavarian mountains. They say that it has some of the most beautiful scenery they have ever had a chance to see.

You probably got my reference to Lowenbrau beer and the mountains in the distance. I sometimes had a lot of trouble thinking of ways of making pertinent references.

Just took time out to deliver a copy of the film. "Two Down and One to Go" to a theater down town. This picture is one which I understand will be seen home as well as being a must for all troops over here. It explains the process of redistribution of armed forces and the basis for discharge of those who have had long service. I check up on my points the other day and decided that 51 is all I can squeeze out. With three children I would be all set or if, if and if. You know how it goes. So I am sweating it out like a lot of the other boys.

Took a trip to Augsbury, the other day through pine and spruce forested foot hills over Hitler's Autobahn. Nice road but getting quite like civilian traffic with speed traps and M.P's watching for unwary speedsters. Augsbury was pretty badly beaten up. When you come right down to it only the medium sized and little town away from the rivers escaped. Those near the rivers which had bridges were somewhat damaged when the retreating Krauts captured them.

Big time in the office this morning. Lots of brass circulating around. One major general, a full colonel, a lt. col. and the general's aide. All was sweetness and light. The general was a prince about the whole thing.

He told us that he was surprised at the excellence of our program. Being an infantry outfit maybe it is surprising. We three fellows in the office are so close to the program that, as Mr. Horton used to say, we have trouble seeing the forest because of the trees. Right now because of the unsettled state of affairs we are continuing with orientation work and news discussions.

Setting up an educational program. Now would be like a school pupil trying to start a school not knowing where the school was going to be, how many students there would be, what courses were planned what facilities were available and a few other minor details. Give me the aspirins.

We got our 45th Div. histories out and I am sending some home so please save them. They aren't what you would call masterpieces but I think they are pretty good.

You have probably heard of the non-fraternization policy which was announced some time ago. Well it taint working. Soldiers are not machines and their glands are just as active as those of others. During the day especially the afternoon we can look out across a wide field and see couples fornicating right out in the open. Some of the more curios have liberated some German range finder glasses and have a lot of fun watching the proceedings like little children peeking through the fence to see the cow being services. Damn it all! A man who has been away from home a long time has to control his thoughts or band his head against the wall. Only when the day is over about 8 in the evening, unless something important come up, we sit around and chew the fat jut like a college bull session. Then to bed and for a while a prayer for sweetheart and all those I love at home and so off to sleep. But every so often my thoughts of you return to many of the nice snooky things you have written me and then I am filled with longing for you. Just as you are probably lying in our great big bed thinking of me. How heavenly it would be to let myself quietly into the house up the stairs and into the room. Then to gather you into my arms and cover your sweet face with kisses and to snuggle down beside you and tell you how much I have missed you these long long months. We both have tightened up so emotionally that I will probably be like a goof and not be able to express myself.

I was certainly surprised by the story you told of Dave's battalion. It isn't very often that such a thing happens. However we have freed a lot our boys who were taken by the Germans. I hope Dave is among them.

Will close now. Remember me to the folks and all my bestest love to you.

From

Chad

P.S. By the way, my rank is technician fourth grade or T/4 which over the phone etc is shorted to sergeant. A T/3 is a technician third grade which is like a staff sergeant. Sorry no 3.1416

Chad

Grunwald, Germany
May 18, 1945

Dearest sweetheart:

Well here's hoping and praying my 38th birthday will be spent where I have always wanted to be right by your side. Days fly by as far work is concerned but they drag out when I think of home. Received pages 1,2, and 3 of letter #308 today. Was stunned by news of Gene Echerty's death. I thought that they had placed him a clerical job.

That makes three of my buddies who lived in the same hut together at McClellen, gone. Will try to write to Wilma but hate the idea of the job.

You can't find words to express how you feel. Catoonah St. must be plenty busy, with so many chicks being brooded. I hope your feet aren't starting to get worse again. This summer will be plenty tough without having them act up. We are now staying in a mansion with fine furniture and deep carpets. I'll tell you more about it later.

All my love.

Chad

Land of Lowenbrau
May 21, 1945

Dearest sweetheart:

This is the first uncensored letters I have written to you in a long long time but the other day we received an order that from now until some change is made letters will go without unit censoring However packages will still be censored.

Mail comes in by dribbles and drabbles. The transportation problem is still a big question. The emphasis is shifting of course to the other theater.

This afternoon we saw the picture "Two Down and One to Go" which explains the working os the redeployment policy. It wasn't very encouraging. The whole business of getting nonessential men back to the states is going to be decided on an individual basis and, since the critical score in points is 85 and I have only 51, it's pretty difficult to tell what is going to happen. At least I am pretty sure now that they won't send the old divisions back to the States. There will be some kind of reshuffling.

At any rate we are nicely fixed now in a private house or perhaps I should say a mansion. We moved from our other quarters to this place and have the entire house to ourselves. It's a big place with lights, water, toilets, electric stove, vacuum cleaner and hot water heater. When we first came in we felt like furniture movers coming in to some place like Wadsworth Lewis. We hardly dared touch anything. But after a while when you get used to it and realize that after all the rich furniture and decorations were probably bought at the cost of other people's misery. We don't feel so awe struck. One room in the down stairs part has 35 paintings. There are all of 50 pairs of antlers and chamois horns hung up in the hall. The owner must have been quite a hunter. There is a garage wing with an apartment for the chauffeur and several downstairs bedrooms for servants in the main house. The master bedroom is huge with an enormous four poster bed with canopy that would make our bed at home look like a crib. Boy what a time you and I could have on a bed like that! Or on the floor or up against the wall for that matter!

We work in the dining room where we set up our work tables and field desks. The walls are covered with gaily painted plates and Dresden China and in the dish closets which are made of hand carved wood there are a lot of crystal glasses and gold trimmed dishes etc. There are clocks all over the place from the 3 grandfather clocks down to little cloisnes (?) clocks. When they strike the hour it sounds like the Anvil Chorus. It takes about an hour to check up on all the clocks to see that they are wound and running. Outdoors there is a large lawn which is rapidly growing into a meadow. We have had so much rain that the grass is growing rapidly. There are lots of lowers some of them I don't recognize. The Columbines are especially beautiful. The owners had a small vegetable garden with potatoes, string beans, lettuce and strawberries which are now in flower.

Yesterday I ran across some slang terms which are being used by the boby socks back in the States. They really tickled my funny bone. An attractive girl is whistle bait, dream puss or a 20-20. A girl with appeal is a blackout girl. Girl crazy is skirt nerts, lap happy, shirty flierty or dame dazed. Boy crazy is shacki wahacky. To be in love is cow-eye-tis. Teacher's pet is Gone Fishing. to be jilted is blow a fuse, defrosted or shot down in flames. Good food is luch mush. My gosh we'll have to learn to talk all over again if this keeps up.

Speaking of talk back in the States I saw an article in Stars and Stripes about an interview with Mae West who said that American men are going to return home sexier thatn they've ever been before. She adds that a lot of loving is coming back from war. Then she finished by saying that a girl needn't worry about holding her man if she realized the surest way to hold him is in her arms. Truer words were never "spoke"! The AMG speaks of millions of European women suffering from mass frustration. Hell, why limit it to Europe? As for us, we have been frustrated for so long I won't know how to start making love to you again. I only hope that I don't shock you too much. But it would be pure heaven just to hold you tight and smell the perfume of your body and gently run my lips up and down your neck and to kiss the sweet hollow in your throat. But enough of that or I'll be laying awake again butting my head against a wall.

Lately I have managed to see quite a lot of what is left of Hitler's old stomping grounds, the birthplace of the Nazi party. One of the fellows who works on the ITE program is set up at the very desk where Hitler and Chamberlain signed the Pact. He sits in Hitler's chair. If that chair could only talk what a story it could tell. The worst place is Nurnberg which is about 90% destroyed Block after block of buildings are nothing but shells with piles of rubble and twisted steel covering the sidewalks and part of the street. Some of the streets were so chocked with debris that bull dozers had to clear a path.

Well, the anvil chorus has sounded and I ought to go to bed. It really is a bed. All my love sweetheart. Take good care of yourself.

Love,

Chad

Ex-land of Beer and Pretzels
May 22, 1945

Dearest Bedie:

Tonight I received V-mails #309, 310, and 311 and was I disgusted to hear that my letters were no reaching you. So I am back to V-mail again in the hope that this will reach you soon and let you know that I am OK and love you more than ever. I know what you mean by saying that you didn't feel much like celebrating V-E day. I won't feel that way until I am sure that it is all over and I am on my way home. However things are still undecided. I was certainly thrilled by the news of Dave Moore's recovery. That was the best news I have had in a long time. Wow! You are certainly going into the chicken business in a big way! I'll bet the chicks you have now are cute little fellers. I can't imagine F.B as a liaison officer for anything. He's too emotional to have the proper, slant on the average G.I's problems. Eichner will make out, allright. He always has managed somehow. I am looking forward to receiving that book of insignia - I have received a lot of favorable comments on the pamphlets you sent me. More on page 2.

Love,
Chad

Two hours later

Dearest Sweetheart:

Time out between page #1 & #2 to experiment with the hot water system. We finally have it working with the prospect of a fine bath in a TUB. Also we have adjourned to the kitchen where the kettle is singer merrily on the electric stove. Coffee soon. You were damning the weather of New England. We have been cussing the weather here too. Cold rain comes down from the mountains and the boys say that there is still plenty of snow there. I hope the package you sent for my Birthday comes along soon because I am really curious. Had a nice letter from Elsa saying that N.A. is practically brooding the chicks. Also that the four footed help in the garden create lots of complications. That reminds me of the row of succatash Mommy Hartmann had in her garden. Here in Germany there are many who have been living on potatoes and spinach for months. Getting late good night my sweet with all my love.

from

Chad

Out in the Sticks
May 25, 1945

Dearest sweetheart:

Received a wonderful surprise yesterday in the form of a registered package with the Thunderbird ring for my birthday present. It was about the nicest thing you could give me because as I wear it I can look at it and think of my sweetheart. I also received a photography Magazine some Newspapers and a big package with socks, candy, and the National Geographic , Insignia Book which I immediately got my nose into and which has already caused a lot of favorable comment.

Thanks for them all Kutsiebug. Today I received a V-mail #312 and boy was I burned to hear that my letter are taking so long to arrive home. You figured my points on the wrong basis. I should be 21 for service, 15 for overseas and 15 for 3 battle stars making 51 with the possibility of 5 more points for an extra battle star to take care of the two parts of the German campaign. Oh well, at any rate, you are right about my chances of getting home soon. My boss is away so I am in charge and we manage to keep pretty busy. Will try in air-mail for the next letter. I hope it doesn't take 15 days coming to the States.

All my love,

Chad

Grunwald
May 29, 1945

Dearest Petunia:

Received V-mail #318 (3 pages) and air mail #320 (May 23rd- my heavens to Betsy a thousand miles a day). That's really traveling! I guess that lowering the discharge age to 35 or even 37 is out of the question for a long time. All the packages received including the swell ring which has caused a lot of envious comment. Also received 2 Life Magazine containing pictures of a lot of the things I have seen including Dachau. There may be some left in America who believe the Germans are a mistreated and much maligned people. They're just the ones to see a place like Dachau where people are still dying from the after effects of the beating and starvation. Look on your map of Germany trace southward up the Isar River about 10 miles and you will see where I am. Beautiful Country. I wish I could take you for a honeymoon up into the Bavarian Alps. Oh, by the way, B and B is Brandy and Benedictine. I haven't had any lately although the nights are cool enough.

All my love,

Chad

Near Grunwald
May 28, 1945

Meine Geliebte:

Yesterday I received #317 and today #316 (written on my birthday) and it's difficult to picture two letters more far apart in morale. The first one written just after coming back from New York was like a light hearted kid tripping along or more like quick silver whereas the next one written just before your going back to work was kinda disgusted with life in general. I know just how you feel, liebschen, because there are lot of days when I go from one extreme to another. I'm just longing for the day when I can get you away from that bank and into my arms where you are going to stay for a long time.

It was wonderful news to hear that you are feeling much better. I am glad that Dr. Morton has been able to really help you . As far as I am concerned my feet are much better because we don't have to walk great distances as we had to do in basic training and in Italy. Since I have been with Service Company and then with I&E my underpinning has been better. However when I went to the doctor for my physical statement I told him about it and he put it down on my record. When I told him my age he remarked that there is very little chance of my being sent to an active theater. That plus the recent statement about men who had been in combat units in both Italy and France and Germany makes me feel a bit more confident.

We have been receiving quite a lot of compliments lately and I feel quite proud of the fact that the S.O.P. which I wrote was highly commended by our Corps and Army I&E officers and came out with the approval of our commanding general.

This A.M.. I had an interesting experience which could happen probably only in the American Army. We had a meeting of the I & E officers and I was chairman. It seemed strange to have a mere technician fourth grade conducting a meeting including a major, a captain and the rest lieutenants.

I am now starting on the ambitious program of learning German. There is a good dictionary in the library of our mansion and i have managed to struggle through a small vocabulary. I can just about manage to say a few simple sentences now and I don't hold any great hopes of being an accomplished German linguist. My happy memories of the liquid and musical tones of French as spoken by various provincial people in France and by the Parisians makes the harsh and guttural sounds of German particularly unpleasant. German names for things are very blunt. For instance the word of suicide is self-murder (Selbstmord).

For the last few days the Bavarian climate has improved and we have had nice sunshine but the nights are still cold. I have to use two blankets every night.

Have to quit now, it's getting late. All my love and take good care of yourself.

Chad

Grunwald
June 3rd, 1945

Dearest sweetheart:

Just received about six newspapers and a small box containing the Career Monographs. I immediately stuck my nose into them and before I knew it the whole evening was gone. We have been quite busy preparing reports and writing up advisory material for our I & E officers. Each day flies by and it's hard to assess our accomplishments. Today was really clear and warm and I was able to get out for a while to toss a soft ball around and loosen up some of my muscles. Lots of the boys are taking tours now and I hope soon to have a chance to visit Oberammergau and see the mountains. All the boys have been admiring my Thunderbird ring. I think it's pretty snazzy myself. I am searching for something to send you for a wedding anniversary present. Out her in the country it is pretty difficult, but I'll find something. I only wish I could make a real present of a second honeymoon. I miss you like everything and love you so much. But being over here is better than being headed for some other places I could mention. Goodnight, my libchen, take good care of yourself.

Love,
Chad

Grunwald
June 6, 1945

Dearest wife:

After work this evening I started plowing through some more Herald Tribunes which came in and among them found some good stuff on the San Francisco Conference. I enjoyed scanning the Ridgefield Press except for two things: a lot of the fellows I had in school have been wounded and a lot of the names in the social news etc. are new ones to me. When I return to the old home town I'll be like a stranger. You mentioned a lot of the Bavarian places which our tours take in especially Oberammergau and Garmisch. Charly went down the other day as far as the Benner Pass. Sort of a vicious cycle to get back into Italy. He says the mountains are wonderful. I thing that on the 15th Mac and I will be able to go. It's something I have been really looking forward to for a long time. Maybe there I will spot something you will like for our anniversary. It will be late but I want you to know I am thinking of you. Only I would give the entire Alps just for our day and night with you at Blue Mt. Lake like June 1934!

Love,

Chad

Grunwald
June 7, 1945

Dearest sweetheart:

This imposing letter head came from the underground shelters or tunnels running out from Hitler's Munich house under the two "shrines" of the 16 Nazis who died when Hitler and his gang tried their putsch in Munich. There are three levels of tunnels and they are filled with all sorts of Nazi rubbish. Looking out from Hitler's house which, by the way, is the billeting are for my old company, you can see the Koenig's Platz which is the area where thousands of Nazis used to gather to listen to and cheer Hitler's speeches. Two nights ago we took a tour around the city and saw most of the famous places connected with Munich's past. Many of the art museums and churches are finished for good. They will have to be torn down before any rebuilding can start. There were about 150 churches in the city and very few of them are left. The old Frauen Kirche or Church of Our Lady with its two very tall towers topped by onion shaped cupolas is heavily damaged. In the center of the city most of the homes are gutted by fire and we were wondering how many people were buried in the endless piles of rubble that can be seen everywhere. On the edge of the city the building were not so heavily damaged. Out where we are on the east bank of the Isar River about 10 Kilometers south of Munich there is very little damage except for brokern windows and doors sprung by the force of bomb explosions. Several evening sago we (Mac, Charley and I) went for a walk along the river. It has a swift current and the water is bold because it comes from the mountains. The water is full of rock flour indicating that some of the tributaries must be glacier fed.

I don't blame you for not being able to find out little town. I guess the ordinary maps don't show it. Don't worry about my wanting to stay anywhere in Europe. The deepest and softest rung and the finest furniture would never be as good as our living room carpet with you spreading out your material to make a dress or Tippie snoozing peacefully but occasionally glancing up over her paws to see that everything was OK.

The third buddy I meant was Henry Kellermeyer who came from Indiana. He was in the same chicken coop with us at McClellan. He got it while on Anzio.

The clipping about F.B. amazed me. I never realized he was such a versatile person. The more I see of the Army and Navy the more I realize how important it can be a good promoter. Some publicity!

Thanks for remembering me to John Hubbard and Eddie Allan.

All my love, sweetheart,

from Chad.

June 10, 1945

Dearest sweetheart:

I received your postal card today written from New York. How I wish I could have been with you at the Hotel Weylin and to have gone to Oklahoma with you! I see in the Stars and Stripes that "Oklahoma" and a lot of other shows are coming over to the E.T.O. That reminds me that I never sent you the autograph I got from Marlene Dietrich when she brought her show to us at Aschaffenburg. We were in a Nazi Training camp where they had lots of loot lying around. As a matter of fact that was where I picked up the little Mauser automatic pistil which I now have. It's the only real German souvenir that i have ever picked up. You probably remember that the Nazi put up a very stiff fight at Aschaffenburg and had to be blasted out with artillery and tank fire. The place was in wild disorder so it was easy to find a lot of loot. One big bldg was a warehouse with thousands of fine cowhide German boots, hob nails, and all. Lots of the fellows sent them home but what they will ever use them for I don't know. Anyone wearing them sounds like a tank coming down the street. To get back to "Legs Dietrich". We had a chance to see the show in an abandoned garage. The troupe was very good. M.D. sang "See What the Boys in the Back Room Will Have" and, of course, "Lili Marlene" the climax of her act was to display her famous underpinning whereupon the wolf howl went up (I don't mean Werewolf). Very nice! And she had a Thunderbird patch dangling from her garter. Supposedly a Morale builder.

I see that the generals are getting quite a reception back home. Men like Patton are OK but that eagle-beaked----. Mark Clark, ought to be farmed out to some newspaper which needs a good press agent. Soldiers in the E.T.O. know him for what he is.

Our wedding anniversary draws nearer and I still haven't found anything really good. Not even a poor forlorn homeless little Toby Jug! I am still not certain about whether I will get a chance to go to Garmisch or not. That territory is the home of some of the worlds best wood carvers so I may find something.

My golly I got a smart wife! Designing dresses and put em together is really something. You make them sweetsie-bug and I'll take 'em off.

Spring in Bavaria gets in my blood and some nights I see a lot of the ceiling before I get to sleep. The weather here is what the Germans call veranderlich and they aren't lying. One day you can get a good tan and the next you need your long handles. We have beautiful roses and all the flowers seem to do well here.

I am not running out of paper. Just too damn lazy, to go get it. Goodnight, Mein Lieb,

Chad

Dearest sweetheart:

This A.M.. I finally succeeded in doing something I have been swearing up and down I would get done. I mailed my packages. Every time I started to get my stuff together to make them up we would move off somewhere or I would have to go off on an errand so it just didn't get done. But she is did now. One package contains a pair of small wooden shoes, a bottle of perfume and some French coins. The other contains a German canteen and belt, a Sicily sketch book (a collector's item now), one "Road to Rome (story of our break out from Anzio), 1 Folies Bergere program, 1 Casino de Paris program, 1 Hist. of Paris, 179th Inf. Coat of Arms, 1 crayon sketch of myself (made in Nancy on the way back from Paris the last time), some German military emblems, 1 Grenoble pin, 1 Notre Dame Rosary and the Paris Medallion for your bracelet. Today I took a trip down the west side of the Isar River south to Lansberg from which you get a fine view of a large lake with the mountains in the background. Not much else that's new. Probably be leaving our mansion before long. C'est la querre! I am OK and feeling fine. I wish I could take you down into the mountain country. What a place for a honeymoon!

All my love,

Chad

My dearest wife:

Here it is the day before our 11th wedding anniversary and I am much ashamed to admit that I still haven't found anything to send home especially for my sweetheart. All I can say, my sweet, is that I send you my love across the ocean and tell you that I miss you more and more each day.

The last few days have been taken up with packing and moving again. We were at Grunwald about 10 kilometers south of Munich on the banks of the Isar River. However somebody with enough rank to get results decided that we should move so that was that! We moved bag and baggage to the fair sized town of Furstenfeldbruck west of Munich. We are set up in two rooms in the town court house. We have a small office and a really fine large room for our reading and news room. We now have a 500 volume reference library containing everything from a cookbook to a Japanese dictionary (not that I am interested in the latter!)

I put up a lot of the colored pictures you sent me and the comments and interest have been gratifying. It begins to look now as though we aren't going to get much of a chance to have an educational program so our main emphasis is on orientation and short on the job training classes with some of the fellows taking correspondence or self-teaching courses.

Mac and I are quartered in a German house on the second floor along with some other fellows in our G-3 section (Plans and Training) We both have fine beds with real mattresses and feather bolsters which are as light as a baby's kiss. I couldn't get used to sheets so I spread my wool blanket out to lie on. I sleep better that way. I wake up every A.M. about 0650 and pester Mac until he wakes up. Then I dress and go for breakfast. Then back to wash up and shave. Then to the office to work. This the army! But I'm not complaining.

I saw the clipping you sent about the fellows with below 85 points getting out of the army but I am not optimistic since I have only 56 points. Not having been wounded or a hero I don't have those extras which would give me the points. Not having any kids I don't get any points there either. I only count myself very lucky for coming through so far and for having a wife back home whom I dearly love and who has given me eleven of the sweetest years of my life.

You asked about the S.O.P. which I wrote for the division. S.O.P. means Standing Operating Procedure an is Army talk for any set of rules which may be set up to guide any Military activity. However, it looks as though our bunch will not have an opportunity use it.

Today I took a trip down to pick up the Stars and Stripes at Tutzing on the Wurn See, a beautiful lake south of Munich. As you got south and descend into Starnberg at the head of the lake you see a fine panorama of the Bavarian Alps in the distance. So far I haven't been down to Garmisch or Oberammergau but hope to when they start up tours again. How I would love to take you with me to one of the lovely inns in the mountains where we could have a honeymoon. Our bed would take a beating I am certain.

It's late now my sweet and I must take myself off to bed where I will dream of my darling and pray for the day when we can be together again.

Your devoted

Chad

My dearest sweetheart:

Our 11th Anniversary has come and gone and still no present from me to mark the event. I am indeed a failure at fining suitable remembrances to send my sweetheart on the one day I should be able to furnish some little reminder of my love for you. Even though I failed in that I want you to know that I was thinking of you and longing for you more than ever, if that is possible.

I received No. 333 today and was amazed at your good fortune in receiving the chicks in such good condition and so speedily. How is the chick feed situation now. The last I remember from your letters about it people were having a tough time getting feed. If you can swing the deal to raise so many chickens it should be quite profitable not mention the source of eggs and meat.

It's an unusual coincidence that just about the same time you were having a bout with cold germs, I was having the same thing. The house or mansion I mentioned at Grunwald was a cold, damp place and it seemed as though we got rain every day so i get pretty thoroughly chilled through and caught cold. It's better now though I have the usual after effects for me, lots of catarrh and plenty of trouble with my sinuses. Aren't I the Calamity Jane though? Lately the weather has improved and I have been feeling much better, I am so sorry that you had a tough time with intestinal trouble and a cold on top of that.

We have had the wind taken out of our sails here because it begins to look as though we will not get the opportunity to set up our unit schools which are planned for those units which will stay in the PTO for some time. I read an article in the news this P.M. stating that eight division have already been picked for Reich duty. They are the 82nd Airborne, 1st armored, 4th armored, 1st Inf., 3rd Inf., 9th Inf., 29th Inf., and 36th Inf. That plus some other signs, begins to make it look as though the old 45th is slated for some kind of moving around. Many men who are no eligible for discharge will probably not be revealed for a year yet. The army has told Congress flatly that it doesn't intend to lower the automatic discharge age below 40. So, here am I with 56 points and only one anchor to the windward, Ike's promise that men who have fought in two theaters will not be asked to fight in a third. Even at that I have my fingers crossed. Come right down to it, I have been around. I have fought in two theaters and have been in three armies., the 5th, then the7th, and now the 3rd.

This letter begins to remind me of the one Henry Aldrich wrote to a girl friend in a neighboring town. He wrote all about his track team and his prowess as an athlete wound up each paragraph with the sentence, "But enough about me, how have you been Lately?" Then he would go on to write more about himself. We heard the program last night over Radio Munich which is now being operated by the Armed Forces Network. We have a swell Blaupunkt radio which is considered by the Germans to be about the best they have. It was given to the Major by a friend of his. Oh, by the way, I liberated a camera and have one roll of German film for it. It's very good because I saw some of the pictures taken with it. It was of mountain scenery in the Bavarian Alps and was as clear as you would want. While we were at Grunwald the Major took some pictures of all of us, Charley Bucknam, Don MacDonald (Mac) and myself. He has promised me a print of it and when I get it I will send it home. It was taken with one of those super-dooper German cameras. I hope it comes out.

Love,

Chad

Furstenfeldbruck
June 24, 1945

My dearest wife:

No mail today except 3 copies of the Press. It was a shock to read about Tom Brady's death. But it was a pleasant surprise to see John Nash's picture on the font page. He look really fit and quite natural standing along side some linotypes even though they are kaput.

Today I went south with the 1 1/2 ton truck to pick up the Stars and Stripes and the Sunday supplements. The weather was fine and sunny with tremendous cumulus clouds piled up on the southern horizon. We had a fine view of the mountains some of which have snow on their sides. Tomorrow A.M. at 0700 I am going on a tour. Yes, at last! The one which was planned back in Grunwald (a southern suburb of Munich) was called off because of rain. So tomorrow we will leave for Garmisch and will go up the Zugspitz from which they say you can see all over the Bavarian Alps on a clear day. At last I have a fairly good German camera and one roll of film with which I hope to take some good views of the quaint Bavarian mountain villages and the mt. scenery. At the top of Zugspitz they have a place where you can take skiing lessons. However I think I'll be too busy with the camera and the scenery to bother with skiing. Remember in Feb. 1934 when I skied up onto your front porch? The night before I had nearly compromised you by staying way late until I just about made it home. Those were the days when you were the one who had the self control for the both of us. Many nights I left your arms with my whole body throbbing and aching with my desire for you. Over here it wasn't so bad while the fighting was going on. We very rarely saw any women except an occasional peasant family or some nuns in Phalsbourg (France) where we stayed for a couple of months. Here in Germany, now that the fighting is over, we see slick chicks riding along the highways on their bicycles with their skirts flying in the breeze and revealing some very interesting and exciting panoramas. These gals do so much cycling that their nether extremities are very well shaped. I confess I am just like the rest of the GI's. My eyes pop open too and my head just naturally seems to turn. However I'll still holding out against the day when I can give my sweetheart a big bear hug and sweep her up in my arms and take her to our nice big soft bed where I can lay her out and investigate the charms that I have missed for so long. To kiss the two sweet blue eyes and run my lips down your funny little nose until I can plant a quivery kiss on your lips and nibble on the little point of your upper lip. Then, not satisfied to travel afield until I am feeling the strong pulse at the base of your throat beating against my lips. To come over between your legs and rest my head on your breast while I kiss two nice nubbins until they rise to points and to feel you quiver in my arms as i run my tongue around those two handfuls of pure delight. Swift fluttery pulsations of joy in your breathing would tell me you were ready for Peter to be laid against the groove he loves to explore. The groove would throb and begin to get moist so that as he pressed up and down his head would slide more easily and rub gently against the little point at the top of the groove. By this time the lips would be swollen and open wide. Peter would stop moving up and down and would rest with his head against a warm and throbbing cavern. So gradually would be push that it would take him several minutes before he was inside the gateway which he sought. But he would be so thrilled by the excitement that he wouldn't be able to contain himself any longer and he would throw a fiery stream of love into the cavern. Then he would rest for a moment, still throbbing. By this time the cavern would be so filled with love that he could easily gain his goal. Slowly at first he would move in and out pausing to rest for a while until he could feel the walls of the cavern throbbing and tightening around him. I would place my hands under you and turning my face so as to taste your kisses would thrust Peter in so deep that his head would be way beyond the ring of muscle. There he would flood the cavern again with his love and rest until we drew apart. Oh my darling wife I don't know how long it's going to be before we can be in each other's arms but I want you to know that I love you with all my heart and soul and miss you more that mere words can tell. I suppose It's foolish in a way to write to tell you what I would like to do with you to show my love and physical longing. It stirs you up and I know it raises hell with me for a while but i feel better after I get it "poured out" on paper. You probably have noticed that I scribble like mad when I am that way.

At last I am able to send you two snap shots of our section. The silly looking goof with the stratospheric forehead is your husband, going right is Charley Bucknam (damned clever fellow with lots of musical ability) then major Lord our boss and one swell person (it takes a long while to get to know him) and last but not least Don MacDonald (I call him Dougal MacDougal) who is a school teacher from Quincy, Mass and an ideal type for advisement work. I will try to get some prints of pictures which the major took at the same time with his super-special German camera. They were taken on the lawn near the "mansion" in Grunwald. Fortunately it was one of the sunny days we had while there.

Will have to close now, my sweet, I have to get ready for tomorrow which will be a long full day.

Give my love to the folks and remember me to the neighbors.

All my love,

Chad

My dearest sweetheart:

Yesterday I finally made the long-awaited trip to Zugspitze and Garmisch-Parten Kirchen. We started out in a driving rain and several times during the day had thunder showers. Bavarian weather is what the Germans call veranderlich (changeable) and how! We went in a big Diesel Mercedes-Benz bus which has a top that rolls back. I was very thankful that we didn't go in a 2 1/2 ton Army truck the way some of the fellows did. We started at 0700 and arrived in Garmisch at 0930. We bought our tickets for 21 marks ($2.10) and started out on the Zugspitz bahn, an electric train with two cars. The RR is narrow gauge all the way for about 2 or 3 miles we were pulled by a small electric engine until we came to the bottom of the range of mountains. There a large engine with a cog wheel attachment hooked on and we began the climb. While climbing the foothills up to 1650 meters alt. We could look out and see vast panoramas of mountain scenery. At a place called Riffelriss, 1650 meters we stopped and took pictures of the mountains and of an emerald green lake which spread out below us. After a 5 min. stop. We got on the train and for 1/2 hour climbed steadily through a tunnel from 1650 meters to 2650 meters alt. My ears kept popping and my head felt light while my stomach felt uneasy. At last we arrived at the Schneefernerhaus a fine hotel just below the Zugspitz peak. This spot is almost 8000 feet above sea level and very cold. We walked through the hotel out onto the terrace from which we could see the whole mountain formation.

We ate lunch in the restaurant and drank watery German beer. Some of the fellows went skiing on the glacier but nicht for me! I explored around the edge of the glacier and took in the scenery through a powerful pair of binoculars they had there. Others took the short cable car ride up to the top of the mountain. Unfortunately for them and for us below who were trying to take pictures, clouds kept rolling up and cutting off the view. There were short intervals of sunshine and took one roll of film which I hope will come out OK. We came back down on the RR to

Garmisch and saw the stadium where they had the Winter Olympics. Then back to Furstenfeldbruch by 8:30 p.m.

On my arrival I found a lot of mail from my sweetheart so I was busy the rest of the evening catching up on your latest news. The Nos. were 332, 334, 335, 336, 337, 338, 339. #339 was mailed the 21st of June. Some fast traveling!

I was not surprised to see that Dave and Jim blew off steam and went on a toot. Dave is releasing steam that has been pent up for a long time. However, if folks will leave us along I can guarantee you that we won't have any trouble staying together. As a matter of fact you'll probably get sick of my hanging on to you all the time. I feel as though I would never want to let you go. If there is any getting splifficating to be done you and I are going to do it on our own. Only I would prefer getting that nice mellow glow that makes everything rosy. Then we would be able to snuggle together and while away the hours just unburdening our hearts and getting reacquainted. Don't be frightened by my brave talk in my letters about what I would like to do with you I realize that for several days after we are together again, you and I will get a lot of enjoyment out of a real courting period. During which we can experience the renewed joy of all the little hundred and one pettings and endearments which we have missed so much. Probably we both will be surprised at how soon you will be emotionally and physically ready for something more strenuous. The one thing in my mind is that no matter how much I may want it. I am not going to rape my wife the way so many blundering idiots do. Besides look at all the fun they miss because when you are relaxed and ready in my arms I feel reassured that I am not hurrying you and you can get that much more enjoyment out of it. As for having intercourse 8 times in 2 days I don't think I am up to that achievement but I will guarantee that what we do have will not lack in quality though it may lack in quantity

I have been wondering for a long time about something and I don't know quite how to say it. But I will put it bluntly. What in hell is Allie trying to do to Jim anyway? Doesn't she realize that he must have some reason for wanting to drink? By panning Jim and nagging him (his puritanical sister doesn't help any there, either, I'll bet) she just makes him seek release in liquor. By avoiding her own duty you get the job of acting as nurse maid. Damn it all, it isn't fair to you.

Things here are in an unsettled state to say the least. Very little is known definitely about what is going to happen. I'll wager though that the old 45th is due for a might over hauling. Normally I would be slated for the Pacific but I am hoping that having fought in two theaters of operations will keep me from heading that way. Nevertheless I am now shucking everything I can possibly get rid of against the possibility that I might have to travel light some day. I am not trying to frighten you but on the other hand I don't want to lull you into thinking that everything is all set for my speedy return home. To many fellows in this Army build up their hopes on things that are promised only to find that the Army has a very unpleasant way of changing its mind. I could mention a lot of things about our I& E program but it would do my blood pressure no good. As far as I know the situation now there are three possibilities. 1- That I may be taken from the 45th and put into another division which will be assigned to occupation duty. 2- I may come home with the division, have a furlough, and then go on eventually to the pacific, or 3- I may come home and because of age or special training be kept in the States. Now you know as much about it as I do. If anything happens which I can tell you, you must rest assured I will let you know.

Another thing, about wives coming over to the European countries. I think that's like a lot of other things that have been aired in the newspapers, it is a lot of talk and promises for political effect. I think that eventually, perhaps after a year has passed and the occupation forces are set up, wives may be brought over. But right now, the food situation is such and the housing problem is so overwhelming (Congressmen who blithely make promises don't know the situation) That it's going to be a long time before wives will be over here with their husband. So please don't send me newspapers (except clippings on a small scale) or any more air mail writing paper or envelopes (I have lots of it). The next few weeks may bring a lot of developments which will clear things up. I hope it's good.

The Charlie I have mentioned several times is Charlie Bucknam from New Rochelle, NY. A graduate of Fordham who specialized in Psych. He is a really fine fellow with a lot of vitality and ability. He is very musical and plays the sax and clarinet very well. He was a riflemen for quite a while until he got a break on Anzio and got a place in the band. Every once in a while he still visits with the boys in the Band and takes part in a jam session.

That Barbitol sounds like bad stuff but i believe the Sulfa drugs have a worse after effect. I know they leave me washed out for days afterward.

I received the Hilltop Dispatch the other day with a note from Zeke. I will write him a note soon.

Dave Moore's story about the long march he had to take reminds me of the American boys I saw in Aschaffenburg. A long train of ambulances was drawn up along the road and we got a chance to talk to some of the patients. I saw one boy I never will forget. He was about 6ft. 1 " tall but he didn't weight more than 100 lbs. His cheek bones seemed to be pushing their way through his skin. He was so feeble that he could just about move his feet and in order to squat alongside the road to have a bowel movement he had to be supported by two medics. The people I will never forget are those I saw at Dachau, the Nazi concentration camp. Many have died there even after our arrival with medical care and food. Even intravenous feeding was not enough to save them.

I told you about the writing on a wall in the center of Munich.

DACHAU BELSEN   BUCHENWALD
ICH SCHAME MICH DAS ICH EIN DEUTCHER BIN HOLPFEL
then some Nazi bastard had the nerve to write in red paint right along side of it
ES SCHAME NICHT

It's going to take a generation to root out this terrible mental sickness.

Dave also mentioned that he came over on the Butner. I rather suspected that he might be on the boat but, though I tried, I couldn't find him. We were pretty well packed in for a small ship.

You asked about Porter or bill as I call him. The last I heard he was clerk for Cannon Co. of the 179th Inf. I haven't seen him in a long time because he is with the admin. center and we were moved to the Division C.P. He is in Munich about 1/2 hrs. drive from here.

I am glad you liked the 45th Div. History. I have sent you a copy of the 6th Corps beach head News which has an up to date history of the 45th with pictures.

You asked about my battle stars. They are 1. Attack on Rome (or the break-out from Anzio) 2. Invasion of S. France 3. Siegfried Line and a new one which is in the works. 4 Central Germany. There is still some talk about the 4th one but I think it is pretty certain to go on our records. I wish they would give one for Anzio too. I will be entitled to the bronze service arrowhead for the initial assault landing at Maxime, France on Aug. 15th. It hasn't been issued to us yet but I am eligible.

My darling, you gave me a terrific thrill when you wrote in letter #339 about how you lay awake on the night of June 19th 1934 wondering what I would be like. I hope I convinced you on that June 20th and in the years that followed that it was worth the trouble of marrying a guy like me, I couldn't love you more, or so it seems now, but I would like to try.

Goodnight with a nice quivery kiss.

From
Chad

Furstenfeldbruck
June 29, 1945

Dearest sweetheart:

Received 3 fat envelopes today containing Life magazine which I read from cover to cover. I am now doing a lot of reading since we received a 500 volume library. As a matter of fact I have my nose in a book most of the time now. Making up for lost time, I guess. Also had a letter from Ralph saying that when I return to the States he plans to have a real binge in celebration. I am still not forgetting our own private binge we promised each other. I don't want to get ossified but I am afraid that it wouldn't take very much to put me under the table. Everything here is in a turmoil with our guys being shuffled around. All the old fellows with 85 points or over will be gone before long. I am shucking down to be able to travel light so please don't send any packages or anything bulky. It won't be too long before we will know what the score is. I am hoping for a lucky break. Take good care of yourself my sweetheart. Give my love to Mother Bedient. All my dearest love to you.

From

Chad

Furstenfeldbruck
July 1, 1945

Dearest Petunia:

In the midst of the rapidly increasing tempo of events here I received your letter #341 today. Your letters seem to be coming through OK but mine must be stymied along the way. Mac says his wife is not receiving his letters as regularly as she should either.

The week you were without mail was probably due to the time we were busy moving from Grunwald. The last couple of days we have been holing out and burning everything we don't want to carry. As far as actual knowledge of what is going to happen is concerned I still don't "know from nuttin!" Men are being shifted around every day and all I know now is that fellows in my category (with two theaters) are being shifted to a division which is slated for occupation.

June Stout was right about the food but lately is has improved. Some days are really bad but, by and large, we are getting better meals now than we were a couple of weeks ago. Don't worry, sweetheart, about my gut and don't send any packages because I don't know where I will be by the time a package would get over here. We get our PX rations of candy and cigarettes and that is really all I need. But one thing you can do for me is to take your vitamin pills and do your best to build up your resistance. Don't try to save stuff for the days when I will be home but use them up as you need them. I want you to get plenty of sleep and put on weight. You are going to need it when I get you in my arms again.

Don't worry about writing me your troubles after all who else should here them but I? My shoulders are broad enough and I know what you have had to put up with. When I get into civilian clothes again I am going to do my damnedest to make you happy and give you a chance to rest up and get your resistance back.

I am sorry to hear that you had the 24 hour flu. It certainly leaves a person pretty weak and washed out. A lot of our boys get the GI's every so often. When warm weather comes they get attacks of Diarrhea. They say it is caused by a germ but actually any number of things may cause it. They use sulfa pills to cure it.

In letter #328 you mentioned eating clams on the half-shell and scallops. You had me drooling because I certainly have missed seafood. Boy! How I could tie into a mess of clams or a nice lobster! How I remember the lobster stew and blueberry pie up in Maine. The other day I was talking to a Mainiac and had him drooling too by describing lobster stew and blueberry pie. That was being really cruel.

You asked about Toby Jugs and the possibility of getting one. When we were in Grunwald we saw lots of priceless Dresden China Figurines but nary a Toby Jug. But the damned military Gov't. had made a complete inventory of everything so there was nothing doing. Where we are now, in a court house in Furstenfeldbruck, there are no souvenirs except German land records and probate books.

Yesterday I received a notice of C. Walker Jr's wedding and a note from Mrs. Walker Sr. I imagine Charley is quite an independent young fellow, if you know what I mean.

If I didn't say so before I should mention that I have the wallet you sent me. I have a zipper wallet which I am using now.

I am having trouble connecting any of my thoughts tonight because Mac is reading the story of Eisenhower's life and keeps telling me about it.

It is a coincidence that you should think of out being married again. I have often thought of it and when you come right down to it, being together again will be like being married all over again. If we can possible arrange it, I want very much to go way with you so that we can have the second honeymoon we have both dreamed about so much during the time we have been separated. It doesn't matter so much to me where we go just so long as we are together away from people who might claim our attention and time. I know that you are afraid that I have changed and that those changes might make it difficult for us to get readjusted. It is true I have change din lots of ways but in the one important thing, my love for you, I have changed only in that I love you more and more as each day goes by. I know that you have changed too, but, knowing that you love me, I am sure that when we are together again, we will have a greater appreciation of our life together. Having been separated for so long we have a keener knowledge of the meaning of our love. I can't say it very well, My sweet, but I know you will understand. Good night, sweetheart, with all my love,

Chad

Dearest sweetheart:

This is probably the most difficult letter to write that I have ever attempted. It has nothing to do with any change in me personally except for the tremendous drive within me to see you again and know that everything is alright between us.

To end the suspense. It begins to look as though I will be coming home before too long. First the background explanation. Our outfit is going through the process of being "redeployed". Men with over 85 points are being transferred out to another division which will eventually come home. They are eligible for discharge. Those with less than 85 points who fought in two theaters (Mediterranean and European) will be sent to a division which is slated for occupation work. These men will probably be over here for a year or two more with very slim prospects that their wives will be able to come over.

I explained in a previous letter about the housing and food shortage as well as the lack of transportation (Even some of the 85+ pointers may have to wait a year before going home). The emphasis is continually being placed on getting men to the Pacific theater as fast as possible. The last group of men, those with less than 85 points and only one theater to their credit will be sent home for training and then to the Pacific. The 45th, as it will eventually be reorganized, is such a division.

Maj. Lord, Mac, Charley and I all thought that be some stroke of fortune we would be regarded as essential enough to stay with the division. We then figured that, being home in the U.S. we wouldn't have to go to the Pacific because of the two theater business. It soon developed that it was no go. We were slated for occupation and I personally, could see month after dreary month stretching out into the future over here in a land that has brought so much misery on the world. It filled me with despair. Events had come to such a point that our names were already on the order to transfer us over to the occupation troops. Major Lord decided to change over to a position of requesting to go with the division and after a lot of anguished thinking Mac, Charley and myself decided to do the same. What we did was to waive our exemption as two theater men in order to stay with the division. Know that this may come as a terrible blow just reading it the way I am putting it down here but I promised to tell you all I could of the truth.

From that point all sorts of surmises can be made. Your guess is as good as the next fellows. Here's the way I have it doped out. By coming with the division I will return to the U.S. much sooner than many of the men who have over 85 points. Once I am in the States my Age, sinus condition and rheumatism in the knees and legs will help me get some kind of job in the States. If, after being in the States for several months training etc. I do have to got to the Pacific the 45th with the longest combat record of any division in the European theater (511 actual combat days) my be in strategic reserve. Last but not least, by staying with Major Lord in I&E work, we would be at the Division Administration Center which is the safest place in the whole division. Well, my darling, I know that I have made a decision which involves a great gamble. I realize that anything can happen to throw a monkey wrench in the whole works but I can't see myself twisting around in a mental prison, like a rat in a cage, rotting away over here in Germany. I would go nuts! If I do have go to the Pacific the chance of being with you gain for a while, being back in the U.S., and getting rid of this uncertainty will be compensation enough. One comforting thought is that the pressure in the Pacific on Japan is mounting daily and now the strength of the United Nations can be concentrated on one enemy and not divided as seemed strategically feasible. Another year surely should see the end of the Pacific War.

In my poor way I have tried to explain to you the things that have influenced me to make the decision I have reached. I hope that you will not be angry or disappointed and will try to understand the things that influenced me to decide the way I did. I could have stayed over here safe and sound in "cold storage" gnawing at the edges of my sanity for a year or two. Or take a gamble and see what happens. Certainly when I get home I am going to try every angle I can to locate something in the States. If you know anyone who has friends in the service who are in positions where they might do me some good, try to get some information for me because I am going to need it.

This is one hell of a way to be telling your wife that you are going to be seeing her soon but that it is the way the Army is.

Our I&E program is now "kaput" because of the shifting personnel. We are now stripped right down to the bare essentials and have had quite a few bonfires doing it. The divisions which are staying here for occupation duty will probably start their unit schools in August. All the fine plans we laid so carefully for setting up our program can be chalked up as good experience. I know I benefitted a lot from it and feel that I am qualified to do this I&E work as well as anyone. As for the present it will be just marking time.

I am feeling OK and have fully recovered from the cold I had while in Grunwald. That was a bitch! The weather was so cold and damp that I got chilled through. We are waring our wool OD's and at night sleep with three blankets over us. This time last year we were sweltering in the hot sun of Italy south of Salerno on the plain below Paestum. I was just getting a taste of orientation work by leading a tour of Pompeii. Remember the letters I wrote describing the red-light district of the ancient city? I found out later from some of the truck drivers that modern Pompeii has a thriving district as well. They didn't say though whether the modern Italian signorinas could demonstrate as many positions as the harlots of ancient Pompeii. I told that we received a 500 volume library from special Service and that I was doing a lot of reading. One of the boys potted a book called, "a Marriage Manual" which goes into some detail about the various positions. The book became quite a popular immediately. This brought on discussions of why it is so important for the woman to bend her knees and pull up her legs before intromission. So you see our bull-sessions are on very elevating topics. Oh! Oh! That wasn't fair.

Well darling, I will have to elevate myself from this chair and get off to bed because it is getting late. So good night my sweet, a nice quivery kiss on your eyelids over your cheeks and an urgent fiery one on your sweet lips.

All my love,
Chad

Furstenfeldbruck
July 5th, 1945

Dearest sweetheart:

The last couple of days I have knocked off early and gone to bed. Nerves, I guess, because my stomach was out of whack and I felt miserable. After the air-mail letter I wrote you explaining my decision I guess I felt all dragged out. Today, after two nights of 11 hrs sleep each, I feel more like myself. Mac and I went over to a beer garden which is being used for the enlisted mens club, drank a couple of beers and listened to the Bavarian music of a hired civilian band. Not much doing now with I&E work except orientation. Lots of new faces of men shifted over from other divisions. One very lucky bread was that we have a new mess sergeant and several new cooks. I almost fell over this AM to find that breakfast consisted of tomato juice, bacon, pancakes, 2 fried eggs, hot cereal bread and coffee. I couldn't believe it at first. It's the first time that every happened to me in the Army. I'll have to watch my waistline. No mail for three days and am lonesome for news.

Chad

Furstenfeldbruck
July 6, 1945

Dearest sweetheart:

Not much to write about tonight because we are still marking time. Probably by now you have seen in the N.Y. Papers that the 45th is scheduled to come home. But any information as to when that will take place is being kept very secret of course. I will be willing to bet that we get home before most of the old fellows of the 45th who were transferred out to join an outfit which will eventually return to the States. The rumor is now that we will receive a thirty day furlough right after reaching the U.S. that would certainly be super ultra to have a month home. I know darn well that the month will seem like about one week but to me over here it seems as though every minute would exist just to have the last drop of joy squeezed out of it. Had an interesting talk today with an old Austrian who was ambassador to Japan at the time of Emperor Franz Josef. He was telling me a lot about the customs of the Japs. He is going to give a lecture to the troops. Good night sweetheart! I hope I get some mail, tomorrow.

Chad

Dearest sweetheart:

By this time you have probably read in the New York papers that the 45th which was scheduled to take the place of the 28th Div. on the list for those coming home, has been postponed for a while. How long, nobody knows. It would be a thrill for me to be able to say that we would be home by your birthday but I guess I won't have the chance.

The mail situation is really loused up this time. None of us in the office have had letters from home now for five days. It begins to look as though our mail has been holed up somewhere along the line. I know just how you feel with no news because it is getting more and more difficult to think of things to write. It's a cowardly trick to play on a wife to keep writing these V-mail letter but I just haven't been able to exercise my imagination enough to compose. Lord knows it would have to be composition, too, because nothing exciting goes on here. I could write you one of those letters you like to snuggle down with but I know you are probably stirred up enough over the news I sent you that I was slated to come home soon.

This morning at breakfast I had the pleasant surprise of meeting one of the boys from G company who was a very close friend on Anzio. He is slated for occupation duty. He had been in London on pass and was surprised as a lot of others were to come back to the division and find that practically all the fellows he knew were transferred to another division. He told me about the fine time he had in London and we both reminisced about the old days back on Anzio. When we go traveling in the States you are liable to see me look astonished and delighted to see some fellow who used to be in my old company in the 179th. Mac and I are both anxious to meet in the States and have our wives get acquainted. Probably that would be impossible during the thirty day furlough we get right after coming home but certainly after this war is over we want to get together for a reunion. During my furlough I want to have you to myself as much as possible.

This afternoon the second anniversary issue of the 45th Division News came out with a complete spread on the record of the 45th and glowing accounts of the deeds of its men. I have saved a souvenir copy and will send it home under separate cover as I did the other booklets which I have picked up from time to time. I was wondering whether you have received the two packages which I sent home from Grunwald. I suppose it's too soon for them to have arrived. One of them contained two bottles of perfume I got in Paris plus some souvenir cards and programs of the Casino de Paris and the Folies Bergers. For about a month now I have been trying to shuck off the things I don't want and make packages of the things I do want to save. I think however, that I will keep my Mauser and my camera with me and bring them home personally.

From the last letters I had from you it looks as though you are going into the chicken business in a big way. I'll bet by now those little chicks are really going for the grass and anything green they can get. How is the fee question now? For a while it must have been pretty tight. I have read that there seems to be plenty of grain so probably it has eased up. Broilers will help out a bit with the meat shortage.

Good night, Sweetheart, I am going out for a glass of very weak German beer, Remember me to the folks and all of my love to you,

from

Chad

Furstenfeldbruck
July 8th, 1945

Dearest sweetheart:

I only hope you are receiving mail from me because something has surely happened to stymie the mail coming here. We were originally slated to be on our way home early this month but evidently we are going to sit around cooling our heels for a while. This PM I went to Augsburg to pick up a couple of boxes of books then spent three hours sewing on a thunderbird patch and a set of chevrons. I missed your nimble fingers Then I started sewing some blue infantry brad on my overseas caps but gave up in disgust. I couldn't get it to look right. Tomorrow AM we have a lecture on Japan coming up. The man giving it is an Austrian whom I mentioned. He is quite the old boy. Very interesting to talk to. He mentioned being in San Francisco the year of the earthquake (1906). Made me feel quite the infant. All our orientation is based on the Pacific theater now and we are keeping track of the daily news events on a big map. The air force is really giving Japan a good dose now and each day it seems to get heavier. More power to 'em!

Good night, my darling with all my love.

Chad

Furstenfeldbruck
July 9, 1945

Dearest sweetheart:

Hooray! I received letter #344 this afternoon. Our mail was held up in the staging area for a while because we were slated to head directly home. I would have been home in August but according to the newspaper tonight the 45th won't be on its way home until September. I hope the weather is cooler because we haven't had any real hot weather since we were at Paestum last summer. Here in Bavaria the days are fairly warm (as a matter of fact the farmers and their families working in the fields are as brown as nuts) but there is always a breeze and the nights are cool. Your description of the heat back home made my tongue hang out. I can just hear you saying "hotter than Dutch love in a strawberry patch."

This AM our Austrian lecturer began his lectures on Japan. He is very interesting and I think he succeeded in holding the interest of the fellows. Anyone talking to a bunch of GI's (who are scheduled for the Pacific probably) who can interest them in Japan must be good.

This PM we took him back to Dachau on business and saw the results of the cleaning up the camp. When I was there last it was shortly after the capture of the territory and the place was a pest home so was declared out-of-bounds or "off-limits" as we call it by the Medics. I did catch a glimpse of about forty RR cars in which corpses were stacked. I have already sent home some pictures of the place which I want to keep as future evidence of German" Kultur". Now the place is cleaned up and visitors are allowed in to see the gas chamber, crematory, dog pens and execution yards. I saw piles of small pits of human bones which had been buried a short distance form the crematory. Even now there is danger of typhus and everyone going in among the remaining ex-prisoners must submit to a thorough dusting with D.D.T. powder. One comical sight I saw was a young fellow and his girl who was very pregnant. They were entering the area so they showed their identification cards. Then the man submitted to the dusting with D.D.T. powder which is done by using a thing that looks like a fly sprayer. The girl shied away but the guard was firm so blushingling she gave in. First she got a couple of puffs of dust up each sleave then the guard put his duster down inside her dress between her breasts and gave the plunger sever vigorous pumps. It must have tickled because she giggled then readjusted her clothing and walked off with her escort.

I must close now and it begins to look as though I won't be able to get a birthday present for you. I haven't seen anything in this area that would make a suitable present. But anyway by that time you will be able to give my love to Tippy. Remember me to the folks.

Furstenfeldbruck
July 12, 1945

Dearest sweetheart:

Hooray! I now have #348 from my sweetheart. I don't blame you for being confoosed by the conflicting newspaper stories about the time of the 45th homecoming. We have been confused too but, my darling, it won't be long now.

We worked today on our shipping boxes. They are made of heavy freshly sawed lumber about one inch thing and are the devil to work with. By tomorrow we will have most of our stuff packed. Then slowly, oh so slowly, the days will pass and we will be on our way to the great assembly Area near Reins. There we will stay for a while to be processed. Then we will be broken up into groups according to the camps in the US. which are our destination. On arrival in the States we will probably stay in the camps for about 24 hours during which time I will have a chance to call you on the phone or send you a telegram. It is possible that the phones will be so busy that I may have to use a telegram. I will have 30 days with you and then I will have to return to the 45th wherever it is stationed. You think your knees are wobbly!

By the way Furstenfeldbruck means Prince's field bridge. Just another example of the way the Germans string words together.

Yes, we are still in the 3rd Army but it doesn't mean we are slated for occupation. It's just that we are in the 3rd A. area. Furstenfeldbruck is about 15 miles west of Munich.

Don't worry about my getting used to sheets and worry about having to sleep alone because you are going to find our big bed awfully snug. I'll be over close to you most of the time. Mac says I am cruel and persistent when I wake him up. I hiss at him. He nods off to sleep for a moment then I pester him until he resigns himself to waking up. I guess I must be a sadist. But when it comes to waking you up I'll raise up on my elbows and lean over you and gently kiss your eyelids then gentle quivery kisses on your lips until you waken, stretch and throw your arms around my neck and snuggle close. Oh Lord, give me strength!

I told Mac about the expensive peas, and he reminded me of the expensive eggs we raised. He has his doubts about the productivity of the Crouchley farm.

If Grace and Kip are married it seems to me the most peculiar way to be married. Maybe they get fun out of it but I know damned well I wouldn't.

It must be hard to keep remembering to soak your feet and rub them but it is very important that you be in good shape when I get home. Then we can go places and do things. We won't be able to spend all our time in bed as much as I would like to. I guess maybe I am getting old, I don't know. The way I feel right now I could hold you in my arms and just keep right on lovin you until you begged for mercy.

I am glad you liked the picture of our I&E staff. I thought I would have some more for you but Major Lord's camera was out of whack and the shutter didn't work right so he spoiled the film. A couple of them would have been really good because Mac dressed up in a Bavarian costume with sporty coat, short leather (chamois) britches and tasseled stockings. He wore a straw hat and had a cigarette in a holder. Since he is 6ft.2" and weighs 250 lbs. he was an imposing sight. We just doubled up with laughter when he strutted out on the lawn in stiff Prussian fashion to pose for his picture. But dam it, the camera wasn't working right so the film was spoiled.

I did have the Leary girl in school and when I looked at the Press article again I realized that the Tom Brady was not from Ridgefield. Tough break for the poor kid! I was just thinking that, even though we have lost many men on the battlefield, there is a greater number of people killed at home from accidents.

I sure want to see those Brahma chicks with their pantelettes. They must be a sight. Aren't they the ones that grow real large?

I have been reading about the newspaper deliverers strike. Also about the trucking strike in Chicago. The Army certainly settled that one in a hurry. People don't realize how important production can be. Maybe you saw that they just admitted a week or so ago that the 7th Army artillery was rationed last winter in Artillery shells. Sometimes the gunners had to fire a whole day's ration in a few minutes. They talk about how rough the Ardennes was. Damn it, it was rough in the Vosges too!

Don't believe too much of that stuff about sending the wives over here this coming fall. There will be plenty of guys with beaucoup points over here sweating out that trip home. The transportation problem not to mention the food problem (which will be worse) will put a crimp in plans of bringing wives over. If I were staying here even for a couple of years I couldn't stand the idea of your being over here where there is still great danger from disease. Then there is the problem of what we could do for Mother Bedient. It would have been a tough situation. But that's all settled. I'm coming home and will be in the States for a while. I don't know how long. Don't worry about my forgetting the phone number. I will seem funny to pick up the phone and call a number stead of saying "Radish please" or some other damned silly code name.

I hope we come home on the Mary or the Elizabeth because they are fast and they usually come to New York. Coming through New York to Shanks or Dix would be so much easier than coming through Boston. Although anywhere in the States is OK by me. It was a pleasant thrill to read about the Acadia. She's quite a boat. I know we had a fine time on board on the Bermuda trip.

Mac and I were going out for a stein of beer but I guess I won't be able to pry him loose from a book he picked up. So I guess I'll go off to bed and dream of holding my sweetheart tight in my arms and just covering her with kisses.

Love

Chad

Dearest sweetheart:

The mail situation is really peculiar. This PM I received letter #342 of June 23rd and #349 of July 7th. It's really difficult to explain how such things happen. Letters that you want to get home before a certain date take much longer than they should then all of a sudden a letter will get home in just a few days. I can't figger it out tall.

You were chiding me about admiring Marlene Dietrick's famous legs. For a man who has been in a desert for a long time to see an oasis suddenly is quite a shock. I'll admit that I had the advantage of going to Paris and seeing some interesting females. Especially those gals who breeze along on their bikes on a windy day. Ma foi!, c'est quelque chose a voir alors! Mais ma cherie, quand vas-tu me permettre voi les james qui sont a moi les plus belles dans toute l'univerce? A cette Lois je serai tres content et je t'embrasswerai avec milles d'embraces. Je gouterai tes douces levres. Je ne pourrai pas quitter tes bras. Now don't say that's what he must have said to sone French gal because I never got the chance. There are two kinds of French girls as far as men are concerned: Those who are really nice and who are sheltered pretty well by their families and those who will take on a man for some kind of consideration whether it's food, clothes, money or fame. The first kind take a long while to get to know and the second kind are bad medicine for any man. So, c'est ca!

Speaking of foreigners I thought I put the accent on veranderlich. I may have forgotten. In the last 15 months I have crammed more foreign words and expressions into my head than any other time. Italian, French and now German. I must admit that my interest in German has dwindled to practically nil now that I am pretty sure of being on my way home soon. I want to hear a certain person call me kutsi bug and hear some spooning talk from my sweetheart.

I saw the pictures of the hurricane in the newspapers and was wondering how it affected Ridgefield. The weather this summer all over the world is damned peculiar. In Russia they are having a heat wave after a very rainy spring.

Your remark about the Jews making big money and buying up places in Ridgefield makes me wonder if the U.S. couldn't do the same as France did. France called in all her currency and issued new. By doing that she caught a lot of black market operators who couldn't explain where their money came from. Also they caught some of the fine upstanding patriots who were doing big business with the Nazis for a long time.

I suppose some wise guy would work out a way of getting around it if they tried it in the U.S.

I am sorry to hear that George Rockwell is slipping. It's not surprising though when you consider how he always threw money around. I don't think he ever really learned the value of money. I mean in a way that he could actually get some enjoyment from spending it.

I received the pipe cleaners and gave them to Mac who is a steady pipe smoker. He appreciated them very much. I am definitely not a pipe smoker. I guess I'm too lazy. That's why I have stuck to smoking cigarettes.

I am glad to hear that Harvey Keeler is now plain "Mr." It must be hard for him to realize. He's been in a long time and, of course, had the advantage of getting two points each month for overseas service. We fellows who came in to the Infantry at Anzio don't have very much time over seas in comparison with those who stayed in England for a couple of years before they actually got into the fighting. Only recently have we seen much credit being given to the divisions who struggled up through Italy, then pushed up through Southern France and finally cut across the Rhineland into Southern Germany. I notice now in the Stars and Stripes that every other day there is a letter from some GI's wondering why a battle star was not given for Anzio. It was just as tough as the Battle of the Bulge in the Ardennes (for which a star was granted) I hope they do give one for Anzio but I guess it's too late now. At any rate I now have four battle stars (Rome, S. France, Rhineland, and Central Europe). I am supposed to get a bronze arrowhead for landing in the assault on Aug. 15th in S. France but so far they haven't given them out. The medal I would like to wear is that honorable discharge button. That's the one that really means the most to me.

This is a devil of a conglomeration to call a letter but I guess I am not very connected in my thoughts any more. I'm thinking about getting home and seeing my sweetheart again.

Love,
Chad

Furstenfeldbruck
July 14, 1945

Dearest sweetheart:

Happy Bastille Day! Isn't that silly? But it is just the way all of us are getting these days. We laugh at the damnedest things now that the prospect of going home has come so close. We start moving very soon now so you had better sop writing as soon as you get this if you haven't already; We are just about finished with the packing are getting ready for a visit of Old Blood and Guts himself tomorrow Probably he will be off somewhere else and some beat-up old Brigadier General will come in his place. Our opinion around here of Gen. P. is pretty low. Of course if you have a good press agent you can get lots of headlines. Give me a general (if I have to have one) like Patch or Bradley. They are real leaders of men. How did I get started on this anyway?

I went to Augsburg today to take back some books which we are sending with the Administration center. The place is like a beehive with plenty of box-making. The weather is fine with bright sunshine and a bit of a breeze. The Germans are really busy now tending their fields. The potatoes and grain they grow now will keep them this winter because Germany isn't going to get any help from us in the way of food as long as French, Dutch, Belgians and others are hungry. Bavaria is probably more fortunate than the industrial parts where they may have to get some help.

I can't thing of anything more to write. I am too excited! The prospect of the not-to-distant future has me dazzled. Just to cuddle my sweetheart in my arms and tell her how much I have missed her. When I do kiss you I will probably feel like the sky rocket which just zooms right up into the sky.

All my love

Chad

PS. Tell Dad, Mother, Ralph & Ruth & Elsa not to write.

Furstenfeldbruck
July 20, 1945

Dearest sweetheart:

This is the last letter I will be able to write from German soil because it won't be long now before we take off. Probably Sunday. We will travel to the Reims Assembly Area where we will live in pup tents for a while until we move to the Staging Area to take the boat. It doesn't seem possible that the time is growing so short. We will be separated into geographical groups. I think Davens in Mass. is the Camp where I will be sent so Mac and I may be together. Oh tempers, please frigit! We have been busy finishing our packing and have everything all set except putting away our typewriter and paper. Last night Mac and I strolled along the banks of the Amper River and discovered the town swimming place. It was very refreshing looking but neither of us quite had the ambition to strip down to our shorts and take a plunge in the cold waters which come from the mountains. Be sure to tell Dad and Mother and the rest of the family to expect me home by late August or early Sept. All my love, my sweetheart.

from

Chad

Camp St. Louis
July 29, 1945

Dearest sweetheart:

After two dusty, hot days we finally arrived in the Reims area where we were assigned a tent city to ourselves. It is a dusty section of France not far from Reims and Chalons. We thought there wouldn't be much to do in I$ E work while here but were sadly mistaken. We've had more distribution work here than we had for a long while at Grunwald or Furstenfeldbruck. The days have been very hot and the nights very cold. It reminds me of North Africa. Getting up in the AM is quite a chore because of the damned cold. We don't know how much longer we are going to be here but are all hoping that we will be on our way soon.

Our mail finally caught up with us and I have received nos. 352-363 all within a few days. Here are a few of the things I wanted to comment on.

It is possible that Lou Price is becoming very "brass conscious" but it may be that he is thinking about overseas duty. He has been lucky enough to stay in the States for a long time. He may be wondering about being sent to the Pacific. I am not trying to be snooty but it is hard to understand why he should be distant and aloof.

You said you had butterflies in your tummy. Would the same treatment I used to give you for your tummy work in this case? In that event I will know just what to do.

The more I read about conditions in the States the more thankful I am that you have stuff put away in the locker. Don't worry about my consumption of meat. I am not a great meat eater and the things I really want are salads, fruit and milk. I feel now as though I could drink gallons of fresh milk. Canned and powdered milk for nearly two years have left a great hunger for real fresh milk high on my food list. I was glad to hear that your ordered the rabbits. They are really fine eating. I remember how fine they were done French Style by our friends at Epival last fall. They made a wine sauce that made the meat taste delicious.

As far as I know 30 days will be all we will get for furlough time. Then we will have to return to the 45th wherever it is stationed. There is all sorts of speculation about the camp but it is dollars to doughnuts that it won't be near New England. That would be too good to be true. I suppose we will be stuck away in some godforsaken isolated spot in Texas.

I was shocked to read about Sid. I thought that marriage and children was just what she needed to get her straightened out physically and emotionally. I am glad you finally received the box I sent with the sketch of my lean and lanky face. But doubt whether it will make much of a decoration.

Pretty soon you will have the real me so you can put the picture away. Be sure to catch up on your sleep because you'll need it. If I am sent to Devens I would like to meet you in Hartford and spend a couple of days before coming home.

I can't understand what happened to my letter explaining my decision to stay with the 45th. Mac and I were comparing notes about the way our mail has gone through and we noticed that several times important news meant for our wives was not received until some friend received a letter with the same news.

I hope you are able to get 30 days leave when I am home for furlough. It would be wonderful to be able to be together for a month. I know the days will fly by but we will be reacquainted at least.

July 30, 1945

The guys got chewing my ear so I couldn't finish this letter and before I knew it darkness had come and I had to tuck the letter away in my dispatch case.

This PM I received letter #364 I still can't understand what happened to my letter waiving two theater rights. As you say it doesn't matter now. However I am glad that you think I did right. Only time can tell the rest. That fried rabbit sounded good. Made my teeth water just to think of it.

This AM we were processed. It didn't take long. It consisted of a check of our physical records, service record, personnel cards and pay books. From now on it will consist of labeling our crates and boxes and checking our equipment.

I am putting together a blot of extra socks, towels, etc which take up too much room in my duffle bag and am making a package of them. I am mailing it tomorrow AM.

My original estimate of late August or early September still stands as far as I can see now. It is amusing to hear the fellows tell about how their folks are keeping tabs on the 45th. The papers and radio must be really keeping track of our homeward progress. Home folks must be doing a good job of scanning the papers and staying up late nights listening to the radio. The boys are getting a lot of movies and U.S.O. shows here as well as music by our bands. Just across the road is a large out door theater which is mobbed every night.

Well I will quit now. Take good care of yourself my sweetheart. Give my love to the folks.

Ton devoue

Chad

P.S. Excuse the pencil my damned pen went flooy for a while. It needs a good bath the same as I do.

Dearest sweetheart:

Still stuck in the dust bowl waiting orders to move and by the way rumors are flying around I may get to see the Danburg Fair. According to the dope I get, transportation is really snafued. Guys who were scheduled to leave Europe early in August will be lucky to get home in September. They dragged us from our area near Munich where we were billeted in houses to this damned God forsaken dust bowl where we breathe, eat, work and sleep in dust up to our ears. But that is the Army and we wouldn't be happy if we didn't have something to bitch about. So enough of my troubles.

Today was quite busy. So far I have seen five movies today all of them orientation films. This AM I had to stick around for two showing of "Two Down and One to Go." Which explains redeployment. After that I delivered some Stars and Stripes. This PM I went to Mourmelon with Capt. Strohm, our acting I&E officer to preview three films for orientation. At least I hadn't seen them before so that was some compensation.

Yesterday I sent home the package I spoke about, the one with towels, socks, photographs, soap, etc. I hope it comes through in good shape. I didn't have very strong twine to tie it with but I guess it will hold.

All of us are interested in the airplane accident in the Empire State Bldg. Old New York must have thought the Japs had unleashed a secret weapon for a while until the smoke cleared away.

Last night I saw Tallulah Bandhead in the "Royal Scandal". For someone who has seen a entertainment movie in a long while I really enjoyed it. The bedroom scenes were well done. You could just see Catherine the Great's ears pricking up when the young lieutenant told her that he had ridden horseback three days and nights to reach her with important news. Evidently one so capable of riding a horse would be able to satisfy the royal need for a rider with endurance. You are not Catherine and I am not a young lieutenant but I'll bet we both are able to ride a good long journey. Fresh, Aren't I?

But seriously my darling little perky nose, I feel as though it will take quite a while before the Devil will be satisfied to rest quietly in hell without moving around to show what in active fellow he is. It is difficult during the relative inactivity of this waiting period to keep my mind from thoughts of cuddling you in my arms and just smothering you with caresses. I remember how you used to like to have me grasp your hands and spread out your arms as Peter slid deeper and deeper into Paradise until you started breathing hard and letting out fully little moans. When I let your hands go you would start beating my shoulders with your fists and pulling at the blankets. You seemed to be reaching the heights of ecstacy and that was what gave my double pleasure. Just the knowledge that my body was yours and was able to make you feels to much delight made me very happy. Each day that goes by brings that all the closer now.

Darling, I love you so much and miss you more and more each day. It is impossible to describe how much but soon I may be able to try to show you and tell you. With all my love,

Chad

Camp St. Louis
August 5, 1945

Dearest sweetheart:

Still sweating it out (and I mean sweating) here in the Dust bowl. Rumors fly as usual but it still looks like September from here. We will be one of the last divisions to be redeployed from the ETO. After us the shipments will probably taper off. We are now going through a siege of worshiping the great god. "Chicken". We have daily inspections of our quarters (squad tents). Charly, Mac and I were all gigged by our esteemed Company Commander for having our wet wash cloths out to dry. That's just a sample of what goes on here. However, it's worse than that back in Germany where I was originally slated to stay. You see some officers feel that they have to justify their existence . The only way they think they can do it is by having inspections and treating grown men like children. We are all following the news from the Pacific with enthusiasm. It really looks good. Oh darling. I miss you so much and am longing for the time to come when I can begin to tell you how much. I love you, my sweet with all my heart, Take good care of yourself.

All my love,

Chad

Dearest sweetheart:

Still at the same old stand although our Dust Bowl has changed to a mud pie. It has been cold and rainy for three or four days. We have had to leave our tent flaps down to keep our stuff dry.

The last three days have kept us in suspense with news coming in concerning the new Atomic Bomb, the entrance of Russia in to the war and now rumors of Japanese peace feelers. We are all sweating out a radio announcement of Japan's acceptance. Everybody was running around the PM trying to check up on the radio. We are all hoping that this Japanese business won't spoil our chances for being sent home.

Last night we saw the Radio City Rockettes. They were in a show put on by the USO. There were about umpteen thousand GI's sitting on the ground while the brass at on their chairs viewing the show. Just heard news flash saying that Stockholm verified the report that Japan had accepted the terms laid down at the Potsdam Conference! I feel like going to church and giving thanks. That is just the way I feel!

To return to the USO show it really was well done with fine scenery and lighting effects that resembled shows back home. A far cry from some of the shows we saw in Italy, France and Germany.

The mail has now definitely tapered off to a blank. As I remember, the last one I had was #365 and I guess that's the last one, I will get in Europe. We were told that our discontinuance notices were mailed out so we will have to sweat out the rest of it without mail. Nobody knows for sure but I think we will start moving in about ten more days and should be in the States by Labor Day. It is possible that we'll get a glimpse of England before we leave. Of course this is conjecture but I think it has a pretty good chance of panning out.

Yesterday I finally mailed the last box of I&E stuff but am keeping my fingers crossed because there is some talk of inspections of the boxes. I'm getting tired of opening and closing boxes.

As the days pass by and our shipping date draws nearer I find myself thinking more and more of home if that is possible. I wish I had some definite information about where to meet you but I don't. I miss you so much it hurts. I love you more and more each day.

Chad

My dearest sweetheart:

This is the fourth rainy day in a row and this miserable sea of mud is really something to navigate in. Yesterday was quite windy and we had trouble keeping our office tent up. The ground was so soft that it wouldn't anchor the tent pins securely. Three of the tent theaters finally collapsed and will have to be put up again. The radio City Rockettes finally had to give up trying to put on shows so they are moving out to one of the other camps. What I did see of them the one night they were able to put on a show was very good. They had all the precision and snap for which they are famous. From a distance they all seemed very good looking (especially the legs) but one of the boys told me that they aren't really so pretty but do have nice figures and legs.

I have this PM off duty so I came up to the tent and am making the most of a rainy spell. Four other fellows in the tent are getting a little bunk fatigue which I will do a little later. You will probably find out that I am a lot more fond of staying in bed since I have been in the Army. Bunk fatigue with you by my side in our big bed won't be hard to take at all.

Just before coming up to the tent I went into the Post Office and purchased two money orders for $100 each. They will probably get home long before I do but you can cash them and put the money aside for anything you want. We may have to use it when I come home on my furlough. Of course things are up in the air now but I doubt if we will be held over here now that we are processed and have our stuff packed. Anything can happen in the Army and usually does so I am keeping my fingers crossed. This AM's paper confirmed the report that the Japs were ready to accept the terms. The Potsdam Conference providing Hiroshito was left on the throne. The United Nations accepted Italy's surrender and allowed Victor Emmanuel to remain on the throne. Maybe they will accept Japans proposition. If the U.N. are able to control Japan's internal policies I can't see much objection to it. I only hope they don't decide that the 45th will be needed for occupation duty in the Pacific.

This is a hell of a life. We live on "ifs", "maybes" and "perhaps" Rumors thicker than French mud and that's saying something.

In my last letter I wrote that I am thinking about you more and more each day Last night I had a wonderful dream about our being together again. The only trouble was that I woke up right in the middle of the best part. You and I had met in some city and I had dropped my duffle bag and had wrapped you up in my arms. We went to a hotel and got a room where I put my stuff aside and when we were all alone I had picked up my sweetheart in my arms and we sat in a nice big easy chair. You were sitting on my lap and had your little nose up under my chin while I held you close and told you how much I loved you. Somehow or other my hands kept caressing your body and before long I could feel your breath coming in quivery sighs. So I have you some quivery kisses to match them. From there on the dream became more and more exciting because then I picked you up and layed you on the bed. Then I took off your clothes with many recesses for quivery kisses along your thighs, over your tummy, and around your nubbins. Next I was pressing my body tight against yours and Peter was throbbing between your legs. He pushed his head against the gates of Paradise and before long his head was inside and was experiencing that warm throbbing feeling that nearly turns me inside out. Then dammit I woke up! By that time I really was stirred up and so was Peter. It was a long time before I could get back to sleep. Oh my darling I muss you so much and I'll never be able to make up to you the mental anguish and the hard work my absence has caused you. I hope and pray that this war will come to a speedy end now. I need you and love you more than. ever.

Camp St. Louis
August 12, 1945

Dearest sweetheart:

Sunshine again after cold drenching rains. The tents are dry again and soon the dust will begin to fly. Today was uneventful except for much speculation about what Japan will do now that the final ultimatum has been given. We feel quite confident that redeployment will continue if it does we will probably be the last bunch to come home with men who are slated for assignment to another theater. A lot of the fellows who are with us now have only a few points. That makes us in the I&E old timers. We are still staying with the thorny problem of boxes. The rules and regulations are quite strict. I suppose they are afraid we may bring a grand piano home with us. As far as I am concerned we could make a big bonfire of the whole damned business! The AM I went out with the stars and Stripes to the units. The paper is very popular now that good news is coming in every day and naturally they all look for news about the fate of the redeployment units. So far we are still slated to start the last part of August so September ought to see us home. I hope that's the right dope. It's getting dark now so will quit with all my love.

Chad

Camp St. Louis
August 17, 1945

Dearest sweetheart:

Still waiting for word to move but it won't be long now. Latest rumor has it that we will leave about the 2nd of September on one of the smaller ships. The boys in hqs. have been preparing big Thunderbird banners to hang over the sides of the ships. Sunday we have our last physical exam which will probably consist of the usual parade I have told you about before. Our I&E work has tapered off to nil now that our boxes are on the train. The arrival of V-J day had us all sweating for a while but we are too far along now to be turned back. Our division just got under the wire! Now the news about discharges from the Army begins to look encouraging they still haven't lowered that age limit enough but I feel that it will be lowered in time. Either that or they will have to lower the critical point score a lot more than it is now. Boy! Am I glad that I volunteered to stay with the division I have had lucky breaks ever since then. I hope by the time I get home you will be able to get way from the bank so that we can be together. Then we would be able to go off somewhere on a trip and really enjoy ourselves I get goosebumps just thinking about it.

All my love, take good care of yourself.

Chad

Camp St. Louis
August 19, 1945

Dearest sweetheart:

   This is the last chance I will have to write you from this camp and I don't know whether we will be able to write from the staging area. Tomorrow we take our train ride of 18 hrs. to the new area and will probably sit around for a week. There we will change our money from francs into that nice green folding stuff that we have missed for so long. We will also have without fail another physical exam which takes about two minutes. Then we will bet on the boat and head for home. We are told that we will probably be sent to the separation center nearest our homes to I hope they don't send me to Ft. Devens but Let me go to a camp near new York then it will be a matter of only a few hours journey. When I reach a camp and find out what the score is I will phone you and we can decide then what to do. I haven't forgotten our telephone number, don't worry. Today is a drab dismal rainy day but those things don't seem to matter now that we know we are going to be on our way. Take good care of yourself, my darling and love.

Chad

Camp Philip Morris
August 23, 1945

Dearest sweetheart:

Last night I went to the Red Cross Club here with the intentions of writing you but the place was so full of GI's that I had to give up. Life here has been just one downpour after another with beaucoups of mud. We traveled here on 3rd lass French cars taking about 18 hours for the whole trip. We got callouses on our buts from the hard wooden seats. The best part of the trip was the efficient system of feeding hot meals. At two different places the train was drawn off on a siding and we went through a chow line which moved very quickly. We detrained at Harfleur just outside Le Havre and went by truck to Camp Philip Morris. The word is now that on Monday we will go to England to get on the boat for the States. It can't be any too soon for us. We are all sick and tired of being shunted along from one camp to another. The news in the papers about fellows 37 or over looks pretty good. I hope that it helps me out. I am reconciled to staying in the Army for quite a while yet because there are so many fellows with high points who have not yet been discharged. Being home in the States won't hurt me however. I am really getting itchy britches now. I hope that this letter won't beat me home by too wide a margin. Give my love to the folks and my special love to you.

from

Chad

Camp Philip Morris
August 27, 1945

Dearest sweetheart:

I am perched up on top of a pile of boxes just outside our tent enjoying the cool of the evening and thinking about how nice it would be to be with you paddling a canoe through the Channel at Wacombus. It won't be long now before we will be on our way again. We will probably start home on the 3rd and I should be starting my furlough somewhere around the 15th. I don't know what my exact status will be when I get back to the States but I feel pretty certain that fellows my age may be screened out for eventual discharge. The fellows with 85 points or more will probably be out by Xmas so I am hoping that after that they will get around to the older fellows. We just got under the wire by being in the 45th. We spend most of our time here getting bunk fatigue, reading, pitching horse shoes or playing volley ball . It's a lazy sort of life and makes a fellow have sticky feet to get under way. I hope everything is OK at home and that you haven't had any more trouble with your feet now. That gas rationing has been lifted we will be able to take some trips. I hope you will be able to get away from the bank. It would be just like a second honeymoon. I am just about aching with longing to be with you again.

All my love.
Chad

Camp Philip Morris
August 30, 1945

Dearest sweetheart:

Time is getting short now so here I am perched up on the old packing case again. By Sunday we will be on the Sea Owl, a converted freighter and probably Monday will be on our way to Boston. I suppose Mac and I will both be sent to Fort Devens before being turned loose but, in any event I will phone you as soon as I can. I'm all excited just thinking of hearing your voice again. I don't know when I will be turned loose for my furlough but I think it will be somewhere between the 12th and the 15th. Whatever you want to do is OK by me. If you think it will be too difficult to get hotel accommodations I will come directly home. By the time I arrive in the States you will probably know what you want to do. The news in the Stars and Stripes today said that with ten days an announcement would be made about lowering the discharge age from 38. So I am really going around in circles today. I've been kidding Mac because he can't remember his telephone number. He's just as excited as I am. Charley's chances of getting out are pretty good too as the I &E section may not hang together too much longer. My darling I miss you so much the days are just dragging. Give my love to the family.

All my love,
Chad

Camp Philip Morris
August 31, 1945

Dearest sweetheart:

Skies are blue, music is in the air and all's right with the world! With a space of ten minutes I received two good bits of news. Your letters 366 and 367 arrived and I devoured them. Then one of the boys told me that our ship is in and we will be leaving soon. Tomorrow AM is our last physical exam and today we turned in our money and got receipts to be exchanged for good old American currency. It will be great to handle nickels, dimes and quarters again instead of paper marks, francs, etc. I was thrilled by the news that we will be able to have a couple of days together in Hartford before coming home. I'm sorry about your staying home waiting for a phone call but our status was pretty shaky for a while. But now we are all set and should arrive in Boston about the 10th and I should be able to phone you as soon as I get into a camp then I'll have definite information about when I can leave to meet you. Try to get rested up sweetheart because we have a lot of getting reacquainted to get caught up with.

All my love to my darling

from
Chad